# PARTY AND GOVERNMENT

# Party and Government

## An Inquiry into the Relationship between Governments and Supporting Parties in Liberal Democracies

Edited by

**Jean Blondel**
*External Professor*
*European University Institute, Florence*

and

**Maurizio Cotta**
*Professor of Political Science*
*University of Siena*

First published in Great Britain 1996 by
**MACMILLAN PRESS LTD**
Houndmills, Basingstoke, Hampshire RG21 6XS
and London
Companies and representatives
throughout the world

A catalogue record for this book is available
from the British Library.

ISBN 0–333–61660–X

First published in the United States of America 1996 by
**ST. MARTIN'S PRESS, INC.,**
Scholarly and Reference Division,
175 Fifth Avenue,
New York, N.Y. 10010

ISBN 0–312–15917–X

Library of Congress Cataloging-in-Publication Data
Party and government : an inquiry into the relationship between
governments and supporting parties in liberal democracies / edited
by Jean Blondel and Maurizio Cotta.
    p.  cm.
Includes bibliographical references and index.
ISBN 0–312–15917–X
1. Political parties—Europe, Western.  2. Political parties–
–United States.  3. Political parties—India.  I. Blondel, Jean,
1929–  .  II. Cotta, Maurizio.
JN94.A979P375   1996
324.2'094—dc20                 96–10705
                                CIP

10   9   8   7   6   5   4   3   2   1
05  04  03  02  01  00  99  98  97  96

Printed in Great Britain by
Ipswich Book Co Ltd, Ipswich, Suffolk

# Contents

# Tables and Figures

# Notes on Contributors

**R.B. Andeweg** is Professor of Political Science at the University of Leiden

**J.W. Björkman** is Professor of Public Policy and Administration at the Institute of Social Studies at the Hague and Professor of Public Administration and Development at the University of Leiden

**J. Blondel** is External Professor at the European University Institute in Florence

**M. Cotta** is Professor of Political Science at the University of Siena

**L. De Winter** is Associate Professor of Political Science at the University of Louvain-la-Neuve

**A-P. Frognier** is Professor of Political Science at the University of Louvain-la-Neuve

**R.S. Katz** is Professor of Political Science at the Johns Hopkins University

**T. König** is Associate Professor at the University of Mannheim

**U. Liebert** is Associate Professor at the University of Heidelberg

**K. Mathur** is Professor of Political Science at the Jawaharlal Nehru University

**L. Morel** is Associate Professor of Political Science at the University of Lille II

**W.C. Müller** is Professor of Political Science at the University of Vienna

**J. Nousiainen** is Professor of Political Science at the University of Turku

**W. Philipp** is Associate Professor at the University of Vienna

**B. Rihoux** is a Researcher at the University of Louvain-la-Neuve

**O. Ruin** is Professor of Political Science at the University of Stockholm

**B. Steininger** is a Researcher at the University of Vienna

**L. Verzichelli** is a Researcher at the University of Siena

for Tess and Raffaella

# Preface

This book follows, one hopes logically, the series of three volumes published by Macmillan since the late 1980s on cabinets in Western Europe, their composition, and their decision processes. These volumes were prepared jointly by a group of political scientists from most Western European countries. It became gradually clear to members of the group that one of the keys to the understanding of the operation of cabinets was provided by the political parties, but that that key was still mysteriously hidden as very little had been done to discover what the true role of parties was in relation to cabinets. The expression 'party government' had begun to be used repeatedly in the context of Western European cabinets, but it was difficult to pinpoint precisely what that expression did cover; it was as a result even more difficult to know to what extent there were differences among countries and within countries when one came to consider the role of parties in government. Some groundwork had been started, in the early 1980s, interestingly at the European University Institute in Florence, under the leadership of Rudolf Wildenmann: the contribution of Richard Katz to this earlier enterprise was so pioneering that our group was led to associate him to the work in which we were thinking of engaging. Yet the analyses which were conducted then had remained essentially signposts: these signposts constituted a further spur to the desire which we had to enter the field.

After a meeting at which we discussed in a broad manner what an empirical analysis of government-party relationships would have to entail, we decided that it was wise, in the first instance, to undertake a survey of these relationships on a country-by-country basis and that a truly comparative study would have to come later. The investigation proved longer and more complex than we had anticipated, but, eventually, the country cases were completed. This book is the product of the bringing together of these country cases.

The volume examines government-supporting party relationships in eleven countries. Nine are Western European; the other two are the United States and India: these two cases are examined in order to start opening a window on two non-Western European liberal polities, the United States because it is the example par excellence of a liberal democratic presidential system, India because it is by far the most populous liberal democracy in the world and because it has had since independence what by most standards has been a highly successful dominant party, the Congress party. These two examples proved most interesting as they enabled us to discover what was and was not universal in the relationships between governments and supporting parties in contemporary liberal democracies. The analysis of these two countries also suggested that similar analyses should be undertaken in other non-Western European liberal democratic countries, an undertaking which is indeed close to the interests of several members of the group.

This study could not have come to fruition, any more than the previous ones in the series, had it not been for the generous support of the European University Institute, the Italian Consiglio Nazionale delle Ricerche, and the research councils of the countries concerned by this study. We wish to thank them most heartily. We are also most thankful to the many researchers who studied the detailed policies on which the conclusions of the country chapters of this book are based. We hope that, as a result, our work is at least beginning to lift a corner of that highly important and yet basically unknown network of relationships between governments and the parties which support them. We also hope that this study will constitute an encouragement for further studies in the field so that it becomes possible to claim, in the coming decades, that we know what parties do when they are involved in government and what governments do when they relate to the parties which support them.

J. Blondel and M. Cotta
Florence and Siena
July 1995

# 1. Introduction
## J. Blondel and M. Cotta

This book is about the relationships between governments and the parties which support them. The problem is an important one: it is at the very root of the idea of 'party government', an idea which is crucial to the theory and practice of modern liberal democratic representative executives, primarily in parliamentary systems, but in presidential systems as well.

Yet the subject has not so far been given the attention it deserves, especially directly and, might one say, consciously. Even in the literature which is devoted explicitly to the subject, little detailed consideration has been given to the matter.[1] Why this should be the case is somewhat mysterious and surely surprising; but at the root of this state of affairs lies probably the fact that the question is viewed as straightforward and at any rate as simple.

Perhaps another reason is the tendency, common in the literature of the 1970s and 1980s, to view governments as almost passive subjects operating under the pressure of a variety of forces, among which parties, but also groups and indeed the civil service play a major part, a standpoint which corresponded to the 'corporatism' period of the analysis of political systems. Indeed, the limited attention given to the relationship between government and parties stems probably from a combination of two views. On the one hand, there is the 'neo-corporatist' model according to which interest organisations dominate the policy-making process, at the expense of democratic institutions such as parliaments, parties, and governments; on the other, there is the tendency in the 'party-government' literature to discuss governments as if they were only tools of the parties and were not independent actors. Thus it has been argued that 'the severely limited role of parties and parliaments in policy-making seems to be a fact which can scarcely be disputed in empirical terms ... To the extent to which policy-making evades political control and guidance, it is determined by the particular interests of pressure groups, large enterprises and bureaucracies, while general and encompassing interests tend to be neglected.'[2]

Quite apart from being simplistic in many ways, this approach has two specific defects in the context of party government. First, it places broadly on the same level parties and other groups, while the insertion of parties in the governmental machinery is manifestly broader and more wide-ranging: ministerial recruitment and ministerial policy are dominated by parties, in many cases at least, to an extent that is not achieved or even attempted by groups. Second, and more importantly, this view of the relationship between governments and supporting parties appears to posit that governments, that is to say specifically leaders and ministers, are not major actors in the process of policy-making and development. At best this is a hypothesis to test, not an assumption to make; as a matter of fact, impressionistic evidence suggests on the contrary that many governments at least are rather autonomous from the party or parties which support them, either because these governments are allowed by the parties a substantial freedom of manoeuvre or because they – and in particular their leaders – control the supporting political parties. What has therefore to be undertaken is an inquiry into the links which exist between government and parties in order to assess where, to what extent, and for what reasons governments are relatively autonomous from or, on the contrary, dependent on these supporting parties.

## WHAT IS PARTY GOVERNMENT?

A serious analysis requires a precise definition of the type of relationships which is covered by the idea of party government. Yet difficulties exist at this level. It has been said, for instance, in a somewhat simplified and rather vague manner, that party government is 'that form of societal conflict regulation in which a plurality of democratically organised political parties play a relatively dominant role both in the socio-political mediation sphere and in the actual process of political decision-making (government sphere)'.[3] Such a 'definition' (if the word applies in this case) says little that can be used for practical purposes, since what is a 'relatively dominant role' is clearly highly debatable; it also seems to assume that a government is *either* party *or* non party, which is manifestly not the case.

Perhaps the most systematic effort is that of R.S. Katz who develops an incremental concept of 'partyness of government' as well indeed as a concept of 'party governmentness'.[4] He mentions three conditions which have to be fulfilled for a government to deserve the title, so to speak, of 'party government'. These are that 'all major governmental decisions must be taken by people chosen in elections conducted along party lines, or by individuals appointed by and responsible to such people', that 'policy must be decided within the governing party, when there is a "monocolour" government, or by negotiation among parties when there is a coalition', and that 'the highest officials (for example, cabinet ministers and especially the prime minister) must be selected within their parties and be responsible to the people through their parties'.[5] R.S. Katz then goes on to note that this definition 'represents an ideal type, rather like but in contrast to Dahl's type of polyarchy. As such, it represents an extreme that may be approximated but is neither realised nor realisable in the ultimate sense. It is also a multidimensional concept. Thus a particular system may closely approximate the ideal type in one respect but not in another.'[6]

R.S. Katz's analysis shows that the problem of defining party government is complex; perhaps even more interestingly, it also suggests that one should look for 'types' of party government. It is to the question of defining such 'types', of examining the dimensions along which these can be analysed, and of determining the political factors which may account for their existence that this book is devoted.

## THE PECULIAR STATUS AND POSITION OF GOVERNMENTS

Yet, for a satisfactory analysis of the relationship between party and government, the approach developed by the 'party-government' literature, which has primarily discussed the effect of parties on governments, should be complemented by an explicit analysis of the other side of the picture, that is to say the effect of governments on parties.

In order to do so, we have to devote first a little more attention to what is less often discussed, namely to what the status and position of governments really are. The fact that governments are so little discussed stems probably from the fact that they are taken for granted or are reduced to something else, for instance to the party in power or the bureaucracy. In reality, governments should not be taken for granted or dissolved into something else in this way.

What, to begin with, is a government? In numerical terms it is constituted by a small number of persons: it is very small if one restricts it to the cabinet as well as perhaps to the close advisers of the prime minister or president, as we shall do in this volume; it is somewhat larger if one includes under secretaries and other second rank ministers, but it remains true that, in all cases, the government is a compact body.

The main point which needs to be made about governments is different, however. It is that these bodies hold a peculiar political and institutional position, which stems from the fact that they are at the crossroads between representation and administration. On the one hand, they are the top echelon of the representative column in a democratic state. On the other, they are the apex of the huge state machine: not surprisingly, they are still termed the 'administration' in some countries.[7]

The historical and political reasons for this state of affairs are well-documented: in most countries of the Continent, governments were set up to assist the monarch in running the bureaucratic machine: this bureaucratic aspect was to remain in some countries the more prominent feature, despite decades during which representative institutions have been in operation. In Britain, meanwhile, the cabinet always had a mixed role: while it was expected to help implement the decisions of the monarch and thus direct the bureaucracy, it was also organised in order to manipulate parliament: from this developed the representative aspect of its role, an aspect which has probably been adopted more fully in the countries which emerged directly from the British tradition. Finally, the more bureaucratic features of the government continued to characterise, or to characterise rather more than the representative features, the cabinets of presidential systems because it is the president alone who shoulders the political responsibility in these regimes.

The position and authority of governments is markedly shaped by the dynamic interaction between these representative and administrative elements; but the role of governments as heads of the state machinery has been further enhanced by the growth of the Welfare State and by the involvement of public bodies in the economic life of countries. The result is that governments have a strikingly higher status than that which they could obtain directly from the fact that they represent or owe their origins to the parties which support them. Moreover, as a result of this increased role, governments have come to be at the centre of a web of relations with the private sector of the economy and society; they are as a result the final destination of demands, inputs, pressures, and messages of all kinds. This has meant in particular that governments have increasingly come to seek and obtain advice from technicians and professionals with whom ministers are directly in contact and thanks to whom they may in part by-pass the regular bureaucratic machine.

The relative weight of the two roles of governments is subject to variations. Traditions differ from country to country and governments are naturally regarded as more representative here, more administrative there. What is the case everywhere, however, is that, because they are at the top of the two worlds of representation and administration, governments are in a position to exercise leadership on a scale which others cannot match.

As traditions vary about the relative role of representation and administration in shaping governmental leadership, a comparative analysis is by far the best way of discovering evidence about the way in which these two characteristics combine to affect party-government relations. One might advance three hypotheses on a preliminary basis. First, it seems plausible to suggest that, the stronger the resources available to the government and the more direct its control over these resources, the greater will be the probability that the government will be autonomous or that it will control the parties with which it is linked. Second, it also seems plausible to suggest that, the stronger the bureaucracy behind the government is, the more this government will be able to impose its views and policies on the supporting parties. Finally, third, one might also state that, the stronger and the more direct the representative basis of governments, the greater will be their influence on the supporting parties, as the character of government-supporting party relationships in Britain seems to indicate.

## THE CONCEPT OF THE SUPPORTING PARTY

The concept of the supporting party is also more complex and less clear than it seems at first sight; a sharp distinction between supporting and 'non-supporting' parties corresponds to limit-cases only, namely those in which the number of significant parties is small, parties are disciplined, and the government has majority support. This concept tends therefore to apply primarily to 'textbook' British or Commonwealth cases. As soon as one deviates from this 'pure' model (including some real-world situations in Britain and in the Commonwealth), what is meant by supporting party becomes less clear.

First, there is a manifest effect of lack of discipline on support. If the party is indisciplined in parliament, should one say that it supports the government or not? A somewhat simplified position has to be taken in practice, but the general point needs to be made. Second, the question of the number of significant parties may not seem in theory to be likely to have a direct impact on the nature of support; in practice, the impact can be large, as, the more parties that are involved in supporting a government, the less this support is likely to be firm. If the partners in a coalition have a high level of cohesion, discipline will none the less be maintained, but there will probably always be a degree of suspicion, with the effect that support will have a conditional and at best somewhat temporary character. One can therefore understand that support is likely to decrease as the number of parties in the coalition is large.

So far we assumed that the party or parties in the government commanded a majority in the legislature, whether in a presidential or in a parliamentary context: this is of course far from being always the case. In presidential systems and in particular in the United States, the fact that the party of the President may not be the party of the majority in the Congress is well-known. In parliamentary systems, the existence of minority governments is by now well recognised, these governments being either near-majority governments or true minority governments.[8] There may be an agreement with one or more parties in order to obtain a working governmental majority; there may be shifting majorities; there may be explicit outside support. All these situations occur fairly frequently.

Finally, there is still a more extreme case, namely that of the support given by opposition parties themselves. In many cases at least, the opposition does not vote systematically and all the time against the government; there may indeed be important occasions (with respect to foreign affairs for instance or in the context of national emergencies) when the opposition supports the government. Indeed, the government may make policy concessions and accept proposals from the opposition parties. These are thus in some way involved in the policy-making process, in a limited manner, admittedly, but not necessarily to an insignificant extent.

The concept of supporting party has therefore to be regarded as being in principle incremental rather than dichotomous: parties support more or less both governmental policies and the government in general. Yet it is not truly practical to go appreciably beyond dichotomies in an empirical analysis which can be concerned only with a limited number of cabinets in an even smaller number of countries. Thus, while we shall consider intermediate cases in specific situations, we shall in general adopt a more 'robust' or simpler distinction, at least in those cases in which the parties are sufficiently disciplined to be deemed to behave, if not always to think, in a united manner.


## PARTIES AS DECISION-MAKING BODIES

The reason why there are problems with the definition of supporting parties stems from the fact that we are concerned here with these organisations as bodies where ideas and policies are generated. What constitutes a party from this point of view is not altogether clear. The matter may be clear in the limit-case of a wholly centralised party, such as a Communist party (of the traditional variety) in which policies are produced by a national executive on a unanimous or near-unanimous basis. If we move away from this limit-case, however, what is to be regarded as a party idea or a party decision becomes more problematic.

The difficulty arises for two reasons, which paradoxically have the opposite effect. First, the more a party is decentralised and indeed factionalised on the basis of ideological, personal, or geographical cleavages, the more it is difficult to determine which decisions can be regarded as party decisions in the full sense of the word, as, in a divided party, a large number of views are aired. Yet, in this case, it is not the party as such, but elements from the party which are at the origin of the policies which the government may come to adopt.

Meanwhile, very decentralised parties are also unlikely to adopt formally many precise and detailed policies; they may not adopt any policies at all, as the example of American parties indicates: in this case, the burden of policy-making is left nearly entirely to the President and to Congressmen, individually or in groups, but not necessarily on a party basis. Thus, while many ideas which eventually become government policy may originate from the party, very few of these ideas can be regarded as having the formal seal of approval of the party as such.

In this respect it is not realistic to adopt an 'all-or-nothing' conception of the nature of decisions in political parties, since these will range from highly centralised to very decentralised. For practical purposes, we need to rely on the 'authoritativeness' of decisions; yet we need to remember that other views, less official, may be of importance and indeed find their way at the governmental level.

Assuming that we know how to assess the ways in which parties support governments, we can then move to an examination of the types of this support. We shall follow the approach proposed by R.S. Katz, that is to say both in terms of the extent to which governments are of a party type ('partyness') and in terms of the relative position which a given government occupies according to a number of possible 'dimensions' of party government.

## THE SPACE OF PARTY-GOVERNMENT RELATIONSHIPS

To do so, we must first identify the space where it is possible to locate all the activities in which parties and governments relate to each other. What then are these activities? For a period at least, the literature on coalition-formation concentrated on the relationship between parties and governments at one level, namely that of the *allocation of positions* among the various parties. This is manifestly insufficient: a *policy component* has obviously to be considered alongside the 'power' component: parties are not only interested in placing some of their members in the government: they have programmes which they wish to see carried out.[9] Conversely, governments may be and indeed are in many cases interested both in placing some of their closest supporters in top positions and in ensuring that the party adopts the policies which it, rather than the supporting party or parties, has prepared.

Yet a further element in this relationship needs to be taken into account: this is constituted by the demands made by parties for *favours and patronage*, which, in some countries at least, play an important part, even if that part is somewhat difficult to measure with precision. Favours can be crucial in two ways: they are means by which the parties can exert influence in the country and thus indirectly become stronger vis-à-vis the government; but they are also means by which the government can have a direct effect on parties, since they are instruments with which they can put pressure on them. They are indeed part of a large set of trade-off relationships in which governments are engaged.

Thus party-government relationships must be considered both from the (more traditional) angle of the possible influence and effect of parties on governments and from the angle of the influence of governments on parties. Such a two-way influence can and does take place with respect to favours, to policies, and to appointments. We need therefore to think of the 'space' of the relationship between parties and governments as being able to cover national policy-making, the composition of the government and of top party organs, and the distribution of patronage. Meanwhile, this space must allow for variations ranging from *dependence of the government on the party, at one extreme, to dependence of the party on the government, at the other.*

## DIMENSIONS OF GOVERNMENT-PARTY RELATIONSHIPS

Let us examine more closely the nature of party-government relationships. To begin with, they have a dimensional character: there can be more or less dependence of one on the other. There is another aspect to be assessed, however, namely that of the absence of any relationship. Governments can be autonomous from parties, in some respects, and correspondingly parties are autonomous from governments in these matters. This means that there are in reality two dimensions, those of *autonomy versus interdependence*, on the one hand, and of the *direction of the dependence*, on the other.

On the one hand, there may be such a limited relationship between the government and the party or parties which nominally support this government that the two can be regarded as being autonomous from each other. Indeed, one of the most important aspects of an inquiry into governments must be to identify the extent to which these governments can act as autonomous agents; but, if the governments are autonomous, the supporting parties are also autonomous. There is indeed a dimension, as there will be areas of autonomy and these will vary from country to country and from time to time. Thus it is sometimes suggested that governments are more often autonomous from parties with respect to foreign affairs than with respect to home affairs.

On the other hand, if there is a relationship of interdependence between governments and supporting parties, this relationship can vary markedly from one extreme of total dependence of the government on the party or parties supporting it to the other extreme of total dependence of the party or parties on the government, with an intermediate point corresponding to equal and reciprocal influence.

These two dimensions are manifestly interconnected, however. If governments and supporting parties were fully autonomous from each other, there would be no direction of dependence, as there would be no dependence of one on the other: at most, in such a case, there would be perfect 'equality' between the two elements, an equality which would stem from the absence of any rapport. Of course, in the real world, there is no 'pure' case of this type. As a result, countries will only be located in a part of the space, this part having the shape of a triangle in which one side is the 'direction of dependence' axis while the other two sides join each other at the autonomy end of the 'autonomy-interdependence' dimension and at the middle point with respect to the 'direction of dependence' dimension. This is another way of saying that the two dimensions are in part interconnected; but they remain distinct. The precise location of countries is obviously impossible to determine at this stage; but the identification of the two dimensions helps to see where in broad terms the countries can be placed at different moments in time.

## PATTERNS OF PARTY-GOVERNMENT RELATIONSHIPS

Let us therefore examine broad patterns of relationships within the triangle which we just defined. Towards the top corner, one will find the executives who have a source of legitimacy of their own, as in some monarchical systems where the government is of a 'bureaucratic' type, in some presidential systems, if the 'party' of the president is in effect sharply distinct from the 'party' which nominally supports the president in the legislature: this case approximates that of the United States and, possibly, of some other presidential systems. A similar situation can be found in parliamentary systems when there is a crisis in the party system and, as a result, a government of technicians is appointed.

The second rather extreme type of government-party relationship is that of the dependent party. This kind of situation can be found in a number of new countries, especially in the Third World, the Mexican PRI being perhaps the best example: the single party is set up in order to help the leader to both mobilise and control the population, although over time the situation may change. If one then moves a little from this extreme position, one can see how changes affect the model somewhat. In Britain, for instance, the Conservative party may be regarded as being still relatively close to the 'government-dominant' end of the dimension. There is in fact 'fusion' of the leadership of the party and of the government, a fusion which benefits the government rather than the party.

Finally, the other bottom corner of the triangle has traditionally been occupied by Communist states, as the party leadership, rather than the governmental leadership, dictated policy and as the former appointed the latter (and indeed appointed, through the *nomenklatura* system, members of the public service well below the governmental level). This system was also a case of 'fusion', as is the case of systems where parties depend on the government, but the 'fusion' is exercised here to the benefit of the party rather than to the benefit of the government or, to use the Communist terminology, of the 'State apparatus'. Meanwhile another type is provided by many of those parliamentary systems which have typically coalition governments and in which both the selection of ministers and the determination of policies are markedly influenced by the government parties; moreover, in several of these countries, though not in all, substantial levels of patronage tend also to be found.

'Central' positions in the triangle are perhaps not occupied because a choice has to be made, ultimately, between 'autonomy' and 'interdependence', leaving some scope for manoeuvre only at the margin. The case of the Fifth French Republic appears interesting in this respect. It was set up on the basis of an ideology of governmental autonomy put forward by De Gaulle, against a background of party dominance over the government in the past. Gradually, however, France moved to a position not unlike that of Britain under the Conservatives and indeed even originally somewhat closer to the 'government-dominant' corner of the triangle. Subsequently, government-party relations moved somewhat from that corner, under the Socialists in particular.

The types and moves which have been indicated here are based on impressions rather than on firm evidence. They suggest that comparisons and contrasts can be made, however; they also suggest that the number of broad categorisations is probably relatively small: it seems therefore possible to look for what may be referred to as 'satellite' sub-types and to describe the moves taking place around each of the types.

## THE POLITICAL FACTORS WHICH ACCOUNT FOR GOVERNMENT-SUPPORTING PARTY RELATIONSHIPS

Having examined the ways in which governments and supporting parties may relate to each other, the next step is to analyse the factors which are likely to affect government-party relationships. These fall into two broad groups. One group includes characteristics of the political system which concern the way decisions are processed in political systems. If one moves from the general to the particular, these characteristics would seem to include, at one extreme, the national political institutions and, at the other, the part played by individual actors and in particular by government leaders and by party leaders. In between, the configuration of the party system, on the one hand, and the characteristics of each of the parties supporting the government, on the other, would also seem to play a major part.

The second type of factors relates to the nature of the decisions which are to be taken: party-government relations may not be the same with respect to all fields (foreign affairs for instance) or over all types of situations (emergencies for example).

## THE EFFECT OF NATIONAL INSTITUTIONAL FRAMEWORK ON GOVERNMENT-PARTY RELATIONSHIPS

To begin with, the national institutions can be expected to have an effect on government-supporting party relationships, an effect which is likely to reduce the strength of these relationships and, at the limit, to weaken them so much that they become almost insignificant.

One of the main reasons why parties exist is in order to provide links between people and government; these links can have an upward direction if parties are primarily representative or have a downward direction if they are mainly 'mobilising'. In both cases, the outcome is the establishment of a close relationship between government and supporting parties. Thus one can hypothesise that constitutional and other national institutional arrangements are likely to reduce the direct links between parties and governments and thus the interdependence between them, as national institutions give authority to the bodies which are set up through them. These bodies acquire as a result (or at least can be expected to acquire, if the national institutional arrangements are legitimate), enough influence to give their members and in particular their leaders the ability to act on their own, to an extent at least. This is what can be expected to occur in 'constitutional' presidential systems, as in the United States, where government-party relationships are reduced in scope because both executive and legislature are strong while the sources of the authority of these two 'powers' are distinct.

We discussed so far the possible effect on government-party relationships of constitutional and other arrangements at the top; but these relationships may well also be affected by the vertical division of powers between centre and regions. That effect is likely to be indirect, however, as what is at stake is the distribution of power within the parties and, in this way, the ability of the party to influence the executive. Thus truly decentralised polities tend also to have highly decentralised parties: this is the case in the United States, in Canada, in Switzerland; in those federal systems which are not truly decentralised, on the other hand, such as that of Austria, the structure of the political parties appears not to be markedly affected either by the constitutional arrangements: the effect on government-party relationships is likely to be correspondingly more limited.

Where they have an effect, national institutional arrangements can affect government-party relationships on all three planes. They can affect policy-making in that the scope for governmental initiatives is large, but such initiatives may also be blocked. At the level of appointments, the composition of the governmental and party elites can be affected, as both the government and the parties are relatively free from each other's interference, while this is not the case in other forms of presidential systems and in parliamentary systems. Finally, while, in most systems, favours and advantages may be distributed by governments to parties, these may be large in presidential systems, for instance to compensate to an extent for the distance between government and party in constitutional presidential systems; the case is not as clear-cut in parliamentary systems.


## PARTY SYSTEMS AND THEIR EFFECT ON GOVERNMENT-PARTY RELATIONSHIPS

The effect of party systems on government-party relationships is also large, though it is mostly indirect: the governmental structure and the decision-making processes are likely to be affected by the existence of a given party system in the country. Some variations are also due to differences in the internal characteristics of the parties, as these can affect the ways in which parties relate to each other.

There are three broad types of situations. One is that of single party majority governments, typically to be found in two-party systems or in systems of more than two parties but where one party is dominant, as in Sweden and, in earlier decades, Norway, as well as, outside Western Europe, for a long period at least, India. The second type of situation is that of minority single party governments in minority coalitions dominated by one party, a situation which has occurred frequently in Denmark and occasionally in Norway. Finally, the third situation is constituted by most types of coalitions, as can be found in Belgium, the Netherlands, Italy, as well as, for long periods at least, Austria.

The effect of the party system on the relationships between governments and supporting parties is not the same with respect to the three planes of these relationships, however. With respect to policy elaboration, there is a substantial amount of governmental influence in single party majority governments and in coalitions with a dominant party: this sole or major party comes to office with a programme, typically adopted previously by the party executive or the national conference; but over time the influence of the government grows. The same is true with respect to the composition of the government and of the top party elite: originally, members of the government emerge from the party, and indeed from senior elements in the party: there is then a true *fusion* between the membership of the government and of the party elite; over time, however, this fusion works to the benefit of the government rather than to that of the party elite. Finally, single party majority governments are probably characterised, by and large, by a relatively low level of distribution of favours and patronage, because of the cohesion of the party and the national character of the electoral contests.

Coalition governments have the opposite characteristics. The membership of the government is typically decided by the party while the government has at most very little say in the composition of the top party elite: ministers tend to be selected by party leaders outside the government and the names are transmitted to the new prime minister. Patronage is often widespread, though this may be further reinforced (or reduced) as a result of the specific power relationships within the coalition parties. Finally, coalition parties often have a major influence on governmental policy, an influence which has tended to be formalised by means of a governmental compact, sometimes very detailed, by which the parties determine in advance the line which the government is to take on most, if not all, issues.

The case of minority single party (or minority coalition) governments is intermediate. First, only the party (or parties) represented in the government play a part in determining the composition of that government: there is thus only partial party influence at this level. Second, with respect to policy elaboration, what begins by a substantial amount of party dominance (including by the parties supporting the government from outside) seems to be slowly replaced by some governmental initiative, indeed even some governmental autonomy, partly reminiscent of constitutional presidential systems: the government proposes some policies and discovers later whether there is support for these policies among the coalition partners.[10] Party dominance appears therefore to be only partial: an 'arms length' situation prevails. Finally, the level of distribution of patronage and favours seems relatively low, in part because the position of the government is rather ambiguous vis-à-vis the supporting parties.

## PARTY STRUCTURE AND IDEOLOGY AND ITS IMPACT ON GOVERNMENT-PARTY RELATIONSHIPS

Alongside the party system, internal party characteristics have an impact on government-supporting party relationships. First, the *ideology* may well play a part, as parties of the Left are more likely to want to intervene in the life of the government which they support than parties of the Right: such an 'interference' is viewed on the Left as a manifestation of 'democracy' and of participation.

Second, the *social base* of the party can also be expected to have an impact. At one extreme, extensive authoritarian parties are set up in order to increase the dominant role of the leadership, but this can be the leadership of the party (in the case of many Communist parties) or of the government (in the case of well-organised parties of the authoritarian Right). At the other extreme, 'representative' parties are likely to attempt to influence governments; but the fact that they have a large social base does not automatically give them influence, as they may be so decentralised and indeed so divided that they are unable to affect the government *as parties*; it is elements in their midst which put pressure and may have influence: this is the case, for instance, with American parties.

Finally, the *party structure* is likely to have an impact on government-party relationships, but this appears to be complex. In 'cohesive' parties decisions are taken primarily at the top, though there may be some consultation of the rank-and-file. Close to that end of the continuum are parties with two power centres, admittedly partly overlapping, these being the parliamentary group and the national executive. Somewhat less cohesive are factionalised or geographically-divided parties: in these cases, decisions taken by the centre are likely to be opposed by a substantial proportion of the local leaders; on some matters there may not be united party positions. Yet there are two contradictory movements: on the one hand, the more cohesive the party is, the more it is able to exercise influence as a party; on the other hand, the more the party displays cohesion, the more the government is able to exercise influence mainly by controlling the top of the organisation.

Thus, where there is no party cohesion at all, there is no real opportunity for either party dominance or for government dominance. There would then seem to be autonomy for the government and for the party; indeed it is not so much the party as such which is autonomous, since this expression covers little reality in such a case: the autonomous agents are the party 'chieftains' who can exercise influence, often because they are members of the legislature. The case of the French Fourth Republic approximated this situation.

Internal party characteristics are thus likely to play a substantial part in determining whether government or party dominates the relationship between the two bodies, although these party characteristics have in most cases to be considered jointly with the party system, in the same way as the effect of the party system has to be examined jointly with the impact of internal party characteristics, and in particular with the level of party cohesion. Thus, while it may be to the advantage of the government and of the party that the cohesion of the party be improved, such a cohesion can also mean that the one who gains from the improved cohesion may not be the one who pushes most strongly for it. In this respect in particular, the members of the political elite can have a large part to play: we need therefore to turn to that element to complete the picture of the general factors affecting government-party relationships.

## LEADERSHIP POSITIONS AND GOVERNMENT-SUPPORTING PARTY RELATIONSHIPS

Major controversies have arisen and continue to arise about the role of leaders of other key actors in political life.[11] This role is clearly boosted or depressed by some, if not all, the factors which we described so far. Thus the presidential system, more than the parliamentary system, gives the chief executive the opportunity to lead the government in an autonomous manner; centralised parties with a high degree of cohesion are likely to have strong leaders while decentralised parties are ruled by oligarchies. To be regarded as being a separate factor in the determination of government-party relationships, leadership must be shown to have a part to play over and above this effect: unfortunately, it is still practically impossible to determine, in a general manner, the part which the personality of leaders may have on government-party relationships. The closest that one can come to such an analysis is to look at the effect of time, although, even on this point there are some difficulties. Thus it is not certain that new leaders are stronger than old leaders;[12] in particular, it is not certain that new leaders can easily shrug off during their first years in office either the party programme or the pressure which the party may exercise on governmental composition. It seems on the contrary that government leaders may be able to grow and acquire over time more autonomy or more influence on party policies and on the composition of the party elite, although this does not always occur.

We have therefore to concentrate on positions held by leaders and see how far government-supporting party relations are affected in the process. Three types of positions of leaders are particularly relevant, those of governmental leadership only, of party leadership only, and of combined governmental and party leadership. The first type can be found in a variety of situations, ranging from presidential chief executives who came to power on the basis of popular, rather than party support, to heads of governments appointed by a president elected by popular vote (French prime ministers in the Fifth Republic, for instance) and to prime ministers in a coalition context. These leaders may have widely different resources, but they all have the same objective, namely to strengthen the role of the government over that of the party. They are therefore likely to stress one or both of two elements, the need for national cohesion and the managerial or technical role of the government. On both grounds, these leaders would appear to want to move government-party relationships away from interdependence and in the direction of greater autonomy.

Party leaders who are not government leaders naturally have the oppposite objective, namely to ensure that the interdependence between government and party is maximised and that this interdependence is exercised to the benefit of the party. A prerequisite is naturally that the party be cohesive: the first aim of such leaders must therefore be to bring about cohesion to their organisation if this is lacking. Moreover, party leaders are also unlikely to be able to exercise strong influence over coalition governments dominated by a party whose leader is also leader of the government, especially if this party has great cohesion. As party leaders exercise their influence indirectly, largely through the ministers of their party, they may attempt to remove many policy matters from the governmental area. Ultimately, the power of party leaders in coalition situations would seem to rest on manipulation and on the threat to bring down the government.

Third, those who are both government and party leaders appear naturally *prima facie* to have the greatest resources, but leaders can exploit this situation more or less. This situation tends to occur in single party governments. These leaders appear to have a choice between two options: they can push government-party relationships in the direction of governmental dominance, though this may lead to discontent in the party; alternatively, they can attempt to realise an equilibrium between party and government by balancing the 'political' demands of the party against the 'technical' demands of the government. This strategy is likely to be the more effective in the long run.

## POLICY FIELDS AND GOVERNMENT-SUPPORTING PARTY RELATIONSHIPS

Finally, there appear to be differences across policy fields, although this may not be primarily due to the substance of the fields but to differences in process and characteristics of the decision. Thus, in the case of foreign affairs, issues related to the European Community have been hotly debated in most Western European parties; the same has been true, in some countries at least and in particular in Britain, of issues related to nuclear disarmament.

Deep down, any difference that exists would seem to stem from the fact that governments and parties have a different *raison d'être*. Governments have to 'run the country'; they have to ensure that the administration functions and that the nation is defended. Parties are primarily interested in policies at the most general levels and at the individual level: they attempt to innovate, on the one hand and, on the other, they take up grievances from members or want to distribute favours.

These fundamental differences in the activities of governments and parties explain why there may be conflicts between the two types of bodies; they explain also why there may be a substantial area of autonomy of governments. Specifically, governments appear to have a privileged position in three types of situations. One of these is constituted by *emergencies*. What takes much of the time and energy of government, often in foreign affairs, but also in home affairs, for instance in the economic field, often does not concern parties at all, unless the matter is politically explosive; in most emergency situations, parties seem satisfied to make general statements and leave the government to decide. Another situation is constituted by *technical* cases, for which parties are ill-equipped. Third, governments are concerned with questions which are either politically non-controversial or which cut across party positions, especially with respect to *implementation*. These issues may be regarded as secondary by parties: governments seem therefore able to acquire some autonomy at this level by default, though on this, too, parties may be somewhat resentful.

Thus autonomy or interdependence are likely to vary markedly according to different types of governmental activities, if not perhaps specifically according to governmental fields. At one end of the dimension are the policy proposals which are presented in the party electoral programme, provided these proposals are truly drafted by the party and not inserted by the government in the first instance. At the other are the measures which the party may have mentioned, but without much enthusiasm, alongside measures which the government proposes and the party endorses or at least does not object to, as well as the measures on which the party has no opinion. Between the policy fields or problems where parties and governments truly intersect and those where the government is autonomous, there is therefore a substantial area of 'semi-autonomy' in which the government may be able to act, largely because parties are not organised to be involved in these matters and indeed do not wish to be involved in them.

## THE LINKS BETWEEN THE THREE COMPONENTS OF GOVERNMENT-SUPPORTING PARTY RELATIONSHIPS: REINFORCEMENT OR COMPENSATION

The three elements which combine to form government-supporting party relationships have a different character: their impact is different as a result. Appointments are made for a period, often a long period, while patronage distribution and policy-making include a succession of decisions, often unrelated to each other. Thus the autonomous or dependent character of appointments has a once-and-for-all character or at least constitutes a block in time whose 'weight' is difficult to compare with a large number of decisions, often small, which characterise patronage or policy-making. The matter is complicated by the fact that there is no guarantee that someone who is a party devotee at a given point in time will remain a devotee for the whole of the period during which this person is in the government. Admittedly, in a context of government dependence on supporting parties with respect to appointments, someone who ceases to follow the party line might be forced to resign and be replaced, but there is only a small likelihood that such an outcome will occur without trouble, immediately, let alone frequently. This of course amounts to saying that full government dependence on supporting parties, even with respect to appointments, is likely to be very rare; but such a point is made as a consequence of what might be regarded as a 'law', namely that even the most loyal party person will gradually acquire some independence as he or she comes to the government, would it only be because of the difference in the roles which the party member-who-becomes-minister has to fulfil.

The relationship between governments and supporting parties takes three different forms. It is therefore natural to ask: in what ways are these three forms *mainly* expected to be linked together? Does a privileged role of the parties in connection with government appointments tend to be linked to a privileged role of the parties in connection with policy-making? There seems to be at least some evidence that such a link is often made: after all, parties tend to claim that they wish to take power *in order* to be able to carry out certain policies. Yet we also know that this does not always occur: many parties send their representatives to the government and are frustrated because their desired policies are not implemented.

Meanwhile, the opposite view has also been put forward, in particular by Strom.[13] This is to say that there appear to be circumstances in which a trade-off takes place between 'seeking power' and 'seeking to influence' or, in our terms, between government dependence on appointments and government dependence on policy-making. Such an interpretation helps to account for cases of minority governments in parliamentary systems, in particular where they are numerous, as in Scandinavia. Some supporting parties may see to it that the government depends on them for appointments, at least to an extent, while others may prefer to obtain that the government depends on them for policy-making only.

This situation is reflected in two broad distinct arrangements between governments and supporting parties. One type of arrangement suggests that there are cases of *reinforcement* (of government dependence on appointments by government dependence on policy-making, for instance); the second suggests that there are cases of *compensation* (for instance of government dependence on appointments by party dependence on policy-making). These arrangements relate naturally to patronage distibution as well: in this context there can be reinforcement if patronage increases the dependence of governments on parties or of parties on governments; there can be compensation for instance if patronage is distributed by governments in order to induce supporting parties to accept appointments and/or policies which these parties might otherwise have opposed. There will tend to be variations depending on whether the distribution of patronage is controlled by the supporting parties or by the government. Overall, therefore, and with respect to appointments, policy-making, and patronage, the distinction between reinforcement and compensation constitutes a major characteristic of the way in which governments and supporting parties relate to each other.

Government-party relationships are a central topic in democratic societies (as well indeed as in non-democratic polities). This central topic can only be examined systematically by going beyond the basic impression that parties develop programmes which, ideally at least, should be implemented by the governments which these parties support. One must examine the relative autonomy and interdependence of governments and supporting parties, however defined, with respect to policies, to appointments, and to patronage and one must look at these matters over time. One can then consider the complex and interlocking factors which account for these relationships. Parties have often been set up to ensure that governments implement programmes which the people are presumed to prefer. In the course of the development of 'party government', governments have been involved in many activities in which parties could not be or did not wish to be truly concerned. Naturally enough, the desire to see parties exercising real pressure on governments persists, since this is a requirement if representative government is to be achieved; but one needs also to discover in what ways and on what matters party pressure on government is most often exercised. An examination of the form which party government takes across parliamentary systems and, to an extent, in presidential systems, such as the one which follows in this volume, will give an idea of the variations which exist in the contemporary world and of the relative success of the different types of relationships.

In order to be both detailed and comparative, this volume is based on country chapters which are structured identically. The countries covered are Britain, France, Germany, Italy, Belgium, the Netherlands, Austria, Finland, Sweden, the United States and India. On the basis of the matters discussed in this Introduction, the country chapters include three main sections, devoted respectively to appointments, policy-making, and patronage. In each case, the extent of autonomy and of interdependence is analysed as well as similarities and differences by party. The introduction to each chapter describes the main type of government (coalition or single party, for instance) and the evolution which might have occurred, while the conclusion considers the overall relationship between government and supporting parties: it examines in particular whether the types of relationships on one plane reinforce or compensate for types of relationships on another; it also presents an overall assessment of the position of the country, at various points of time if necessary, in the space of autonomy and interdependence.

## NOTES

1.  The literature on party government as such is relatively limited. The most systematic presentation of the problem appeared in the first two volumes on 'The Future of party Government' edited by R. Wildenmann, *Visions and Realities of Party Government* (F.G. Castles and R. Wildenmann, eds, 1986) and *Party Governments: European and American Experiences* (R.S. Katz, ed., 1987) published by De Gruyter (Berlin) as part of the European University Institute Series.

2.  F. Lehner and K. Schubert, 'Party Government and the Political Control of Public Policy', *EJPR*, (1984), vol. 12, 131–46, p. 134.

3.  A. Mintzel and H. Schmitt (1981) 'How to investigate the future of party government' (unpublished), quoted in R.S. Katz, 'Party Government: A Rationalistic Conception', F.G. Castles and R. Wildenmann, eds, *op.cit.* (1986), p. 42.

4.  R.S. Katz, 'Party Government: A Rationalistic Conception', in F.G. Castles and R. Wildenmann, eds, *Visions and Realities of Party Government* (1986), Berlin: De Gruyter, pp. 42 and foll.

5.  *ibid.*, p. 43.

6.  *ibid.*, p. 44.

7. See J. Blondel, 'Ministerial careers and the nature of parliamentary government: the cases of Austria and Belgium', *Eur. J. of Pol. Res.* vol. 16, (1) (1988), pp. 51–71. P. Flora and A. Heidenheimer, eds, *The Development of the Welfare state in Europe and America* (1981), New York: Transaction Books. A. King, 'Executives', in F.I. Greenstein and N.W. Polsby, eds, *Handbook of Political Science*, Vol. 5 (1975), Reading, Mass.: Addison-Wesley, pp. 173–256.

8. See K. Strom, 'Minority Governments in Parliamentary Democracies', *Comp. Pol. Stud.* vol. 17 (2) (1984), pp. 199–228. See also K. Strom, *Minority Government and Majority Rule* (1990), Cambridge: Cambridge U.P.

9. On this problem, see among others, R.L. Peterson *et al.*, 'Government Formation and Policy Formulation', *Res Publica*, vol 25, (1983), pp. 49–82.

10. See in particular K. Strom, 'Deferred Gratification and Minority Governments in Scandinavia', *Legislative Studies Quarterly*, (11), 4, November 1986, pp. 583–605.

11. For a summary of these controversies, see my *Political Leadership* (1986), London and Los Angeles: Sage, *passim*.

12. The particular strength of new leaders was stressed by V. Bunce, *Do New Leaders Make a Difference?* (1981), Princeton, N.J.: Princeton University Press.

13. See K. Strom, *op. cit.* vol. 17 (2) (1984), pp. 211.

# 2. Britain: A Textbook Case of Government-Supporting Party Relationship

## J. Blondel

### INTRODUCTION

The study of the relationship between government and supporting party(ies) in Britain is among the simplest and indeed probably *the* simplest which can be found in Western Europe. In parliamentary terms at least, Britain has been a two-party or near two-party system throughout the second half of the twentieth century. The attempts by the Liberals (later Liberal Democrats) and by the Social Democratic Party to break the two-party parliamentary 'stranglehold' have been basically unsuccessful, except to a limited extent in two relatively short periods, both of which occurred in the 1970s. At the February 1974 General Election, no party had an overall majority: Labour had most seats and formed a minority government, the first to be set up in Britain since 1929. After a few months, the prime minister, Harold Wilson, dissolved the Commons and obtained a (small) overall majority; that overall majority was wiped out three years later as a result of by-election defeats, both to the Liberals and to nationalist parties in Scotland and Wales. The government then entered into a pact with the Liberal Party, the first such arrangement to take place in Britain since the early part of the century: this pact stipulated that the prime minister (then James Callaghan) would discuss proposed legislation with the Liberal leader and indeed that consultations would take place periodically between them. This pact lasted about two years, after which, under pressure from the rank-and-file of the party, the Liberal leader denounced it. The Callaghan government survived for a few more months and was eventually defeated on a vote of confidence, also the first such event to have occurred in Britain for decades. The prime minister then dissolved the Chamber; the Conservative party was returned under Mrs Thatcher in May 1979 and the long period of Tory rule began.

The analysis of government-supporting parties in Britain which is conducted here covers the period 1974–90, that is to say from the return of Labour to power to the resignation of Mrs Thatcher. The first five years (1974–9) constitute the third period of Labour in office since the end of World War II, under the premiership of Wilson (for the second time) between 1974 and 1976 and of Callaghan between 1976 and 1979. As was pointed out earlier, this period consists of first, the minority Wilson government (Feb.–Oct. 1974), second, the majority Wilson government (Oct. 1974–Mar. 1976), and third, the Callaghan government (1976–9), first of a majority then of a minority character. The last eleven years of the period correspond to the successive Thatcher governments, all of a majority character, indeed supported by a massive majority between 1983 and 1987; these governments were often reshuffled and were basically reconstructed after the elections of 1983 and 1987.

The British governments of the period considered, indeed of the whole post World War II period, are thus all of the single party type; they are even of a single party majority type, except for part of 1974 and from 1977 to 1979. The challenge launched by the Liberals had indeed the converse effect to the one which had been sought in that it reinforced the dominance of the Conservative party during the 1980s and made single-party majority government even stronger than it had been previously; as a matter of fact, it took two general elections (1987 and 1992) for the Labour party to return to a position in which it could begin to be a credible alternative to the Conservatives. The long period of Conservative dominance can thus be directly linked to the relative success at the polls of Liberals and Social Democrats, this success being in turn attributable, in a Downsian manner, to the 'extreme' policies and postures of a substantial segment of the Labour rank-and-file, a point to which we shall return in the section on policies of this chapter. Thus the electoral system, combined with the markedly geographical character of the areas of strength of the two main parties (broadly the South for the Conservatives, the North of England, Scotland and Wales for Labour) contrived to render inoperative the Liberal and Social Democratic challenge.

This chapter is therefore devoted almost exclusively to the relationship between the Labour government and the Labour party (between 1974 and 1979), on the one hand, and between the Conservative government and the Conservative party (between 1979 and 1990), on the other. The pact linking the Labour government (and especially the prime minister) and the Liberal leadership had a very limited and almost exclusively negative effect on policy-making; it had no effect at all on appointments and almost none, as far could be ascertained, on patronage.

## APPOINTMENTS

As is well-known, the prime minister plays a key part in the British political system and specifically in the structure and composition of the government.

The point has been established by all students of British politics; it has indeed been established for both major parties, even if one can denote some differences between Conservative and Labour in this respect.

The role of the prime minister is enhanced by the fact that he or she is in practice always the leader of the party in power. There have been some exceptions in the past, often because the prime minister was chosen by the monarch before being appointed leader: this was possible in the Conservative party before 1965 as there was no clear mechanism to appoint the leader, but can no longer occur since a procedure involving Members of Parliament was adopted in that year. The fact that the prime minister is also the leader of the 'supporting party' or, more accurately, of the party which forms the government, means that the question of the relative power of government and party with respect to appointments is somewhat difficult to disentangle and, at the limit, cannot be entirely determined. The situation is particularly difficult to define in the Conservative party where the leader has more appointment powers, as we shall see. Thus it is to an extent arbitrary to speak of 'autonomy' or of 'dependence' in the context of the prime ministers; there are even difficulties in using these concepts with respect to ministers.

Within this general framework, the situation is none the less somewhat easier to describe with respect to appointments in the cabinet than it is with respect to appointments in the party.

**Cabinet appointments**

First, the leader is elected in effect by the parliamentary party in the Conservative case (though Tory peers have some formal ratification role), while all sections of the party participate in the election of the Labour leader since the 1980s: trade unions, constituency representatives, and socialist societies thus play a part alongside the parliamentary party in the process. To this extent, there is a substantial apparent 'dependence' of both leaders, and in particular of the Labour leader, on the party at large; but, in most cases, the leader is elected before (often a long time before) the party comes to power. The leader then subsequently becomes automatically prime minister when the party obtains a majority of seats at the general election.

Second, a somewhat peculiar situation, which is neither one of dependence nor one of complete autonomy, exists with respect to cabinet appointments, with few differences between the two main parties. In both the Conservative and Labour cases, first, the prime minister can exercise considerable discretion with respect to the appointment of ministers with the very important reservation that these ministers must in practice be drawn from within the parliamentary party and that some attention must be paid to a variety of sub-groups in the party (geographical, gender, and even ideological). However, the prime minister is not formally constrained to choose the ministers from among any elected body *within* the parliamentary party, for instance from the 'parliamentary committee' elected every year; it is only that, in practice, both Labour and Conservative prime ministers tend to appoint to the cabinet, understandably, colleagues who had been in their Shadow Cabinet on coming to office after a period of opposition, although they can and often do change the posts which these occupied and indeed appoint some ministers from outside this group. As the Conservative Shadow Cabinet is entirely appointed by the Leader of the Party, this means that Conservative prime ministers are only bound by decisions which they made themselves previously. In the Labour case, the Shadow Cabinet is composed in part, though only in part, of members of the parliamentary committee elected by the whole parliamentary party: to this extent, Labour prime ministers operate under some constraints, but these are not in practice appreciably more severe than those under which Conservative prime ministers operate: most of those elected to the Labour 'parliamentary committee' are the 'friends' of the leader.

As time passes, the picture changes a little with reshuffles taking place. These are frequent in Britain (typically once a year); they are also occasions for prime ministers to display a substantial freedom of manoeuvre, though they tend to draw new ministers from among the members of the rest of the government and have to draw them from within the parliamentary parties.

Appointments to the cabinet are therefore of two types. When a party is returned to office after a period in opposition, there is, so to speak, a 'lateral transfer' of what was hitherto the leadership of the parliamentary party to the cabinet. The situation resembles that of an orchestra which moves from one (smaller) auditorium to a larger one, the conductor being able to make some changes in the process. This 'lateral move' suggests that appointments to the government are not made autonomously; but one cannot speak of 'dependence' either, since the leadership of the party effectively disappears from the party as such.

In the subsequent phases, as the prime minister can exercise more choice, the selection of ministers becomes a more autonomous act on the part, if not of the cabinet, at least of the prime minister, although choices have still to be made from within the parliamentary party. Admittedly, the process by which the prime minister acquires more autonomy over appointments has tended to be more visible and complete in the Conservative than in the Labour case; but this is probably because Conservative prime ministers have had more time to acquire and exercise their authority: the Conservatives had two spells of government of thirteen years or more, while the Labour party never was in power more than six years consecutively. This process of acquiring greater autonomy is not without risks, however: there have been serious consequences for the Conservative prime ministers (Macmillan in 1962, Thatcher, over the years) who used too readily their power to sack and replace ministers.

## Party appointments

While appointments to the cabinet in Britain are therefore based, in both parties, first on 'lateral transfer' and, second, on autonomy, appointments to the party leadership differ significantly among the two parties. Three elements have to be distinguished, the parliamentary party, the 'representative' party in the country, and the party 'secretariat', generally known as 'Headquarters' or as 'Central Office' in the Conservative party. In the Labour party, all three are independent from the government, appointments to party headquarters being controlled by the 'representative' party in the country; in the Conservative party, the first two of these three elements are also independent from the government, but appointments to party headquarters are controlled by the prime minister, this control being exercised by the prime minister by virtue of the fact that he or she is leader of the party.

With respect to the parliamentary party, the situation is identical in the two parties: when they are in power, Conservative backbenchers and Labour backbenchers elect a committee independently from the government. Indeed, there is scarcely any interchange of personnel between these backbench committees and the government. During the period under consideration (1974–90), no member of the cabinet subsequently became a member of the parliamentary committee of either party; no move towards the cabinet took place either, though a small number of members of the parliamentary committee did become junior ministers in the Conservative government.

The situation is broadly similar in the two parties in the context of the leadership of the 'representative' party in the country, though this independence manifests itself in a different manner in the two parties. The Conservative 'National Union' is officially and to a very large extent really a body distinct from the parliamentary machine of the Conservative party. It must be regarded as being, in a sense, an association of the 'friends' of the Conservative party in parliament: it is therefore logical that it should be independent. Moreover, the power structure of the National Union is pyramidal: members of the top leadership tend to be selected because they hold a position of office at a lower level in the Union; hence the part played by leaders of areas (regions which include a substantial number of constituencies) in the top leadership of the party: some importance is also given to leaders of functional bodies, such as the Women's organisation. The turnover is also rather rapid: chairmen and vice-chairmen are usually appointed for one or at most a few years, vice-chairmen typically replacing the chairmen. These leaders of the National Union tend therefore to be members of the local or regional Conservative establishment: there are few national politicians among them, except to an extent among those who are 'Presidents': but the position of President is more honorific than substantial and it is held for one year only.

Independence between the party in the country and the cabinet is also achieved in the Labour case, but for different reasons and in a conflictual manner. The Conservative leadership is content to leave the National Union alone, so to speak; the Labour leadership, on the contrary, always wanted, perhaps because of the established view that the party in the country represents the rank-and-file, to exercise influence on the decisions of the National Executive, of its sub-committees, and of the Annual Conference. When in government the Labour leadership did therefore endeavour to obtain the support of at least the majority of the National Executive and of the Conference votes.

As the Executive Committee and the General Purposes Committee of the National Union, the National Executive of the Labour Party is a 'confederal body': it includes representatives of trade unions, of socialist societies, of constituencies, of women, together with two representatives of the parliamentary party (the Leader and the Deputy Leader). The representatives of trade unions are elected by arrangements among groups of unions: the leadership of the Labour party has little say, even informally, on the selection of these representatives, although, by and large, that section of the National Executive has tended to be supportive of Labour governments. Contests are on the contrary the norm in the other sections. Constituency representatives and women representatives are elected by ballot, quite independently from the government: in the case of women representatives, all sections of the party have a vote and trade unions have therefore the biggest say by far; in the case of constituency representatives, only the constituency delegates have a vote. Since the 1950s, the majority of constituency representatives have been drawn from the Left of the Party and have tended to be against the government when Labour is in power. In 1974, for instance, there were only two government supporters out of seven constituency representatives, while one of the others was Tony Benn who, though he was in the cabinet, was in continuous opposition to the majority of that body; there was only one supporter of the government among the five women's representatives. The 1945–51 Labour cabinet had been able to exercise successful pressure on the nominations and appointments to the National Executive, not just among constituency representatives, but in all the sections: the desire may have still existed in the 1960s and 1970s, but the ability was not there and the majority of the National Executive of the Labour Party can therefore be said to have been fully independent from the cabinet, although a minority did represent the views of the cabinet and although the cabinet could, by exercising pressure, obtain votes in its favour at least in a substantial number of specific policy cases.

Thus both parties are autonomous, in terms of appointments, with respect to the leadership of the parliamentary parties and of the party in the country; there is a major difference between them in relation to appointments to party headquarters, on the other hand. The Labour headquarters are subordinated to the National Executive and its sub-committees: appointments are controlled by the National Executive. In the Conservative case, the 'Party' *stricto sensu* is entirely in the hands of the leader and is no way responsible to the National Union. Appointments to headquarters and in particular the apppointment of the Party Chairman are controlled by the Leader of the Party, and, therefore, by the prime minister (but not by the cabinet as such) when the Conservative party is in power.

This difference has a direct effect on who can draft and issue policy documents. In the Labour party the National Executive has this authority, although manifestos are in practice prepared by a joint body including both cabinet and National Executive representatives. In the Conservative party, these documents are drafted by headquarters on behalf of the Chairman or of the Leader of the Party. As a result, while no document can be issued in the Conservative party with which the Leader of the Party disagrees, this can and indeed does occur in the Labour party. While the Labour government may have to fight to obtain the documents it wishes to obtain, oppponents to the leadership in the Conservative party would have to fight in order to see to it that their views come out in print as official Conservative documents. This major distinction has a substantial effect on the power relationships between party and government in the Conservative and Labour parties.

The Conservative party is thus only in part autonomous from the government: its parliamentary and 'representative' wings are autonomous, but this autonomy will be effective in terms of policy outputs only after battles have been fought successfully at the level of Central Office; conversely, the Labour party is fully autonomous and Labour cabinets can achieve what they desire only by exercising pressure in order to ensure that Party Headquarters publish documents with which they do not disagree.

These characteristics of the two main parties have not appreciably changed in the course of the second half of the twentieth century. Thus, in Britain, appointments to the cabinet take place first by 'transfer' from the top of the parliamentary party and, second, by a gradual process of increased autonomy. Appointments to top party positions are autonomous, except for the important fact that, in the Conservative party, Central Office is the machine of the Leader, appointments being made at his or her discretion.


## POLICIES

Whether the government can or cannot exercise full control on party pronouncements and in particular on the content of the election manifesto, the government has a power which parties do not possess, namely that of being able to implement policies or on the contrary to refuse to implement policies. Parties are thus always constrained to exercise pressure from outside in order to achieve their goals.

The process by which policies develop is long and tortuous; much of this activity occurs outside the parties and outside the government. Yet, even if we concentrate on the relationship between the cabinet and the party or parties supporting the government, there is, there too, a long and tortuous process. Given the main points at which ideas for policies can emerge in large parties such as the British parties, it is obviously impossible to determine with precision the path which each idea has taken before being adopted and implemented by the government; but it would be equally wrong to concentrate on formal moments in the development of these ideas and in particular to consider exclusively the manifesto or the party programme. The fact that a proposal is in the manifesto is no indication of its origin; policy development does indeed take place both before and after the manifesto has been adopted and issued.

The only way to analyse concretely who, of the government or of the party, is responsible for policy development is to examine interaction processes in the context of specific policies. In the British case, eight policies were thus selected, four for the Labour party and four for the Conservative party. They cover different fields of government; they have been regarded as critical both by the cabinet and the rank-and-file of the party concerned. They give therefore a broad idea of the extent to which government and supporting party take account of each other in practice.

The four Labour cases relate to industrial policy development (specifically the question of 'planning agreements'), to industrial relations (the question of the appointment of workers' representatives to company boards), to economic policy (the question of wage restraint), and to Europe (the question of the 'renegotiation' of British entry and subsequent stay of Britain in the EEC). The four Conservative cases relate to industrial relations (the curbing of the powers of trade unions), to economic matters (denationalisations and privatisations), to local government finance (the abolition of the rates and the eventual setting up of the Community Charge, more commonly known as 'poll tax'), and to Europe (the renegotiation of the Common Agricultural Policy and of the budgetary contribution of Britain to the EEC). In all cases, the analysis relates to a substantial length of time in order to make it possible to discover fully how the interaction between government and party took place, even if this means covering more than one parliament and, especially in the case of some Conservative policies, including a substantial number of Acts of Parliament.

The two main 'actors' in both parties are the government and the party at large; the parliamentary parties occupy an intermediate position in both cases. They were not responsible for the initiation of any of these policies; they were involved at subsequent stages and then played a part, but in practice a somewhat limited one. In the Labour case, the fact that the parliamentary majority was small or even non-existent led to greater compactness: parliament constituted a key element inasmuch as the Liberal party might cease to support the government on a given issue; indeed, the fact that the Liberal party would not support the government on a matter was used as an argument to postpone or bury some proposals. On the Conservative side, the euphoria of victory in 1979 first tamed the parliamentary party, but discontent then set in; however, the surge in popularity of Mrs Thatcher as a result of the Falklands war led to the huge victory of the party (in seats) in 1983: conflict between the government and the backbenchers was reduced as a result.

On the other hand, and in both parties, albeit more in the Labour party, the formal structure of the party at large has always made it easy, especially by comparison with many Continental parties, for debates over governmental policy to take place and for strong pressure to be exercised on the cabinet. The reason why this is the case is that both parties (indeed the Liberals as well) hold an Annual Conference, in the early autumn, lasting about a week, at which the main issues of the time are debated. Admittedly, the Conference has always been regarded as a much tougher test for Labour governments than its equivalent for Conservative governments. Moreover, in view of what was pointed out earlier about appointments and the position of party headquarters, the National Executive of the Labour party is markedly more intent to control the cabinet than corresponding bodies in the National Union.

Yet the greatest difference between the two parties is perhaps more at the level of tone and attitudes than of results. Not enough distinction is typically made between *climate* and *outcomes*. The Annual Conference of the Labour party is more often an occasion for frustrated 'extremists' to vent their discontent than it is a place for truly anti-cabinet resolutions to be passed, although this does occur. Conversely, while the climate of the Conservative

Conference is one of a rally to which one goes to display one's loyalty to the Party, not only are criticisms voiced but repeated pressure can achieve some policy changes.[1]

## Policy initiation

The relatively greater role of the Labour Conference than of the Conservative Conference seems ostensibly to receive empirical support from the fact that only one of the four policies examined here was initiated by the party at large (the policy on local government finance); however, in two other cases, those of privatisation and even more of trade union reform, there was agreement between Conference and cabinet, as had been earlier the case between the party at large and the Shadow Cabinet: these policies cannot therefore be regarded as being of the cabinet alone: cabinet and party were strongly united. As a matter of fact, on trade union reform, party demands were more sanguine, at least for a few years from 1979, than the measures which the government was prepared to take at the time. Thus only one policy, that of the reform of the Common Agricultural Policy and of the budgetary contributions to the EEC, can be said to have been fully government-initiated.

On the Labour side, two of the four policies were clearly of party origin: the National Executive and its sub-committees wanted planning agreements and they wanted workers' representatives on company boards. On the other hand, the policy of 'renegotiation' of the EEC was a compromise which the party had reluctantly adopted under leadership pressure, while the policy of wage restraint originated from the leadership and was passively supported by the rank-and-file.

Thus while Labour policies originated ostensibly rather more in the Labour party at large than Conservative policies in the Conservative National Union, the difference is not as large as might have been expected. There are marked similarities between the two parties, moreover. In both cases, distinctions can be made among fields, social matters coming more frequently from the party at large and economic and foreign policies coming more often from the government leadership, although one must not exaggerate the contrast. More importantly, also in both parties, the leadership (to become the cabinet) proved to be at least as important as an initiator as the party at large: the sharing of initiation is therefore a characteristic feature of party-government relationships in Britain.

## Policy development

It is of course impossible to describe in detail here the complex evolution which nearly all the policies selected followed over the years. One can, however, discover broad patterns in the toing and froing of ideas between government and party, both in the country and in parliament; one can also examine what the final outcome was and thus determine who won, if there was a conflict or, alternatively, whether an amicable arrangement was found.

### Labour policies

In the Labour case, all four policies gave rise to substantial, indeed major conflict; all four policies also led to a victory of the government, though these victories may be regarded as having been temporary since, in three of the cases, what would have happened had Labour won in 1979 was quite unclear; moreover, the Labour defeat of 1979 may be attributed in part to the worry which many electors had about the policies which the Labour party would have pursued had it won.

The nature of the 'victory' of the Labour cabinet over the rank-and-file differs markedly between the policies. First, in two cases, the government won in the sense that it succeeded in blocking party initiatives: neither the proposal to introduce planning agreements nor that to introduce some representation of workers on company boards was implemented, though, for a year or so in the first case and for about three years in the second, the government did appear to at least pursue these ideas. In the case of the planning agreements proposal, it was clear very quickly that the cabinet (and especially its leader, Harold Wilson) wanted to limit drastically the effect of the policy, for instance by making the agreements voluntary rather than compulsory; the shifting of Tony Benn from industry to energy in 1975 did mean that very little, if anything, would henceforth be achieved on this front. On the policy of workers' representation on boards, on the other hand, the cabinet appeared more serious in wanting to give a concrete content to what was a relatively vague manifesto proposal. A committee was set up to look into the matter: this reported favourably; the cabinet seemed to want to go ahead, except for the fact that, having by then lost its overall majority, it had become clear that the policy could simply not be enacted by parliament any longer, at least unless the provisions were markedly watered down.

The reaction of the party to these delays and to the increasing realisation that little, if anything, would be done, was, somewhat surprisingly, one of passive acceptance. At the beginning, in 1975 in particular, the Party Conference strongly pressed for the implementation of these policies and especially for planning agreements, which were Tony Benn's key project.[2] Subsequently, the temperature seemed to diminish, perhaps because many activists became convinced that nothing 'radical' would emerge from that Labour government: there was the (clearly unwarranted) expectation that a new Labour government would implement a radical programme. All the hope seemed placed in the future, the present being perhaps more bearable as a result.[3]

The Labour government thus succeeded in blocking the two policies initiated by the party which are analysed here. Meanwhile, the government did succeed in implementing the other two policies which are examined and which it had initiated and initiated to a large extent against the party at large and even to some extent against the parliamentary party.

In the case of the EEC, the government clearly won the day against the party. The 'renegotiation' had been limited in scope; the party at large complained that little gain had been made. The new accord was indeed rejected by a substantial majority at a special Conference of the Party early in 1975; but the cabinet went ahead with the referendum, which the party had previously agreed would take place. In the event, the cabinet won in both parliament and country, admittedly with the help of the votes of Conservatives and Liberals. Party activists were stunned to discover that two-thirds of those who voted had accepted the EEC: this limited the extent of opposition for a period at least; only as the end of the term of parliament approached did anti-Common Market voices begin again to be heard, though to no practical effect.[4]

The cabinet also won a victory on the 'social contract' and on wage restraint against large sections of the party, but that victory was less complete. There were indeed three phases in the process. At first, the cabinet was subjected to virulent attacks among activists.[5] Later, however, having succeeded in obtaining the support of many trade unions, it managed to reduce inflation and even checked unemployment somewhat: as a result, party opposition became less vocal in the middle period of the parliament. In a third phase, however, attacks started again, while trade unions withdrew their support. Although the government maintained its policy, it only did so by flouting Conference in October 1978 altogether in a context of considerable tension.[6] By then the government no longer had a majority in Parliament; there were soon to be prolonged strikes which destroyed much of the cabinet's credibility. Whether the government truly won the day on the issue is therefore somewhat doubtful. Yet it had been able, not merely to initiate, but to carry out a policy for a number of years and for a while to roll back opposition within the party. To this extent at least, as on European matters, Labour governments must be viewed as having played a key part in policy-making, while the effective part played by the party at large was less significant and indeed rather limited.

*Conservative policies*
Somewhat surprisingly perhaps, the Conservative rank-and-file was able, on the other hand, to achieve at least some results by pressurising the government in the one policy area which it had initiated, the reform of local finance, and

even probably to obtain more radical measures on trade union reform than might otherwise have taken place; meanwhile, with respect to the other two policy fields, the leadership was clearly dominant.

On European matters, the government easily won support in parliament and in the party at large: interest in the 'renegotiation' of EEC arrangements was limited. Indeed, there was to be limited interest later when the Single European Act was discussed and signed, despite the fact that this measure extended significantly the role of the EEC.[7] One has to go beyond the period analysed here to find major divisions in the party over Europe: the Maastricht Treaty was strongly opposed by a significant section of the party; but the battle took place essentially in Parliament, not in the party at large and it is questionable as to whether the battle would have be so fierce had not Mrs Thatcher, by then out of the government, chosen to attack her successor on this issue.

On privatisation, the rank-and-file was generally content to follow the lead of the government. Originally, support was rather passive; indeed, the government itself was cautious during the lifetime of the 1979–83 Parliament, while being clearly the initiator: it paid only little attention to the specific proposals made in the manifesto; it denationalised or privatised both more and less than had been promised.[8] Meanwhile, the party at large was content to accept what the government was doing. Only later, after 1983, when the policy of privatisation proved to be both politically and economically successful was there enthusiasm among the rank-and-file. Policy developments in this field were thus entirely due to governmental action: the party followed and applauded.[9]

Things were somewhat different in the other two policy fields. On the matter of local government finance, pressure was continuously put on the government for the abolition of the rates. The cabinet's response was to refuse: being pressurised at Conference successive ministers explained that no viable alternative could be found. A committee had suggested earlier the introduction of a local income tax, but the idea had pleased no one. The cabinet tried to defuse the issue by stressing its efforts to reduce local expenditure: but this was regarded as insufficient by activists.[10] The government finally did change its mind, ostensibly because of an outcry resulting from changes in the valuation of property in Scotland: it announced the end of the rates and the introduction of a 'Community Charge' (*alias* 'poll tax'). The rank-and-file had therefore won against a very reluctant government embattled for a number of years. Yet, ironically, the new tax quickly proved highly unpopular; it was to wound mortally the Thatcher government and it was subsequently repealed.

The rank-and-file also exercised successful pressure on the cabinet on trade union reform. The first governmental proposals were regarded by many in the Party both in the country and in Parliament as too tame.[11] More radical measures were introduced after the first Secretary for Employment J. (later Lord) Prior, who believed in a cautious approach, was replaced by N. (later Lord) Tebbitt. Mrs Thatcher clearly also supported the radical view which many in the rank-and-file wanted to see adopted. Thus, while the cabinet constantly kept the initiative in the development of policies in the field, it was none the less pushed in the direction of increasingly severe actions against trade unions by substantial sections of the rank-and-file.

The Conservative party at large has therefore had some influence on both the initiation and the development of policies: in one case at least, the government lost control and was probably obliged to agree to a change of policy. However, such a result was obtained only after several years of pressure, during the second Conservative parliament, when the majority (in seats) was huge and Mrs Thatcher's popularity was at its peak. The comparison between Conservative and Labour cannot be wholly satisfactorily conducted on the matter, since Labour never remained in office consecutively for more than six years and effectively beyond the election of one full parliament.

Three points can be made, however, with respect to policy-making. First, the cabinet, whether Labour or Conservative, exercises considerable influence on both policy initiation and policy development. Much of what is in manifestos comes from the government or from the leadership group of the opposition which subsequently becomes the government if the party obtains a majority. Second, views of the rank-and-file which the cabinet opposes can typically be blocked for long periods, even if it seems that, in the end, the government may have to give in. Third, the true difference between the two parties is one of climate and of atmosphere. It is not that the Conservative rank-and-file is entirely lame; it is not that the Labour rank-and-file achieves much: it is that the Labour rank-and-file harasses Labour governments, although the result of such a harassment may well be the demise of Labour from office rather than a change of policy of the Labour government.

## PATRONAGE

Patronage is not very extensive in Britain, although its full extent is not well-known. It seems to be confined essentially to two sectors, the distribution of 'honours' and the membership of Boards of State bodies and of 'quangos'. Honours have been known for generations to be a key instrument by which at least the top echelons of political parties and of party sympathisers were recompensed for services rendered to the 'cause'.[12] The Labour party was originally and still is to an extent reticent since the distribution of honours implies the recognition of inequalities of status and the officialisation of a kind of snobbery. Yet the party had to be realistic on the matter; it has accepted to distribute honours and in particular peerages, especially after life peerages were established in 1963, as the question of party strength in the House of Lords was at stake. Conservatives have never had any reservations on the matter and it is clear that honours are widely distributed to recompense supporters at all levels, whether in parliament, in Central Office, or in the National Union.

Honours are officially decided by the prime minister of the day (who acts also, by agreement, on behalf of the Leader of the Opposition in the case of the main opposition party as well as on behalf of the Liberal party). Although the prime minister is of course not at the origin of the all the decisions taken in his or her own party, a close supervision is maintained, even if proposals naturally come often from various sectors of the party. Overall, the distribution of honours and titles is regarded as a key means of helping to hold the party together. It is a manifest form of patronage, but one which is diffuse rather than directed at a particular issue or policy.

The second type of well-developed form of patronage relates to the appointments of party influentials and party faithfuls to Boards of companies and to quangos. Not all these jobs are distributed on a strict party basis, admittedly, but large numbers are. For instance, the chairmanships of nationalised industries have often been given to well-known party figures, ex-ministers in particular, though this has of course not always been the case. A similar tendency emerged as a result of the privatisation programme: a substantial number of ex-ministers or other prominent members of the Conservative party have been appointed to the Boards of the newly privatised firms. The same has occurred with quangos.

On the other hand, there is no or very little influence of political parties in the recruitment and promotion of civil servants. There are even very few advisers attached to ministers or even prime ministers, although the tendency to appoint such advisers has increased somewhat since the 1960s. There is therefore no significant form of patronage in relation to the machinery of government itself. This is true even in the foreign service where the number of political appointees, for instance among ambassadors, has always been very small.

While patronage relating to honours and to what might be regarded as 'post-political or public career' jobs is relatively well-known or at least not hidden, the extent to which patronage exists in relation to business contracts is appreciably less publicised. Favours of this kind are probably distributed to a limited extent only, but the occasional discovery of scandals suggests that they can occur. The fact that large numbers of firms subsidise the Conservative party is well-known and indeed part of the public record; but it seems that some of this financing is hidden and that indirect mechanisms are used to conceal some donations. Why this should be the case leads to some speculation about purpose, given that there are no legal limitations in Britain to the amounts which can be given to parties (while there are severe restrictions to the expenditure of candidates during election campaigns). It is also well-known that some leaders of large public works firms figure prominently among the donors to the Conservative party. Moreover, gifts are also probably made at the local level: it would be surprising if some advantages were not occasionally asked for in return; there have also been scandals in relation to housing, in part in order to ensure victories in certain electoral districts.

What the extent is of the favours distributed in this way is impossible to say on the basis of the existing evidence. That there is some patronage of this kind seems seems highly probable; indeed, the fact that such activities exist is not new in Britain. It is also highly probable, given the way business distributes its support, that the Conservatives are relatively more involved in such a distribution, although the cash given by business to the Conservatives is primarily designed to help the party to secure a victory at the polls and is not related to what might be regarded as patronage in the strict sense of the word. Meanwhile, the distribution of positions to ex-Labour ministers and other Labour politicians as well as the emergence of occasional scandals at the local level suggest that patronage, however limited, also plays some part in the Labour party.

CONCLUSION

The relation between the government and its supporting party in Britain is thus primarily characterised (1) by a *transfer* of the party leadership to the cabinet when the party regains power, (2) by a *considerable autonomy of the prime minister* in choosing ministers subsequently, (3) by a *predominant influence of the government on policy initiation and development*, and (4) by a *limited amount of patronage* which, at the central government level at least, is closely supervised by the prime minister. There has seemingly been no significant change in this pattern over time, except in terms of cyclical movements during the life of a parliament and during the period when the same party is continuously in power.

There are also few differences between the two main parties, except essentially in two ways. First, the Labour leader does not control Party headquarters: this means that the opposition within the Labour party is freer to publish documents which can be damaging to the Labour government. Second, the tone of the Labour Conference and the atmosphere in the Labour National Executive and in its sub-committees is appreciably more conflictual than in equivalent bodies of the Conservative National Union. Labour has never been in power for sufficiently long periods to make it possible to appreciate whether, in the long run, such a difference in atmosphere affects markedly the power equilibrium between government and supporting party. On the other hand, the fact that Labour has never been in power for long periods has been due in part to the atmosphere prevailing in the party at large: the postures of the National Executive and of Conference may well have contributed to a diffuse feeling among the electorate that a Labour cabinet would not be able in the long run to control these bodies and that power would eventually fall into the hands of an 'extremist' segment of the party.

If one takes together appointments, policy-making, and patronage, the overall conclusion to be drawn is that, in Britain, *there is no or very little compensation*, except perhaps within the field of policy-making. There is no or very little compensation between patronage distribution and policy-making: what patronage there is appears designed to ensure that the faithful are rewarded for their past activities, thereby also indicating to those who are currently faithful that they will be similarly rewarded in the future. There is no compensation either between appointments and policy development.

One might be tempted to analyse the relationship between appointments and policy-making in terms of *reinforcement*: the party might be regarded as sending its 'delegates' to the government in order to ensure that the preferred policies are implemented. Yet a more careful examination of developments shows that this is not the case. Policies are largely selected by the members of the cabinet; the manifesto is in large part the product of the cabinet in that it is written, especially in the Conservative party, at its instigation. Ministers proceed from Parliament, but they acquire such an independent status and authority that they can in no way be described as party 'delegates'. They are not entirely autonomous, to be sure; but they constitute a group apart, the group of the leadership, which, under the strong direction of the prime minister, comes to be at a substantial distance from the party at large and even from the bulk of the parliamentary party.

The cabinet can induce the party to adopt the policies it suggests; whatever amount of patronage exists at the central government level is firmly controlled by the prime minister; ministers are appointed by the prime minister with a considerable degree of autonomy. On the basis of these characteristics, it must be concluded that, in Britain, cabinet-supporting party relationships are relatively *close to the 'government-domination' area* of the 'triangle' of government-supporting party relationships, with a substantial extent of party 'autonomy' prevailing only with respect to appointments.

NOTES

1. On the Labour Conference, see in particular L. Minkin, *The Labour Party Conference* (1980), Manchester: Manchester U.P. On the Conservative Conference, see R.N. Kelly, *Conservative Party Conferences* (1989), Manchester: Manchester U.P. See also J. Ramsden, *The Making of Conservative Party Policy* (1980), London: Longmans.
2. Labour Party Conference Report, 1975, pp. 213 and foll.
3. See for instance, for 1977, Labour Party Conference Report, 1977 pp. 188 and foll.
4. Labour Party Conference Report, 1978, pp. 303–11.
5. Labour Party Conference Report, 1975, pp. 188–205.
6. Labour Party Conference Report, 1978, pp. 214.
7. There was no debate specifically on Europe at the Conservative Conferences of 1987 and 1988.
8. The Conservative Manifesto of 1979 merely said: 'A Conservative government would also try to sell back shares in the recently nationalised aerospace, shipbuilding and National Freight operations' (quoted in D.Butler and D. Kavanagh, *The British General Election of 1979* (1979), London: Macmillan, p. 156. In fact, the 1979–83 government did not denationalise shipbuilding; on the other hand, it denationalised British Airways, Sealink and BR Hotels, none of which was mentioned in the Manifesto.
9. No resolution on the subject of privatisation was discussed in 1980. On the other hand, in 1982, a fiery speech was made by N. Lawson, then Minister of Energy and the 1983 Conservative Manifesto made very strong claims for privatisation.
10. See T. Travers, *The Politics of Local Government Finance* (1986), London: Allen and Unwin, pp. 124: 'Ministers and others had spent some time nurturing grievances about the rates ... Having done so, they were forced to produce a Green Paper which suggested that the problems associated with other taxes were greater than any imagined difficulties with the rates'; and p. 125: (there was) 'little expectation in or outside government that an alternative would or could be found.'
11. As evidenced by Resolutions passed by the Conservative Conference in 1980 and 1982. In 1980, the Resolution stated that (the Conference) 'urges HM Government to continue the review of the privileges afforded to the trade unions ...'; in 1982, the Resolution stated that '(t)his Conference now looks forward to further legislation ...'
12. There was a well-publicised scandal after World War I when it was revealed that Lloyd-George, then prime minister, had sold honours to help his political career.

# 3. France: Party Government at Last?

## Laurence Morel

### INTRODUCTION

France is well-known among other European countries for the weakness of its parties. While the mass-party model was spreading everywhere in the 1950s, the only French party which resembled this model was the Communist party. The Socialist party reorganised by François Mitterrand in 1971 expanded its structure to some extent, but only to the point of becoming 'a small engine under a big bonnet' (Dupin, 1991). In a similar way, the new Gaullist Party led by Chirac had activists but remained, as indicated by its name, Rally for the Republic, a 'rally' around its leader. The Union of Democratic Forces (UDF), finally, is a confederacy of relatively small parties mainly organised around presidential hopefuls.

Moreover, the role and importance of a party depends on whether that party is in the majority or in the opposition. The party of the president, in particular, tends to become rapidly amorphous, while opposition parties, although not able to influence policies, strengthen their organisation and constitute springboards for presidential candidates (Braud, 1988; Thiébault, 1993).

These general impressions about French parties need to be made more precise; the extent to which parties benefit from belonging to and supporting the government must be ascertained. These impressions have also to be assessed in a context in which, against a general and well-publicised trend of party decline in liberal democracies, and in comparison with the past, France came to have relatively organised parties in the 1980s.

As elsewhere in this volume, the analysis of this chapter is based on three types of relationships between parties and governments, those which emerge in the context of appointments, policies, and patronage. Four cabinets are studied, covering a period of ten years (1981–91). The first is the Mauroy cabinet (1981–4) which was supported by a large majority based on the Socialist party (PS) which alone had a majority in parliament; yet the Communist party (PC), the Centre-Left Movement of the Left-radicals (MRG), and the small Extreme-Left United Socialist Party (PSU) were none the less associated to the government. The second cabinet is that of Fabius (1984–6), the Communists having by then left the government. The third is the Chirac cabinet (1986–8), constituted after the 1986 general election was won by the Right; the cabinet was a coalition between a well-organised party, the Gaullist RPR, whose leader was the prime minister, and the much less structured UDF, which was to have only a secondary role in the government. The two years of the Chirac cabinet were the first example in the history of the Fifth Republic of what came to be known as 'cohabitation' between a president of the Republic of the Left and a prime minister of the Right. The fourth cabinet is that of Rocard (1988–91): it was a minority government, following the 1988 election at which the Socialist party obtained a relative majority only; the cabinet included a number of UDF and other Centre politicians as well as members recruited directly from the 'civil society'.

## APPOINTMENTS

The overlap between the membership of the government and the membership of party executives is rather small, as Table 3.1 shows.[1] This is more the case

Table 3.1: *Overlap between government and party executive (1981–91)*

|  | Government members | Party leader in government? | Government members in party executive |
|---|---|---|---|
| **Mauroy and Fabius** | 53 | | |
| PS | 45 | no | 0 |
| PSU | 1 | no | 0 |
| MRG | 2 | no | 0 |
| PCF | 4 | no | 1 (MS*) |
| **Chirac** | 31 | | |
| RPR | 15 | yes (PM) | 1 (PM) |
| UDF–PR | 5 | yes | 5 |
| UDF–CDS | 4 | yes | 2 |
| UDF–PSD | 1 | no | 1 |
| UDF–RAD | 2 | yes | 2 |
| **Rocard** | 39 | | |
| PS | 21 | no | 0 |
| MRG | 2 | no | 1 (MS) |
| UDF–CDS | 2 | no | 0 |
| UDF–PR | 1 | no | 1 |
| UDF–RAD | 2 | no | 0 |

*MS = minister of State
PM = Prime Minister
PR = President of the Republic

of 'mass' parties, such as the PS (whose constitution prohibits the joint holding of government and party posts) or the RPR than of 'cadre' parties such as the UDF. With eleven ministers (ten from the UDF) belonging to their party executive, the Chirac cabinet thus contrasts sharply with the Socialist cabinets. Yet, when informal influence and previous positions are taken into account, the difference is not as large.

There are also substantial variations in the mechanisms of party appointments. Parties of the Left elect their secretariat and their executive; in parties of the Right, the secretariat is appointed by the leader. When the Right was in power between 1986 and 1988, the appointment of the general secretary and of the executive of the RPR and of the UDF secretariat were thus fully government-dependent. Moreover, in the RPR, an undefined number of members of the executive are chosen by the party president. There are also *ex officio* members, as in the executives of the parties which compose the UDF.[2]

Table 3.2: *Origin of government members (1981–91)*

| | Government members | Party leader has entered government? | Government members directly coming from their party executive |
|---|---|---|---|
| **Mauroy and Fabius** | 53 | | |
| PS | 45 | yes (PR*) | 13 |
| PSU | 1 | yes | 1 |
| MRG | 2 | yes | 1 |
| PCF | 4 | no | 1 |
| **Chirac** | 31 | | |
| RPR | 15 | yes (PM) | 7 |
| UDF–PR | 5 | yes | 5 |
| UDF–CDS | 4 | yes | 2 |
| UDF–PSD | 1 | no | 1 |
| UDF–RAD | 2 | yes | 2 |
| **Rocard** | 39 | | |
| PS | 21 | yes (MS) | 12 |
| MRG | 2 | yes | 2 |
| UDF–CDS | 2 | no | 0 |
| UDF–PR | 1 | no | 1 |
| UDF–RAD | 2 | no | 0 |

The practice differs from the rules in many respects. To begin with, the selection of members of the government tends to be made primarily by the president of the Republic and the prime minister, except in cases of 'cohabitation'; only then is the president constrained in the appointment of the prime minister (Mény, 1992:290).[3] Similarly, rule and practice differ with respect to the prime minister's dismissal: formally the prime minister resigns; in practice the president has always been able to force the prime minister to go, as was shown in particular by the brutality of Rocard's removal in June 1991. There has been no similar example in the 'cohabitation' context.

The appointment of ministers does not always follow the constitutional requirements either. In principle the president of the Republic nominates and dismisses ministers on the proposal of the prime minister: this was the case during the 'cohabitation' period, but not in other cases, as the president was directly involved; on the other hand, during the 'cohabitation' period, the influence of the prime minister was markedly restricted as it was effective only with respect to Gaullist ministers: the choice of the UDF ministers was to a large extent the result of negotiations between the prime minister and UDF leaders.

## Appointments in cases of 'fusion' between government and party executive

### Socialist ministers in the Mauroy cabinet

The relationship between the Socialist party and the Mauroy cabinet seems on the surface to be one of autonomy, as socialist ministers did not sit on the Socialist executive. Yet there had been a transfer from that executive to top governmental positions which went to the most prominent members of the socialist executive elected at the 1979 Congress: Mitterrand became president of the Republic, Mauroy prime minister, and Rocard, Chevènement, Defferre, and Mme Questiaux ministers of State.[4] Overall, thirteen members of the executive joined the government in May 1981.[5]

The 1981 governmental elite had thus a strong party background; that elite also formed the real executive after 1981, even if it did not belong formally to the executive. Rocard, Chevènement and Mauroy were the heads of three important sections of the party, while Jospin was the head of what had been the Mitterrand section: the president of the Republic remained indeed until 1986 the party's real leader, with Jospin, appointed first secretary in January 1981, taking his orders from him (Portelli, 1992: 113). Moreover, the national secretariat and the executive both comprised a majority of Mitterrand men, while the president of the Socialist group at the National Assembly, Pierre Joxe, was also close to the president. Indeed, it has been suggested that the composition of the socialist executive was decided by Mitterrand himself between 1981 and 1986 (Avril, 1981; Thiébault, 1993).

Thus not only was the division between party executive and government rather artificial during the Mauroy cabinet, but the independence of party appointments was also more formal than real. Ministerial appointments were decided exclusively by the president, because of his influence over the prime minister. Appointments to the Socialist executive and to the government were thus made by a 'nominator' combining government and party background. The Mauroy cabinet, on the whole, was therefore a case of *fusion* between government and party executive.

### Gaullist ministers in the Chirac cabinet

Another example of fusion is provided by Gaullist ministers in the Chirac cabinet. Chirac, who was the effective government leader during the 'cohabitation' period, also retained the position of party president. Rules and practice thus coincided. With Chirac being the only member of the RPR executive, fusion is analogous to that which obtained in the Socialist party in 1981, the only difference being that the Socialist leadership was oligarchic, while that of the RPR was 'monocratic' (Schonfeld, 1985).[6] The structure of the Chirac cabinet was also more 'monocratic' than that of the Mauroy cabinet, as showed by the appointment of only one minister of State,[7] leaders of the UDF entering the government having been appointed as 'ordinary' ministers: this contrasts with the 1981 situation, when ministers of State were appointed to represent the main political forces supporting the government.

As unchallenged and sole leader of the winning party of the coalition, Chirac can be said to have appointed himself. Once appointed, he decided, in his dual role as government and party leader, the appointment of all the Gaullist ministers.

Within the Gaullist party, Chirac was easily re-elected party president in 1987, being, as usual, the only candidate. In accordance with party rules, most appointments to the executive were decided by him. One of his close followers, Toubon, was appointed general secretary, as Jospin had been appointed by Mitterrand at the head of the Socialist party in 1981. Appointments of both RPR ministers and of members of the party executive during the 'cohabitation' period were thus decided almost exclusively by Chirac, who combined party and government leadership.

### Fusion in the UDF: the Republican party, the Centre of Social Democrats, and the Radical party (1986–8)

Fusion between party and government also characterised three of the four parties which formed the UDF confederation. Most ministers of these parties belonged to their party executive. Moreover, their leaders (Léotard, Méhaignerie, and Rossinot) entered the government. Appointments to the

UDF executive bodies were largely under the influence of their party leaders in the government. As in the case of the RPR, part of these bodies was directly appointed by these leaders and their authority over their party accounted for the other appointments. Léotard was unanimously elected general secretary of the Republican party (PR) in June 1986 and party president in November 1988, while Pierre Méhaignerie became president of the Centre of Social Democrats (CDS) when he was minister in the Chirac government.

The selection of other UDF ministers was more complex. While Chirac forced the UDF leaders to enter the government, as a condition of becoming prime minister himself, both Chirac and Mitterrand played some, admittedly limited, part in the selection of a number of ministers and even in the allocation of portfolios. Thus Mitterrand prevented Léotard and Lecanuet (the president of the UDF) to become respectively ministers of Defence and of Foreign Affairs: non-political appointments were made to these posts. The appointment of other UDF ministers, meanwhile, was the result of negotiations between the prime minister and the UDF party leaders. Chirac had little power to decide who was to be appointed, but he did exercise some influence in the distribution of portfolios: indeed, in spite of numerical equality of positions between RPR and UDF, Gaullists occupied almost all the key posts.

**Appointments in the case of a government-dependent party**

*The Socialist Party under Fabius and Rocard*
Government dependence characterised the Socialist Party during the Fabius and Rocard cabinets; the move from fusion towards government dependence was mainly due to ministers having lost their party roots. Thus Mitterrand reappointed most ministers and these therefore no longer came directly from the party as had been the case in 1981; the same development occurred in practice in 1988. Admittedly, there was, as in 1981, a transfer from the socialist executive to the government: twelve ministers[8] came from the national secretariat or the executive bureau, but most of them had already been ministers in 1981–6; they had spent too little time in opposition to have acquired a party viewpoint again. Although he was by then less of a party man and indeed was no longer the socialist leader, Mitterrand was the true nominator of many ministers, as can be seen by the fact that his men were appointed to the most important ministries (Cabannes, 1989:195).

Meanwhile, the characteristics of appointments to the socialist executive had changed by 1988. It was no longer the case that these were decided by one person: there were a number of leaders, all of whom were influential as a result of their previous participation in the government. Moreover, the fact that Mauroy and Fabius played a part in appointments to socialist executive does not reduce the overwhelmingly government-dependent character of these appointments, as, in both cases, the persons concerned deliberately chose to be in the party only and to wait in the 'wings' rather than to be 'downgraded' to being 'mere' ministers in the Rocard government.

## Autonomy of appointments in both party and government

There was autonomy of appoinments in both party and government in the 1980s in two types of cases. One type is that of parties supporting the government without being needed for the majority to exist: this occurred between 1981 and 1986; the other is that of the minority Rocard cabinet of 1988–91, during which the support of the Left radicals and of members of the UDF was necessary for the government to remain in office.

*Autonomy between government and supporting parties between 1981 and 1986. The role of the PCF (1981–4), of the PSU (1983–6) and of the MRG (1981–6)*
The Communist party was invited to join the government in 1981 and obtained four portfolios. These tended to be filled by second-rank politicians: three out of the four did not belong to the executive and had no great influence in the party; the fourth belonged to the executive, but was close to Marchais, the party's secretary general.[9]

The Communist leadership was thus involved in the choice of ministers; Communist ministers were also maintained in a strict dependence on the party during their tenure of office; they were forced to resign when Marchais decided to end Communist participation in the government in July 1984. Yet ministerial appointments were not party dependent: as Communist support was not needed by the government, the president of the Republic could still autonomously decide to appoint and dismiss ministers from the party, although a deterrent was the ability which the party had to mobilise part of the left-wing electorate.[10]

The president was also autonomous with respect to the Independent Socialist party (PSU), one of whose ministers entered the government in 1983, first as junior minister and then as full minister in the Fabius cabinet. Matters were different in the case of the Movement of the Left Radicals (MRG), which had actively participated in Mitterrand's election. There was no negotiation between the president of the Republic and the MRG; the leader of the party, Crépeau, decided on his own to enter the government and abandon the party leadership.[11]

Conversely, appointments to the executive bodies of these parties were fully autonomous during the Mauroy government. In the case of the Communist party, this was so because the party leader was not in the government and was the true nominator to the party executive. In the case of the other two parties, leaders had to resign their party position on entering the government: they might have kept some influence, but this was not decisive.

*Autonomy between government and supporting parties between 1988 and 1991*[12]

Neither the Movement of the Left Radicals nor the UDF interfered in the appointment of their ministers in the Rocard government. The MRG leader, as in 1981 and as all party leaders which entered the government in the period, decided freely to enter the government. In the case of the other ministers, lack of party discipline accounts for government autonomy. The decision of some members of the UDF to enter the government was taken independently: the executives of the parties forming the UDF neither backed such a decision nor supported the government; but none of the persons concerned held an important position in the party.

## POLICIES

### Initiation

Socialist support for governmental policies was high during the Mauroy cabinet. In 1981–2 the government actively implemented the Socialist platform known as the '110 proposals', priority being given to structural reforms such as nationalisations and decentralisation (Ross, 1985:153–4). Indeed, in July 1981, the president of the Republic specified that there would be full implementation of the programme of nationalisations (proposal 21) and not partial implementation as some members of the government had wanted.

Admittedly, the '110 proposals' were Mitterrand's platform for the presidential election: the party programme was the 'Socialist Project' of 1980; but both texts had been elaborated by the CERES, a left-wing section of the party whose views reflected the prevailing mood in the party at the time (Portelli, 1992:111). Mitterrand's platform had therefore been easily approved in January 1981 by an extraordinary Congress of the Socialist party. The platform was more moderate than the 'Socialist Project' or the 'Common Programme of the Left' agreed with the Communist party in 1972 (Ross, 1985:152; Portelli, 1992:111); but it followed the main socialist line: on nationalisations, for example, the only difference between the 'Common

Programme' and 'Proposal 21' was a slight reduction in the number of firms to be nationalised.

Yet the fact that governmental policies had been elaborated within the party does not mean that the party had a real power of initiation during the period. In a message to parliament, in July 1981, the president of the Republic stated that the government programme was based on the '110 proposals', thus implicitly saying that the powers of initiative of the Socialist parliamentary party would be small (Avril, 1981:117; Charlot, 1983:30–31). Indeed, only six per cent of the laws adopted between 1981 and 1986 were initiated by parliament. The Socialist executive strictly controlled the parliamentarians and that executive was in turn controlled by the president as a result of this body being composed of a majority of his supporters.

The nuclear issue illustrates this point as early as September 1981. Party and parliamentary party were both favourable to a reduction of nuclear energy production, in accordance with the 'Socialist Project'; but this reduction was not mentioned in the '110 proposals'. It was opposed both by the president and by the prime minister. The party secretary's refusal to side with the party was decisive and the request was abandoned. Thus the governmental programme was based on the '110 proposals', not on the 'Socialist Project' (Avril, 1981).

Moreover, by and large, the fact that the government implemented the '110 proposals' was not the result of party pressure. The need to fulfil pledges, to begin with, was politically important in the case of a party which had long been in opposition, had campaigned for radical change, and had a detailed and ambitious platform. Another factor, paradoxically, was the inexperience of ministers, also due to the long period in opposition.[13] Experts who came to be personal aides to ministers were also keen to implement a programme which they had previously drafted.[14]

As the election became more distant and ministers more experienced, governmental action dissociated itself gradually from the '110 proposals'. Indeed, after 1983, the Socialist Party ceased to be able to propose policies. This was in part because many experts entered the government; this was even more because of the U-turn of March 1983, when austerity was introduced and Keynesian demand-stimulating economic policy abandoned. This U-turn was decided by Mitterrand alone, without involvement of the party (July, 1986).[15] From that point in time, the party programme ceased to be the blueprint for governmental action.

The factors accounting for programme implementation in 1981–3 – strong party penetration in the State and an election recently won on the basis of a detailed platform – also obtained in the context of the 1986 Chirac cabinet. This cabinet, as the Mauroy cabinet earlier, undertook, especially in its first six months, a large number of reforms based on the electoral platform. Typical in this context are the privatisation measures. A bill approved by the cabinet in April 1986, three weeks after the formation of the Chirac government, was passed by parliament in July. As Duverger commented in *Le Monde* (10 May 1986): 'Faithfulness to the programme now pushes the Right to make a move which parallels the one made by the Left in 1982 out of the desire to remain faithful to the election progamme. In both cases, ideology dominates.'

As the '110 proposals', the UDF-RPR platform was elaborated by party experts: it was the result of a large programmatic and ideological effort of the party elite, especially of the Gaullist elite, from 1983 onwards. The two policies examined here, both of which were part of the twenty 'central commitments' of the UDF-RPR platform, illustrate this point.

Privatisations were the ideological banner of the Right in 1986. The issue was given special prominence in the general context of the new liberalism personified by Thatcher in Britain and Reagan in America and in the special context of Socialist nationalisations. Yet the move did not mobilise the Right in the same way as nationalisations had mobilised Communist and Socialist parties in 1981, a difference which the Gaullists did not see.

The reform of the nationality code was also an idea of the party elite which was thought likely to mobilise the UDF and RPR rank-and-file by proposing an answer to the problem of immigration. After the failure of the more liberal approach to the problem attempted by the Socialists between 1981 and 1983, the positions of Left and Right on immigration had become similar. Meanwhile, the reform was one of the favourite themes of the Extreme-right: it had figured in the National Front's platform since 1972. To show an interest for the problem seemed to the classical Right a way of limiting the expansion of this dangerous competitor while reactivating differences with the Socialists. Yet to question the ease with which one could become French was in opposition with past attitudes on the Right.

On the surface, the reform of the nationality code can be regarded as an instance of the party being able to force an issue on to the government. The government was lukewarm as there were difficulties with respect to the precise content of the reform (the election platform indicated only an intention to abolish the right to obtain French nationality automatically) and as a law on immigration had caused an upheaval. Thus the proposal would have been blocked in the ministry had not National Front and a number of Gaullist deputies presented a private members' bill. Yet the decisive push did not come from parliament, but rather from parts of Right-wing opinion. Nor did the part played by parliamentarians reflect strong party 'power' in the same way as corresponding measures would have done among parties of the Left.[16] The higher proportion of private members' bills adopted between 1986 and 1988 (18 per cent of the total) does not therefore mean that the party as such had major influence in initiating legislation.

At the 1988 election, Mitterrand's 'Letter to all the French', which was used in both the presidential and parliamentary 1988 election campaigns, was not elaborated in the party and did not specifically reflect its views: it was written by the president of the Republic with the help of a few collaborators. It merely proposed to continue the policies of the Fabius 1984–6 government. It was also too vague to provide a basis for a governmental programme: it could indeed easily be transgressed, as was to be the case with the refusal by Mitterrand to allow either new nationalisations or new privatisations, although in pratice Rocard was forced in 1991 to undertake partial privatisations in order to finance the State deficit.

If the 'Letter' did not constitute a programme, this was in part because the Socialist party had not used its two years in opposition to draw the lessons of its experience in government. As a result, although the party was very critical towards the Rocard government of 1988–91, it was not able to produce many counter-proposals. Moreover, the cabinet was a minority government and it needed the support of at least part of the Centre. There were thus only a few examples of Socialist party pressure, a successful one being a private members' bill to reform rent legislation; the bill was successful because the government was divided on the issue, because Mitterrand unofficially supported the idea and because the backbencher was able to make a truly expert case.

Differences between cabinets with respect to parliamentary initiatives stem therefore largely from the presence or absence of a detailed and recent party programme and/or from the ability of the party to supply the government with policies worked out in detail by experts. Thus a party having ended a long period in opposition is more likely to have a strong programmatic bent than a party which has spent many years in government or, as the Socialist party in 1988, only a few years in opposition. A large parliamentary support, as was the case during the Mauroy and Fabius governments, also increases the chances of implementation of the party programme.

## Elaboration

Consultation was permanent between government and party during the 1981–6 parliament; this consultation took the form of 'Tuesday morning breakfasts' and 'Wednesday noon lunches', attended by the president of the Republic, the prime minister, and the party's main leaders. This was a new development in the Fifth Republic which resulted from the coming to power for the first time of a highly structured party. It even seemed in 1981 that the party might replace the prime minister in his traditional role of leader of the majority (Portelli, 1985:238): thus, in cases of conflict between government and parliament, the prime minister had to negotiate with the Socialist executive; individual ministers had direct contacts with party organs and the president of the Republic had such a special relationship with the Socialist party that this relationship was described as a 'parallel Constitution' (Avril, 1981). The prime minister was often by-passed, as over private schools (Dupin, 1991:98).

The primary aim of this regular consultation process was to ensure both parliamentary and popular support for the government. This last aim was fulfilled less successfully after 1983 (Ross, 1985). Yet the loyal support of the party was never in question: this was in part because, as was noted earlier, the strength of the party's organisation was more apparent than real. It was typically sufficient to convince a small group of national leaders to obtain the following of the rest of the party; moreover, party leaders could all the more easily be convinced that, as was also mentioned, top leaders had gone to the government, while the executive was overwhelmingly composed of Mitterrand's men.

On the whole, the party's influence in the early stages of legislation was limited; this was made easier as legislative details were rarely mentioned in Mitterrand's platform, either because there were divisions of opinion or because these details had not been anticipated. On nationalisations, for instance, the party had to accept the reform to be 'softened' in a number of ways, as on the fate of subsidiaries owned by the nationalised firms, on the minimum level of deposits required for a bank to be nationalised, on the nationalisation of cooperative banks, and on the postponement of the nationalisation of banks not quoted on the Stock Exchange. Not surprisingly, some sections of the party felt frustrated by the final result.[17]

The ability of the party to amend policies was larger during the parliamentary stage, because of the poor drafting and technical inadequacies of many bills, especially in the early years. Yet the changes which took place did not alter the basic structure of government bills, while the parliamentary party had to abandon many amendments because they would have amended those bills too drastically (Avril, 1981:119).

The first public conflicts occurred in September 1981 over private radios and nuclear energy; but the true test was at the end of 1982 on the matter of granting amnesty to those who had been involved in a failed 'putsch' during the Algerian conflict in the early 1960s.[18] The party secretary, Jospin, had previously always been able to elaborate compromises between government and party: on the amnesty issue, however, he opposed publicly the government, as did Joxe, the chairman of the parliamentary party. It should be noted that the issue was not mentioned in the '110 proposals' or in the government programme; it came to the fore only as a result of a speech made by Mitterrand to a group of French Algerians, the substance of it being subsequently repeated in a letter to an association representing them.

The bill immediately led to a sharp conflict between government and party. An amendment, excluding all army officers from the amnesty, was adopted in the National Assembly by 266 Socialist MPs out of 286; in the Senate, however, where the old generation of Socialists was less intransigent, a draft close to the government's text was adopted. When the bill returned to the National Assembly, the prime minister made it a question of confidence and the government won.

During the Chirac government of 1986–8, regular meetings between ministers and party leaders also took place; a formal liaison committee was set up. As in 1981–6, party influence remained limited to the early stages of the drafting of bills. Yet the debate on nationality shows that this influence was stronger when the government had no clear ideas about what to do. In that case, as was pointed out earlier, pressure first came from the National Front and Gaullist parliamentary parties. The text was then modified somewhat in a liberal direction under Centrist influence; subsequently, when the Council of State expressed reservations about aspects of the draft, further changes were asked for by Centre deputies. The government bill only emerged at that point, but it was not proceeded further in view of substantial opposition to the bill and because of the death of a young Arab victim of police violence during a demonstration on a different topic, namely university reform.

The privatisation bill was drafted by the government without any party or parliamentary interference. It was almost completely rewritten by a special committee and on the floor of the House. To speed up the process, the government made the matter a question of confidence. As in 1981–6, the influence of parliament was due to ministerial inexperience and to overhasty drafting. Nor should this influence be overestimated: the policy content of amendments was limited; often the government introduced them itself and rarely did it accept important changes, except insofar as amendments were close to the text of the electoral platform. On issues such as university reform, taxes, social security, terrorism, criminality, or New Caledonia, which were the main bones of contention between the government and its supporters in parliament, the government remained firm. The UDF group, by far the most critical of cabinet action, often complained about the systematic use of procedures to defeat opposition or to speed up the process. The 'blocked vote', which prevents in effect parliamentarians from having any oportunity to modify a bill under discussion, was used 68 times in two years (as against only ten times between 1981 and 1986); the confidence motion was used eight times (as against eleven times in five years between 1981 and 1986).[19] The discipline of the majority was also due to the specific conditions of the 'cohabitation' with a Socialist president and to the narrowness of that majority. The main effect of the forthcoming presidential election was also to unify the coalition in view of the second ballot of this election.

Although the consultation process between the Socialist party and the government was again highly developed between 1988 and 1991, it was less formalised than between 1981 and 1986: there were no regular place of, time of, and participants at the meetings. This situation reflected in part the greater autonomy of the Socialist party both from the president of the Republic, who did not have on the new secretary Mauroy the influence he had once on Jospin, and from the prime minister, who was not very popular in the party; but the situation was more due to the party's extreme fragmentation (Dupin, 1991).

Moreover, the 'Rocard method', ostensibly based on intense negotiations, consisted more in explaining government action to the party, especially the concessions made to the Centre, than in consultation. Rarely did the government take into account party views in the preparation of bills. This was clear in connection with the budget, although it was always examined at length by the Socialist executive. In September 1989, for example, party reactions to the draft budget were highly critical: much conciliation was undertaken in the prime minister's office; but the party obtained little. In particular, the reduction of company tax, which was regarded by the party as a provocation, was none the less maintained; similarly, the government paid little attention to party views when drafting the bill on the minimum income (named '*Revenu Minimum d'Insertion*' or RMI), ostensibly because there was urgency, since, immediately after Mitterrand's re-election in May 1988, it was announced that the matter would be treated as having absolute priority. The aim was to pass the bill before the end of 1988, so that people could receive money before the winter; but it was also likely that the government wanted to implement quickly this aspect of the programme as the parliamentary election was to be held in June. Yet the bill was a complex measure including 52 clauses.

As in 1981–6, conflicts between the Socialist parliamentary party and the Rocard government were referred to the executive of the party, whose advice was binding, according to the statutes (article 52). Sanctions could be imposed if voting discipline was breached or amendments presented without permission of the executive (article 17). Yet the executive had no means to force the government to follow its decisions and, in practice, it scarcely did so during the Rocard government; concessions were generally over details and they were made in exchange for more important concessions by the party (Payen, 1992). Indeed these concessions were sometimes taken away, as happened with the reform of local taxes, which had been forced on the government by the party, but whose application was postponed. Often the promise to study a proposal made by the party or to evaluate the effects of a policy that it did not want (as on the law on temporary employment) was sufficient to obtain party support. In the case of the minimum income bill, the party apparently succeeded to obtain more during the parliamentary than during the pre-parliamentary stage: the minimum income was guaranteed and in effect became a right; on the other hand, the parliamentary party was unable to obtain any change on the issue of the distribution of the income by local authorities: the State remained the distributor.

From Mauroy to Fabius and to Rocard, the Socialist party's capacity to modify legislation regularly decreased. The contrary might have been expected in 1988: there was hostility to Rocard among large sections of the party; there was greater distance between the president and the party; indeed Mitterrand's known antagonism to Rocard could have made of the president a precious ally of the party, as he indeed proved to be occasionally, but not always. On the other hand, the minority status of the government undoubtedly played a key part in restricting the margin of manoeuvre of the supporting party: confidence was sought by the government 39 times between 1988 and 1993, more than during the first 30 years of the Fifth Republic. Moreover, as under Fabius, the experience acquired by ministers and the decline of party organisations after many years in power helped the government to retain the upper hand.

## PATRONAGE

### Appointments

Appointments concerned mainly three kinds of posts, those for which there was discretion and whose beneficiaries are nominated by decree, those of top administrators, and those in the personal staff of ministers, known as *ministerial cabinets*. In theory, party penetration in public posts can be a means of securing the implementation of policies or of enabling the minister to be surrounded by a team he is used to working with: yet it is often only an opportunity to share power, prestige, facilities, including that of raising funds (Suleiman, 1991:58; Mény, 1992:312). Appointments and resources are thus closely connected.

About one thousand posts belong to the patronage category (Quermonne, 1991:237). Some turnover already took place in 1974, with the election of Giscard d'Estaing; the Socialists operated a much greater 'purge' in 1981: the Right responded in kind in 1986, which gave the impression that a French spoils system was born. Rocard was keen to limit such changes to a minimum in 1988, but the trend towards a politisation of the administration seemed to be maintained (Quermonne, 1991:234–7). It is widely believed that there are two circles in French administration, the inner circle, which participates in power, and the outer circle, which waits to return to power and is increasingly in the private sector (Mény, 1992:110–3).

What was new under the Socialists, however, was the fact that most people appointed were party members: they included 59 per cent of those who belonged to *ministerial cabinets* in 1981 as against only 9 per cent who declared themselves apolitical: this was a sharp break from previous practice (Dagnaud & Mehl, 1987). Moreover, a large proportion of the posts went to party officials, two methods being used. One consisted in opening the competitive examination to the National School of Administration (ENA) to locally elected and trade union officials, as well as to active members of associations, a reform which was abolished by the Right in 1986 but reintroduced in 1988 in a less 'militant' form to people with eight years of professional experience or in local government; as a matter of fact, the reform had limited numerical significance and the appointment of party officials at the top of the civil service was mainly achieved by increasing the number of posts, including at the top of nationalised industries,[20] while the decentralisation measures increased the number of posts in local government.[21] The second method consisted of increasing the number of top civil service posts ('*Grands Corps*' posts) open to external recruitment; the Right, on its return in 1986, passed a bill to check this increase, but there was no return to the previous situation. Meanwhile, the number of members of *ministerial cabinets* doubled between 1980 and 1982; but the increase was not stopped by the Chirac government and it continued under Rocard: it was checked only subsequently. The role of these *cabinets* also increased (Quermonne, 1991:238).

Ministerial cabinets are perhaps the best illustration of what has been called the 'PS-State' in 1981 and the 'RPR-State' in 1986 (Dagnaud and Mehl,1988:16). 28 per cent of the members of the cabinets between 1981 and 1986 were party activists and 15 per cent were party officials, a clear contrast with the situation under previous governments: studies of the composition of ministerial cabinets before 1981 do not mention any party officials at all among them (Dagnaud & Mehl, 1987:140–1).[22] The phenomenon was repeated in 1986 in almost identical proportions: 29 per cent and 14 per cent of the members of the ministerial cabinets were then respectively party activists and party officials.[23] As under the Mauroy and Fabius cabinets, these party men and women occupied the most sensitive functions in the staff of ministers.

The reasons for such a party penetration in *ministerial cabinets* are numerous. In 1981, after 23 years in opposition, the Left was naturally worried about what its links would be with the top civil service; naturally, too, the Right was anxious to replace these people in 1986. The politisation of the administration is thus a side and perverse effect of alternance. Yet a more important reason is constituted by the type of party organisation characterising the Socialist party in 1981. The high number of activists, their important contribution to the victory, their capacity to mobilise the electorate, all these were elements which could not go without some counterparts. The professionalisation of the RPR organisation, largely due to the need to compete with the PS but also resulting from five years in opposition, provides a similar explanation in 1986. By 1988, on the other hand, the Socialist party had ceased to play an important part and the party officials who had invaded the *ministerial cabinets* in 1981–6 had become professionals. The direct transfer from party to government was therefore more limited, or, as with ministers, it was a transfer of people without a pure party background (Dagnaud & Mehl, 1989).

**Party finance**

Money is the second type of patronage resource distributed by governments to supporting parties. Some of these parties benefited markedly from the secret funds legally placed at the disposition of the government: this was the case of the UDF when it was set up. Yet the main source of funding, in the 1980s, was private firms, who exchanged money for contracts or licences. One clear example relates to the authorisation to build supermarkets. Every request must be referred to a commission of twenty composed of nine small shopkeepers, nine locally elected officials, and two consumer representatives. This system has led to various kinds of trade-offs: often the authorisation is granted in exchange for the building of public infrastructures; but, more secretly, a political cost has to be paid. Deals also take place at national level, the minister of Trade being competent on appeal from the decisions of the commission. Thus, in the period studied, there were strange correlations between the high number of authorisations produced and the proximity of an election (Mény, 1992:264–5).

The ways used by parties to obtain private funding are diverse. Traditionally, Right-wing parties received regular donations directly; the Left, on the other hand, not having such good relations with business, invented a system of forced contributions in connection with the granting of contracts or licences: this was done by means of fictitious bills paid in exchange for imaginary work to go-between companies which then transferred the money to the party. The best documented case has been that of '*URBA-Conseil*', a real estate consultancy company set up in 1972, which was for years the main supplier of funds of the Socialist party.

Associations also constituted an important source of income or of services in kind for parties in the 1980s, largely as associations are subjected to almost no control. Socialists were linked to the largest scandal, that of the '*Carrefour du Développement*' set up by the minister of Cooperation in 1983, to 'sensitise public opinion to the economic, scientific, cultural and technical problems of developing countries'. This body spent 81 million francs ($ 16 million) in three years for a variety of shady deals, not all of which have been elucidated. Yet associations have been most prolific at the local level. They often serve as screens for the promotion of the mayor or his party, the mayor himself often being the president. In some large cities, the network of associations financed by the municipality is complex and involves very large funds, the most corrupt case being undoubtedly the 'Systeme Médecin', established by a previous mayor of Nice.

The Left may seem to have benefited more than the Right from these patronage resources: in reality, it may merely have been caught more often. The Socialist party, imitating the Communists, centralised its funding network, as the URBA affair showed. This was part of an effort to enable parties to control directly the resources drawn from their participation in the government, key actors having often been individual politicians in the past, particularly at the local level:[24] what was gained in efficiency was lost in security, however. Meanwhile, the Left was in power for most of the period studied here. Moreover, in order to end the scandals of Socialist party finance, the Rocard government sent a bill to parliament which granted an amnesty to corrupt practices having taken place before 1990: investigations which could have involved the Right, especially those dating back from the 1970s, cannot come to light. Indeed, various affairs which took place in the 1990s show that it is probably illusory to establish distinctions between Right and Left.

The likelihood is that all supporting parties, at local or national level, have benefited substantially from their participation in the government. The sums involved greatly increased in the 1980s. As in relation to appointments, this increase coincided with the strengthening of the party organisations, while it is also the consequence of rising campaign costs. Yet other factors played a part: one is alternance, which led not only to the politisation of the administration, but also to a kind of tacit agreement regarding corruption: 'All political sides partake of the system and hence no strict controls have been put into place' (Suleiman:1991:59). According to Mény, another reason is the decline of ethics which characterised the 1980s; this author further suggests that control mechanisms have been weak, in large part, paradoxically, because of the very excess of detailed controls, political actors being in effect constrained to acting in part illegally.[25] The ineffectiveness of the controls results from the extreme concentration of power in the French political system. At the national level, this concentration is increased by the politisation of the administration; at the local level, it is helped by the fact that the same person can hold several elected offices, and in particular be a mayor and an MP. Opposition is also generally weak in local assemblies. Thus the local level appears to be the ideal place for corruption to develop.[26] Decentralisation, by increasing the powers and resources of local authorities without establishing effective control mechanisms at the same time, is thus in part a cause of the apparent increase of corruption in the 1980s. In such a context, the legislation introduced since 1990 to secure transparence, limitations, and public contributions in the field of party finance is likely to have only a limited effect.[27]

## CONCLUSION

The relation between government and supporting parties in France can thus be characterised in the following way:

(1) There is a large transfer of party leaders to the government. Ministers and members of party executives are appointed by people who have a mixed party-government background, but who become increasingly, over time, purely governmental.
(2) There is a predominant influence of the government in policy initiation and elaboration, and
(3) There is a substantial amount of patronage, mainly with respect to appointments and to finance.

The limited influence of parties over policies is mainly the result of the weakness of parties, both in terms of their structure and in terms of their links with the society. Party weakness is further increased by the move of leaders to the government and the appointment of party staff to *ministerial cabinets*. Supporting parties become empty shells and their leaders-cum-ministers direct them from the government, through regular meetings and by having loyal nominees on executives. This move to the government is not so much a cause but a direct consequence of party weakness: few in France think in terms of a party career; politicians want to be in or near the government. This was shown for instance by Jospin's decision in 1988 to cease being Socialist secretary in order to become a minister. There is a kind of vicious circle: people leave parties because they are not centres of power but parties are not centres of power because people use them merely as springboards to the government.

Party influence over policy is subject to time variations, however. Time spent in government appears to be the main reason for the difference between the power of the supporting parties during the Mauroy and Chirac cabinets, on the one hand, and the Fabius and Rocard cabinets, on the other. Time changes the effect of the massive entry of party men and women to key national positions. At the beginning there is a manifest tendency to implement the party programme; gradually, politicians become increasingly likely to put forward their own policies. If a party returns to power after only a short time in opposition, as was the case in 1988, there is not even any party dominance at all: in 1988, most of the Socialists appointed to the government were experienced ex-ministers and the Socialist party presented no real programme at the two elections of that year. Similarly, in May 1995, the RPR leaders, who had returned to power in 1993, claimed to have a project, not a programme.

Party weakness must not be exaggerated, however. The fact that governing parties obtain many appointments and much patronage shows that these parties do have some bargaining power. This is indeed the great political innovation in France in the 1980s. The access of better organised parties to power, largely as a result of more political competition and of alternance, did not entirely transform the influence of governing parties in policy-making, but the share of appointments and patronage became larger. These developments may be the clearest manifestations of the increase of the role of parties in the country. Thus the role of parties in France, even if it is still limited, is more similar today to the role played by supporting parties in other Western European countries: there is unquestionably in this respect a major change in the nature of French politics.

NOTES

1. The government includes the president of the Republic, the prime minister, all ministers, and delegate ministers. Typically party executives include the national leader, the 'secretariat', the 'bureau' or 'political committee', and the heads of parliamentary parties. These bodies have generally about forty members.

2. French parties differ in the way they elect their leaders. This is done by the congress in Right-wing parties and in the MRG and by a more restricted body in Left-wing parties.
3. According to Duverger (1990:261), the president of the Republic had a margin of manoeuvre in 1986; in our opinion, a different choice would have caused a rebellion in parliament and would also have been unpopular.
4. Ministers of State have formally no more power than ordinary ministers. The title was sometimes used in the past as a consolation prize.
5. Including Mitterrand, Mauroy, Fabius, Rocard, Chevènement, Joxe.
6. The monocratic style of the RPR was strongly criticised after two years in government and the Chirac government can be said to have changed this style, with different 'sections' having emerged.
7. Balladur.
8. Including Rocard, Jospin, Chevènement.
9. Fitermann.
10. Or change their position.
11. The other MRG minister, Maurice Faure, participated only one month in the government in 1981.
12. The Social Democratic Party (PSD) also enters into this category.
13. Only Jobert had been minister in the Fifth Republic; Mitterrand and two others had been ministers in the Fourth.
14. 42 per cent of the members of *ministerial cabinets* between 1981 and 1986 were PS experts (Dagnaud & Mehl, 1988: 60–1).
15. S. July, *Les années Mitterrand*, (1986), Paris: Grasset.
16. According to Toubon, general secretary of the RPR at the time, the order of importance was government-parliamentary group-party at large (interview with the author).
17. Eight of the nine industrial firms scheduled for nationalisation were indeed nationalised as well as the main branches of the armament and steel industries; the main omission was insurance.
18. Partial rehabilitation was made possible in 1974, after an amnesty for crimes had been passed in 1968.
19. For a comparison between the use of such mechanisms in 1981–6 and 1986–8 see Bigaud (1988) and Mendel-Riche (1986).
20. The number of ministers also increased in 1981.
21. Privatisations achieved by the Right also created opportunities to favour political friends.
22. Figures from Dagnaud & Mehl, 1987.
23. Among whom 42 per cent came from the RPR and 33 per cent from the UDF.
24. Mény states that this constitutes a substantial difference from other European countries (Mény, 1992: 315).
25. The alternative is the blocking of the system. See M. Crozier, *The Stalled Society* (1973), New York, N.Y.: Viking Press.
26. According to Mény, local governments contribute more than the national government to party finance, a matter which is difficult to evaluate. Others insist that the biggest funds are at the national level (Suleiman, 1991:60).
27. The law of January 1995 prohibits donations from corporations.

# 4. Sweden: From Stability to Instability?

## O. Ruin

### INTRODUCTION

Sweden has long been known for its political stability. The same five-party system existed for 70 years, that is to say from the moment parliamentary government became fully established after the First World War up to the late 1980s. One of the five parties, the Social Democrats, had alone or together with other parties governed the country from 1932 to 1976 without interruption except for 100 days in the summer of 1936. Both in terms of the parties and in terms of the structure of government, this stability has declined, however.

The five parties that traditionally constituted the Swedish party system were the Social Democratic party, the Conservative party, the Liberal party, The Agrarian party (later called the Centre party) and the Communist party (later called the the Left party). Conservatives, Liberals and the Centre party have usually been called the 'bourgeois' parties whereas the Social Democratic and Left parties are known as 'non-bourgeois' or socialist. This division into bourgeois and socialist parties respectively introduced a kind of two-party distinction into Swedish political life although the country had a multiparty system. Since the 1970s in particular the bourgeois parties have grown closer while the traditional antagonism between Social Democrats and Communists diminished.

This long-standing party stability did not exclude substantial electoral movements. These were particularly large among the bourgeois parties, as each of the three of them dominated successively that side of Swedish politics. The Conservatives' moments of strength were at the beginning and at the end of the period, in the 1920s and in the 1980s; the Liberals won a striking victory at the 1948 election with the charismatic leadership of Bertil Ohlin, a future Nobel prize winner in economics, and the party continued through most of the 1950s to draw more than 20 per cent of the votes; the Centre party had its moment of triumph in the 1970s when it obtained 25 per cent of the votes cast. Meanwhile, the Social Democratic party did not experience similar fluctuations in electoral strength from the beginning of the 1930s up to the end of 1980s: they never obtained less than 40 per cent of the votes or appreciably more than 50 per cent (which they did obtain on five occasions, this being in itself a remarkable achievement in a multiparty system). In the 1990s, however, the Social Democratic party fell to 37 per cent of the votes cast at the 1991 election but it recovered three years later, in 1994, when it obtained a more traditional 45 per cent (Larsson, 1994).

The stability of the Swedish five-party system ended in the mid-1980s and the hitherto solid structure began to fragment. To be represented in the Riksdag, parties must receive at least 4 per cent of the votes overall or 12 per cent in one constituency; if they meet one or the other of these conditions, they are guaranteed full proportionality of seats in relation to votes. At the 1988 general election one new party, the Greens, succeeded in crossing the threshold; it failed three years later but returned to the Riksdag in 1994. In 1991, when the Greens were defeated, two other new parties entered parliament, the Christian Democratic party, which had been founded more than twenty years earlier, and New Democracy, an organisation of a populist character which had been very recently set up: this last party was eliminated at the subsequent election three years later, but the Christian Democrats succeeded in remaining in the Riksdag by a very narrow margin. This coming and going of new parties has been interpreted as a sign of a worldwide phenomenon, namely that party loyalties have weakened and voter mobility has increased, as a result of a decline in the trust in parties and politicians.

Whether stable or not, Swedish political parties have a strong and elaborate organisation (with the exception of some of the new parties): this organisation reflects the political organisation of the state. At the top level, which corresponds to the Riksdag and to the national government, parties have congresses, executive committees and national leaders. Congresses tend to be convened every three years in most parties, one of their central tasks being to elect the leader and the executive committee, a body which varies in size and importance from party to party. Further down, parties have regional and local bodies corresponding to the regional and local structure of the Swedish state. A great number of committees, concerned with different policy areas are also linked to the parties. Finally, in parallel to the party organisations proper, there are nationwide organisations catering for one segment of the party membership only, for example women or the young. The parties represented in the Riksdag also naturally have their own parliamentary structure (Bäck/Möller, 1990).

Governments have also been extremely stable up to the mid-1970s: this stability has been epitomised by the long reign of the Social Democrats, the existing constitutional order having been conducive to this stability. Until 1970, the Riksdag was composed of two chambers which had in principle the same powers and equal importance; the term of the indirectly elected First

Chamber was eight years and that of the directly elected Second Chamber four years. The electoral system was proportional, but it favoured the Social Democrats as they were the largest party. When the Social Democratic party was in coalition with other parties, the cabinet could count on solid majorities in both of the chambers of the legislature: during the Second World War a four-party national government was set up and both before and after the war the Social Democrats formed a two-party coalition government with the Centre party for some years. During most of the four decades of their continuous rule, however, the Social Democrats formed single-party governments, usually with a majority in the indirectly elected First Chamber but not in the directly elected Second Chamber, where the small Communist party tended to support them.

The governmental situation became more unstable after 1970. As a result of the constitutional changes of that year the previous bicameral Riksdag was replaced by a unicameral legislature, the terms of eight and four years were replaced by a shortened term of three years only, and the proportional election system favouring larger parties was replaced by a strictly proportional system (Ruin, 1988). In parallel to these constitutional changes, as was already mentioned above, the party structure and the relations between these parties also underwent changes.

From the late 1960s to the mid-1990s, Sweden had ten different governments, which are identified here by their leaders and by the parties on which they were based. These are:

| Government | Tenure dates | Months | Party/parties |
|---|---|---|---|
| Palme I | 69–76 | 84 | Social Democrats |
| Fälldin I | 76–78 | 24 | Con/Lib/Cent |
| Ullsten | 78–79 | 12 | Liberals |
| Fälldin II | 79–81 | 18 | Con/Lib/Cent |
| Fälldin III | 81–82 | 17 | Lib/Cent |
| Palme II | 82–86 | 41 | Social Democrats |
| Carlsson I | 86–90 | 48 | Social Democrats |
| Carlsson II | 90–91 | 18 | Social Democrats |
| Bildt | 91–94 | 36 | Con/Lib/Cent/Ch D |
| Carlsson III | 94– | | Social Democrats |

As can be seen from the table above, the Social Democrats remained in power after the constitutional changes of 1970 for six more years until the general election of 1976. Their parliamentary position was already weakened after the 1970 election compared to what it had been during the previous decades; when they returned to power in 1982 they had continuously to form minority governments. Meanwhile, the bourgeois parties did succeed in forming a majority cabinet in 1976. This government lasted for two years only, however, and a second attempt in the autumn of 1979 to form a new majority government lasted one and a half years only. The other three 'bourgeois' governments of the period have all been of a minority kind. Two of them – the Liberal government of 1978–9 and the Liberal-Centre party government of 1981–2 – had a marked minority character whereas the four-party 'bourgeois' cabinet formed in 1991 commanded a substantially larger share of the seats in Parliament although it was also of a minority type. At the 1994 election the Social Democrats were returned to power, though once again not on a majority basis: they obtained 162 seats out of 349.

Whatever the parliamentary situation the relationships between supporting parties and government have always been close in Sweden. This closeness is shown most clearly by the fact that those who serve as party leaders are also expected to be members of the cabinet, when their party is in power. The tradition was established in the 1920s and has been maintained ever since with one exception only, namely when the chairman of the Centre party resigned from the four-party bourgeois government in June 1994 because of a disagreement over the question of building a bridge across the Sound to Denmark, while the other Centre party cabinet members remained in office. The raison d'être for this fusion of party leadership and cabinet membership has been to facilitate smooth relations between government and supporting parties or, to put it differently, to reduce the risk of tensions developing between the two sides. The burden may be heavy, however, particularly for the person who serves as prime minister while remaining party leader.

## APPOINTMENTS

Closeness and interdependence between supporting parties and governments can be seen with respect to appointments. Appointments have typically been made on the basis of party consideration with respect both to the cabinet and to a number of positions in the ministries. There is in Sweden a rather original division between relatively small ministries and central agencies independent of these ministries: currently the total staff of all 12 ministries is about 2500; but there are over 300 central agencies with a significantly greater number of employees than the ministries (Ruin, 1990:2).

Since the 1990s at least, Swedish cabinets have had twenty members or more. The four-party bourgeois cabinet of 1991 had 21 members and the 1994 Social Democratic cabinet 22. Cabinet members are not by law or parliamentary practice required also to be members of Parliament: however, a clear majority of them have had such a double membership since World War I: in the 1991–4 four-party bourgeois cabinet only six of the 21 ministers did not have a seat in the Riksdag; on the other hand, in the 1994 Social Democratic cabinet, as many as 11 were, rather surprisingly, recruited from outside the legislature. However, irrespective of Riksdag membership, most cabinet members have tended to belong to the governmental party or the parties: only one of the 21 members of the 1991 bourgeois cabinet was not a registered member of any of the four governmental parties although she was said to have 'bourgeois' sympathies in general; it had also previously been the case that one or two cabinet members, often with high judicial competence, did not have a clear party affiliation. All the members of the 1994 Social Democratic cabinet were members of the party at the time they took office; but two of them had earlier in their careers been members of other parties: this is something exceptional in Swedish parliamentary life.

The prime minister, who is the leader of the cabinet, is formally appointed by the Riksdag: the nomination is presented to the Chamber after negotiations with the different party leaders by the Speaker and not, as in other parliamentary countries, by the King, who is the head of state, as the King is not involved at all in the process. Formally the newly appointed premier has in his turn the right to appoint other members of the cabinet, but this right varies in practice depending on whether the government is of a single-party or coalition character. In one-party governments the process of selection is clearly in the hands of the prime minister: in modern times almost all governments of this type have been Social Democratic and all the three successive leaders of the party in the post-war era – Tage Erlander, Olof Palme and Ingvar Carlsson – have chosen themselves their cabinet colleagues. While a few influentials have been asked for advice, no party organ has been involved. Being the leader of a team, the prime minister must be allowed – this is often emphasised – to make up the team himself. In coalition governments the situation is necessarily different: the prime minister still retains the formal right to appoint members of the cabinet, but this appointing power is effectively limited to choosing the cabinet members of his own party although he might have views about the members proposed by the other parties. Indeed, the prime minister has sometimes explicitly objected to candidates put forward by one of the other coalition parties, but the norm has been for ministers of the other bourgeois parties to be selected by their respective party leaders, although the type of advice sought by the leader varies from party to party.

Cabinet ministers are not only recruited by a party leader; they tend also to have held key positions in their party. There are differences between the bourgeois parties and the Social Democrats in this respect, however.

In the three-party bourgeois government formed in the autumn of 1976 exactly half of the members of the cabinet – 10 out of 20 – were at the same time members of the executive committees of their respective parties. This group included the three party leaders and a number of top members of the parties concerned; in the 1991 bourgeois government the proportion of ministers with strong party ties was even higher as the need was felt in each of the four parties of the coalition to include top party influentials: thus 15 of the 21 ministers were also members of the executive committees of their parties.

In the Social Democratic cabinet of 1982 led by Olof Palme 12 of the 19 ministers were also members of the (rather large) executive committee of the party. This committee had a nucleus of eight persons – 'verkställande utskottet'. Five of these were members of the cabinet, as well as two of their alternates. Roughly the same ratio of top influentials to more ordinary members can be found in the 1986 cabinet led by Ingvar Carlsson after the assassination of Olof Palme. In the 1994 Carlsson cabinet half the ministers were members or alternates of the 'nucleus' of the Social Democratic executive committee.

Whether cabinets are bourgeois or Social Democratic, the close ties between government and supporting parties extends to the personnel in the ministries. The formation of a new government in Sweden usually means a shift of around 150 office holders at the level immediately below the cabinet proper. Those who come and go with the change of government are regarded as political appointments, the most important among them being the under-secretaries of state ('statssekreterare') who are in effect assistant ministers; while in the past some of them were chosen without regard to their political views, this is no longer the case. There are also experts, coordinating agents, and press secretaries, all of whom tend to belong to the same party as the minister whom they are serving or at least share his or her political values. They might indeed have themselves held high elected positions in their party or have been employed at party headquarters.

Below the level of the ministries (which, as was pointed out, are very small), appointments are occasionally made bearing in mind, not just general qualifications but the political background. We shall return to this point in the context of patronage.

## POLICY-MAKING

The relationships between governments and supporting parties with respect to policy-making are influenced by a number of factors, of which three need special mention. First, the structure of the policy-making process has long been divided into sharply distinct phases in most policy areas. Usually, after an issue has been placed on the agenda, a commission is appointed to investigate the issue and make recommendations. Such commissions are appointed by the cabinet or, for less important matters, by an agency of the central government. Between 200 and 300 cabinet appointed commissions have been set up every year during the post-World War II period. They include, in varying combinations, not only politicians who speak for their respective parties, but also representatives of different interests, civil servants, and independent experts. The parties represented are both the opposition and the government parties. The general aim of these commissions, as is emphasised by their composition, is to obtain consensus on the recommendations given, a goal which is not always reached. The commission system has been regarded as an important instrument in the build-up of the spirit of compromise which has traditionally characterised Swedish politics (Johansson, 1992).

After the commission has presented its report the government submits it to a number of public authorities and to relevant interest groups for their comments (the 'remiss' system). Thereafter the government might be ready to draft a bill on the basis of the commission report and the reactions to the report. The Riksdag reaches its decision after a committee deliberation. Finally, detailed regulations are drafted within the civil service to implement the law.

This process is obviously time-consuming: it was not uncommon earlier for six to eight years to elapse between the referral of a problem to a commission and the drafting of new regulations in the problem area, which then had to be implemented. This process has been progressively speeded up, however (Ruin, 1982). Less time tends to be devoted to the different stages in the process; more than before, important policy decisions are taken directly by cabinet and Riksdag. There are a number of reasons for this change: elections to the Riksdag take place every three years instead of four since 1970; the impact of international politics on Sweden is greater and more rapid, the reaction has therefore to be more rapid; the mass media also create a climate of nervousness as they investigate matters and tend to jump from one problem area to another. Thus the classic stability of Swedish politics has been weakened.

Second, the relationship between governments and supporting parties is also in turn influenced by the relationships within the supporting parties, for instance between the parliamentary party and other groups. By and large, the tensions which have been found to exist in other parliamentary systems between the party in parliament and the rest of the party have not developed in Sweden. There is a degree of overlap between the executive committee of the parliamentary party and the executive committee of the party as a whole.

On average, since the 1970s, somewhat more than 40 per cent of the members of the parliamentary party executive have been members of the party executive (Isberg & Johansson, 1993). There has not been either much debate in Sweden about the respective part to be played by the parliamentary party and the other key organs of the party. Yet the Social Democrats did stress more than the bourgeois parties stressed the superior status of the party at large and of its key representative bodies, that is to say primarily the congress. The fact that the Social Democrats held this view but that the party also was in power without interruption for more than forty years has meant that meetings of the congress every four years (every three years after 1970) were important political events which had consequences for the relationship between the government and the supporting party.

Tage Erlander, who served simultaneously as Social Democratic leader and as prime minister for the record time of 23 years (1946–69), was a master in cajoling the party congress in order to keep party and cabinet in tune with each other. For him, the cabinet and the parliamentary party (of which he was also chairman) had to follow the decisions of the Congress. Yet he also succeeded in seeing to it that the decisions of congress remained general rather than detailed, thus leaving the cabinet some room for manoeuvre. He worked both openly and behind the scenes to achieve his aims. He chaired the committee of congress whose task was to consider the various proposals which were raised and then presented the recommendations of the committee on these matters to the congress and defended them. The double goal was to respect the mood of the assembled congress delegates and to keep the ultimate decisions rather vague (Ruin, 1990:1).

Third, the relationship between governments and supporting parties has also been affected by the fact that the parties have increased their production of policy statements, although there are differences in this respect, but not necessarily as a result of parties being in government or in opposition. Increased party activity has taken many forms. There have been more motions presented to party congresses concerning concrete policy areas; there have been more policy statements adopted by congresses; the number of party committees in charge of working out policy programmes for different issue areas has also grown. This development is both an answer to demands for more internal party democracy and a consequence of the increased financing of party activities.

Since the 1970s, the relationship between government and supporting parties has been diverse with respect to policy making. A key distinction is the one between bourgeois coalitions and Social Democratic single-party cabinets. Differences relate both to the formation and the day-to-day running of government. A comparison will be made here between the bourgeois three-party and four-party cabinets, formed in 1976 and 1991 respectively, on the one hand, and the Social Democratic one-party cabinets, formed in 1982 and 1994, on the other (Bergström, 1987).

The formation of these four cabinets took place immediately after general elections; there were also some governmental changes between elections during these two decades but they will not be considered here. In all four cases two and a half weeks elapsed from the moment when the election result was declared and the Thursday when the Riksdag voted for the prime ministerial candidate presented by the Speaker to Parliament two days earlier. During these 18 days discussions were held not only to decide which parties were to form the government and who would be the members of the cabinet but also on the programme of the new government. That programme was presented to the Riksdag by the prime minister the day after his election together with the list of cabinet appointments.

The programmes of the bourgeois coalition governments were, naturally enough, objects of intense negotiations between the parties of these coalitions during the short time available. During the 1976 election campaign each party had campaigned separately for its programme: there had been no common policy platform. Fifteen years later, during the 1991 election campaign, two of the prospective coalition parties, the Conservatives and the Liberals, defended a common programme which had been elaborated in advance; this programme was then the basis on which negotiations took place for two weeks among the four potential coalition partners. The bourgeois party leaders were the key actors in these negotiations, both in 1976 and in 1991; they were also all to become members of the government. To assist them they had both advisers from their own parties and small groups of representatives from all the parties, all of whom were attempting to discover common solutions on the various issues. Issue area after issue area was examined. As the negotiations went on, viewpoints and support were sought from the parliamentary parties as well as from the executive committees of the supporting parties. The degree and intensity of the relationship between party leadership and central party organs varied, the Centre party leadership being in this respect the most active and the most ready to pass on information.

The 1976 negotiations were more difficult and uncertain than those of 1991. In 1976 the bourgeois parties had no experience in forming a coalition government or in working out a common programme, whereas they could profit from such an experience in 1991. Moreover, in 1976, one issue, that of nuclear power, was particularly controversial; it did indeed lead to the break-up of the coalition two years later. In 1976 as in 1991 the aim was to include in the programme both policy questions on which each party of the coalition felt strongly and questions on which the parties had originally disagreed but had been able to find a common ground. The hope was that if a coalition programme was rather specific, including on matters on which there had been disagreement earlier, the task of the government would be facilitated and the risk of deadlocks reduced. The highly detailed wording of the governmental programme even prompted observers to believe, forgetting how unpredictable political life tends to be, that the work of a cabinet, based on a fairly detailed programme, would primarily be one of implementation and not one of repeated negotiations between proponents of different views.

The programmes presented by the two Social Democratic governments which followed the bourgeois coalition governments – the government of Olof Palme in 1982 and of Ingvar Carlsson in 1994 – were not based on bargains as the bourgeois programmes were. They were also on the whole less specific in their wording; nor had they been explicitly approved by the parliamentary party or by the executive committee of the party. They had been drafted, under the supervision of the future prime minister, by a small circle of close assistants. However, most promises and declarations included in these programmes had already been made during the previous election campaigns and in turn been both discussed and approved by the relevant organs of the party before they were made public. One very important decision made by the Palme government immediately after it was set up had naturally not been discussed during the election campaign: this was the devaluation of the Swedish crown by 16 per cent; yet the future minister of finance had prepared the ground by discussing the issue with key party influentials (Bergström, 1987).

The day-to-day running of the government, regardless of the party composition of the cabinet, requires continuous coordination. Ministers tend to move in different directions. The main coordinating actors in the Swedish government, as well as in the governments of other countries, are the prime minister together with the minister of finance. Moreover, in Sweden, coordination is also achieved as a result of the fact that all cabinet members have lunch together every day and that the bills to be presented to parliament are regularly scrutinised by representatives of the different ministries (Larsson, 1986).

In the bourgeois multi-party coalitions, a further mechanism was added to ensure coordination and to counter the fact that, despite the existence of a common governmental programme, the parties tend to move in different directions according to the way in which they rank and evaluate issues. Cabinets then become arenas where views need to be continuously scrutinised and even full-scale negotiations between the parties take place. Arrangements needed to be introduced to facilitate the working of these governments.

In the 1976 three-party government, cabinet members from different parties were often given portfolios in one and the same ministry and thereby expected to scrutinise each other's policies as a matter of course. In the Ministry for Education, for instance, a Liberal was responsible for universities and culture whereas a Conservative was in charge of primary and secondary education. In the 1991 four-party government the arrangement was the converse one: it consisted of letting representatives from one party wholly control a department. In the Ministry of Education both the minister in charge of universities and the minister responible for primary and secondary education were Conservative (culture came to constitute a separate department on this occasion). Similarly, with different fields of competence, two Liberals ran the Ministry of Social Affairs and two members of the Centre party the Ministry of the Environment.

Formal coordination arrangements between the coalition parties were also different in the 1976 and 1991 governments. In 1976, each of the three party leaders – one being the prime minister and the other two being in charge of departments – had a group of advisers whose task was explicitly to examine with similar groups around the two other party leaders whether the policies to be pursued by the cabinet were acceptable to all the coalition parties. In the 1991 four-party coalition, coordination was concentrated in the office of the prime minister, where each of the four parties had a number of representatives whose task was to iron out differences and to supervise cabinet policies from the point of view of the various parties.

Beyond these arrangements, the party leaders constituted a final appeal mechanism within the cabinet if differences between the coalition parties still had to be solved. This group of three in the 1976 government and of four in the 1991 government constituted a kind of inner cabinet. Since they remained leaders of their party after they had entered the cabinet, they were in close contact with key politicians and with opinion prevailing within their respective parties. The way they kept in touch with their party varied but the result was that the job of keeping the cabinet and supporting parties in tune with each other was facilitated.

The two single-party Social Democratic cabinets of the period did not have the same coordination problems as the bourgeois governments. Yet they needed to keep cabinet policies in tune with opinions in the party and to find a common ground when there were conflicting views. The two Social Democratic prime ministers, Olof Palme and Ingvar Carlsson, were both former disciples and assistants of their predecessor Tage Erlander: one lesson given by Erlander was to listen always to the party and to try by all means to keep it intact. Erlander had used a richly developed network of contacts to maintain unity between cabinet and party. Every week, when the Riksdag was in session, he met with the Social Democratic parliamentary party which he also chaired; he had frequent meetings with the party secretary and the party treasurer; he convened the party's executive committee at least once a month; he conferred regularly with the editors of the Social Democratic newspapers; he appeared before a multitude of organisations within the party, local organisations, women's organisations, youth organisations, district party congresses, union congresses etc. This was done as part of an effort both to explain and provide information about governmental policies to party members and to learn about and subsequently transform the wishes of party members into practical policies carried out by the government (Ruin, 1990).

Olof Palme and Ingvar Carlsson continued in principle this bridge-building line of the prime minister-cum-party leader, but such a line was becoming more difficult to follow than at the time of Erlander. Social Democratic congresses developed an appetite for passing resolutions on various political issues and in making these resolutions specific (Pierre, 1986). Because of their acceptance of the doctrine of the superiority of organised party opinion, Palme and Carlsson came to feel somewhat more shackled by these expressions of opinions than Erlander had been. One way of dealing with the problem consisted of increasing the involvement of the executive committee of the party and particularly its nucleus of eight – the highest ranking party bodies between the congresses – in preparing governmental policies. Ingvar Carlsson had been more prepared to obtain the backing of the party before governmental decisions were taken, whereas Palme tended more often to act more independently. The Social Democratic parliamentary party also showed a somewhat greater propensity to be independent vis-à-vis the government than before, in part because it had become accustomed to greater 'freedom' when the party was in opposition and in part because, as many other groups within the Social Democratic party, it did not feel so strongly duty-bound to remain loyal to the party and to the government based on it on all matters (Ruin, 1991).

Moreover, there were limits to Ingvar Carlsson's willingness to seek the explicit backing of the party before important governmental decisions were taken during his first period as prime minister. At least in two instances sudden changes in traditional policies led to discontent among the party rank-and-file although these changes had been approved by the party's inner core. One instance concerned the reform of the high marginal rate of tax in the early 1990s. At fairly short notice a deal was concluded with the Liberal party despite the fact that in a preceding election campaign the Social Democrats strongly had attacked that party for holding views to which they were now ready to subscribe: the deal was attacked by many Social Democrats. The other and even more striking reversal of old policies took place in the autumn of 1990 when the Social Democratic government suddenly, in the shadow of an acute economic crisis and the new foreign policy situation resulting from the fall of the Berlin wall, announced its readiness to apply for membership of the European Community. Social Democrats had for decades argued against such a membership; nor had the new line been explicitly approved by the party Congress which preceded this surprising turnaround. Gradually resistance grew among the rank-and-file against the decision and it persisted even after the subsequent party Congress had adopted a pro-EU stance. In the referendum of November 1994 on the European Union, which finally resolved the issue, almost half the Social Democratic electors appear to have voted against membership.

Tensions between Social Democratic governments and the supporting party with respect to cabinet policies have often involved the Confederation of Trade Unions (LO). This body has always been considered to be a key part of the workers' movement: as a rule, the leader of the LO has had a seat on the core group of the executive committee of the Social Democratic party. Difficulties have arisen over attempts at coordinating cabinet policies with the wishes of LO. In the 1970s, for example, LO decided to press for what was to be known as 'wage earner funds', a proposal regarded as too extreme by many Social Democrats (including Olof Palme) and which was to be a burden for Social Democratic governments until a watered-down proposal was aproved by the Riksdag in 1983 (and repealed when the bourgeois parties came into power in 1991). In the 1980s conflicts arose between the cabinet and LO over economic policies; there was even talk of a 'war of the roses' within the Social Democratic party (Feldt, 1991). The source of this type of conflict is the fact that LO is a trade union acting on behalf of a limited if very large group of people and tends therefore to have a narrower mandate than the government.

Thus the relationship between Swedish governments and supporting parties over policy making have been characterised by a high degree of inter-dependence. A cabinet can neither be wholly dependent on the supporting parties nor be wholly autonomous. On the one hand, it is never the case that the leadership of a party in government stands beside the cabinet and issues directives for the cabinet to implement: there is fusion between party and cabinet leadership when a party is in power. On the other hand, the cabinet cannot take decisions on important political issues without consulting, if time permits, at least key influentials in the supporting parties, although this consultation process does not guarantee that party views will be in tune with the governmental policies pursued.

There are none the less variations around this broad type of relationship. One type of variation concerns the first phase of a cabinet's life. In multi-party governments the formation process is particularly important in terms of policy-making: this is the stage when the supporting parties are directly involved in discussing the programme which will constitute the basis of the cabinet's work. In one-party governments – which, as we saw, are more frequent in Sweden than coalition governments – this phase is far less crucial. Another type of variation in the policy-making process relates to the parties: although all of them emphasise the value of close relations between government and supporting parties, Social Democratic and Centre party ministers appear more inclined than ministers of other parties to involve their party in important decisions. Finally, a third variation in the policy-making process results from the issues themselves: those which are particularly sensitive from the point of view of the party tend naturally to be those in which close contacts are kept with the supporting party before a cabinet decision is taken.


PATRONAGE

Whether there is patronage in Sweden is largely a matter of definition. First, the financing of party activities can be regarded as bordering on patronage. Swedish political parties are supported by the state to a substantial extent: between 75 and 90 per cent of their budgets is publicly financed. Yet this support, which originated in the 1960s, is not dependent on the existence of a special relationship between a particular party and the government, since the money allocated is strictly distributed in relation both to the number of seats in the Riksdag and of votes at the general election. There is no scrutiny of these appropriations: the parties themselves are solely responsible for the use of the money, most of which goes to personnel, housing and election campaigning. In accordance with the principles of openness characterising Swedish public life, the way the funds are used is made public (ESO, 1994). A similar transparency applies also to the salaries of members of parliament, and of ministers: these are indeed determined by public bodies separate both from the parliament and the cabinet.

Another aspect of Swedish politics which borders on the question of patronage stems from the fact that newly-formed governments are regarded as having a responsibility to provide jobs in the public sector to those who held a key position in the outgoing government but do not want to carry on in politics. This practice developed since the 1970s, as there were frequent changes of parliamentary majorities in that period. Those entitled to such a special treatment are former cabinet members and former under-secretaries of state ('statssekreterare'); the types of jobs offered are mostly leadership positions in the public sector such as those of county governor, head of a central board or agency, or ambassador. Positions of this kind are also occasionally offered, even though a change of government has not recently occurred, when a leading politician wishes to move out of active politics. The constitution explicitly states that people are to be appointed to positions in public administration solely on the basis of 'merit and skill', but involvement at a high level in politics is regarded as adding significantly to the skill of a future public servant and has therefore been considered to be constitutionally acceptable. When former politicians are thus recruited to posts in the public sector, the principle is that the favours should be spread fairly evenly among the main parties.

Another aspect of Swedish politics which might also be considered as patronage is constituted by the appointment of former or active politicians to the many boards, councils, and committees of the public sector. Thus the central agencies, which are formally independent of the small ministries, often include laymen on their boards and advisory committees; universities and other institutions of higher learning also have boards which include persons who do not belong to the institution. However, those who are appointed by the government to bodies of this kind are not only politicians: there are also representatives from other walks of life; moreover, the politicians who are appointed do not belong only to the parties supporting the government but also to the opposition parties. Key positions in these elaborate networks – for example chairmanships – are often filled by people from parties supporting the government, however, although other views are also represented. Finally, these appointments to boards, councils, or committees within the public sector are not only rewards for services rendered but must also be seen, from the point of view of the government, as mechanisms of control and as means of obtaining different viewpoints.

Swedish governments, as most governments, pursue from time to time policies which tend to benefit a particular group or locality only: the regional dimension is important in Swedish politics, for instance. Symbolically enough, in the plenary hall of the Riksdag members are not seated according to their party affiliation but according to their residence. Rather frequently representatives from the same area belonging to different parties work together on common regional questions. These might relate to the setting up of a new college, the moving out of a public agency from the capital to the region, or the defence of a regional army regiment threatened with closedown and so on. Although such regional requests may be supported by the government, this type of support probably should not be classified as patronage.

Swedish political life, including the relations between governments and supporting parties, has so far been exempt from corruption. There are few examples from the parliamentary history of the country of politicians found guilty of taking bribes or having benefited financially from political activity. A sense of justice and political decency has prevailed, based on a constitutional tradition which goes back hundreds of years. The decline in trust for parties and politicians mentioned earlier which has developed recently does not seem to be due so much to an increase in improper behaviour of politicians as to the difficulties encountered in delivering what has been promised or in shortcomings in effective communication with the electorate. There is some worry, however, that these rather idyllic characteristics of honesty might come to an end and that the trend towards political corruption visible in other parts of Europe might spread also to Sweden.

## CONCLUSION

The relationship between governments and their supporting parties has been close during the period during which parliamentary government has existed in Sweden. This closeness has above all been epitomised by the fact that leaders of governmental parties supporting the government have been members of the cabinet, either as prime ministers or as heads of important departments. One side has not been superior to the other nor has one enjoyed full autonomy vis-à-vis the other. Some changes have occurred during the past decades, however, but these point to somewhat different conclusions, as each side seems to have gained in relation to the other.

Parties have expanded in a variety of ways. Their personnel has grown, partly as a result of public financing; internal activities have increased, for instance in terms of proposals presented to the party congresses; there has been a greater desire to elaborate specific party programmes for different policy areas. Loyalty toward the government seems also to have been somewhat reduced in the supporting parties: the parliamentary parties, as well as the executive committees of the parties, have displayed a greater tendency than in the past to argue against the cabinet. Moreover, signs of crisis in the party system have also been visible not only in Sweden but also in many other Western countries. Among citizens at the grass roots there seems to be less willingness to engage in regular party work, less interest in all-encompassing party programmes and platforms, more concern for single issues, and less trust in parties and party politicians.

Swedish governments, meanwhile, with some differences, have acquired a somewhat greater autonomy vis-à-vis supporting parties. In terms of appointments, prime ministers have tended to recruit cabinet ministers somewhat less from among parliamentarians, a tendency which was particularly noticeable in the October 1994 Social Democratic government where only half of the ministers were parliamentarians and some of the others had not played a particularly active part in the life of the party. With respect to policies, governments have more than before taken key decisions which, partly because the rhythm of politics has become more rapid, have not been solidly based on the views of members of the supporting parties. Finally there has been somewhat more patronage in that governments have been expected to provide jobs in the public sector to key individuals from previous governments who did not wish to stay in politics.

It is difficult to interpret these changes in the relationship between governments and supporting parties; meanwhile, a wholly new dimension has to be considered, as a result of Sweden's decision to join the European Union from 1995. In the debate preceding that decision the future relationship between parties and governments was discussed. The fear was expressed that governments would be further strengthened as a result, as they might not have enough time in the future to consult their own supporters in policy areas where the final say rests with the European Union and where complex negotiations with other European governments would have to take place. Two points were emphasised in reply during the public debate in this respect. The first was that new institutions would be established to facilitate regular contacts at home between government and parliamentary parties; the second was that the parliamentary parties themselves would be drawn into transnational European networks that would give them perspectives and insights matching those of the cabinet.

Yet, while it is difficult to predict the consequences of the Swedish membership of the European Union on the relationship between parties and government, as well as to determine precisely the nature of the changes in this relationship which previously occurred, the main conclusion does remain: the relationships between the two main sides of Swedish political life, governments and parties, have been and continue to be characterised by a high degree of interdependence.

# 5. Germany: Party Influence or Chancellor Rule?

## Thomas König and Ulrike Liebert

### INTRODUCTION

The distribution of power between government and supporting parties in Germany does not depend only on party characteristics, on the party system, or on cabinet cohesion; it has been also influenced by four further factors. (1) Governments have always been supported by relatively substantial parliamentary majorities (see Table 5.1); (2) parliamentary parties in the *Bundestag* have been characterised by marked party discipline, this party discipline being enhanced by the financial support enjoyed by candidates and by the nomination procedures; (3) there has been a moderate multi-party system with a further tendency – until at least 1980 – towards concentration; (4) finally, parties have come to dominate and control increasingly positions and resources in the public sector and even in many parts of the private sector.

Meanwhile, the dependence of governments on supporting parties has been significantly counterbalanced by three characeristics which have strengthened governmental autonomy or even dominance vis-à-vis their supporting parties – the powers of the prime minister, the nature of coalitions, and the special features of federalism.

Governmental leadership is institutionally anchored in the powers of the chancellor. He alone is elected by parliament and he alone appoints ministers; he can create new portfolios and change existing ones: the number of cabinet ministers thus expanded over the years, as well as that of state secretaries. On the other hand, ministers direct their departments independently and not under the guidance of the chancellor; indeed, although they are not legally empowered to initiate bills as the cabinet is a collegial body with every member having the same voting rights, it is normal practice for each minister to be responsible for the bills which come under the jurisdiction of their department.

All German post-war cabinets have been supported by a majority coalition, normally closely-knit although there have been exceptions, as in 1963, when the FDP left the CDU-led government, or in 1982, when the FDP left the SPD-led government. Between 1949 and 1994 most governments have consisted of three-party coalitions led by the CDU together with the Bavarian

78

Christian Social Union (CSU) and the FDP; the only exceptions have been the early period of the Bonn Republic, when the party system was not yet stabilised, the 1966–9 'Grand coalition' of CDU/CSU and SPD, and the 1969–82 period of SPD-FDP government.

Table 5.1: *Cabinets in the Federal Republic of Germany*

| No. | year | prime minister | supp. parties | parl. support |
|-----|------|----------------|---------------|---------------|
| 1 | 1949 | Adenauer I | CDU/CSU/FDP/DP | 51.7% |
| 2 | 1953 | Adenauer II | CDU/CSU/FDP/ DP/BHE | 68.4% |
| 3 | 1957 | Adenauer III | CDU/CSU/DP | 57.7% |
| 4 | 1961 | Adenauer IV | CDU/CSU/FDP | 61.9% |
| 5 | 1962 | Adenauer V | CDU/CSU/FDP | 61.9% |
| 6 | 1963 | Erhard I | CDU/CSU/FDP | 61.9% |
| 7 | 1965 | Erhard II | CDU/CSU/FDP | 59.3% |
| 8 | 1966 | Kiesinger | CDU/CSU/SPD | 90.1% |
| 9 | 1969 | Brandt I | SPD/FDP | 51.2% |
| 10 | 1972 | Brandt II | SPD/FDP | 54.7% |
| 11 | 1974 | Schmidt I | SPD/FDP | 54.7% |
| 12 | 1976 | Schmidt II | SPD/FDP | 51.0% |
| 13 | 1980 | Schmidt III | SPD/FDP | 54.6% |
| 14 | 1982 | Kohl I | CDU/CSU/FDP | 56.2% |
| 15 | 1983 | Kohl II | CDU/CSU/FDP | 55.8% |
| 16 | 1987 | Kohl III | CDU/CSU/FDP | 54.1% |
| 17 | 1990 | Kohl IV | CDU/CSU/FDP | 60.1% |
| 18 | 1994 | Kohl V | CDU/CSU/FDP | 52.0% |

The federal structure of the country limits the extent to which parties can dominate the governments they support: this may indeed be a recipe for inaction. In policy areas in which the 1949 Basic Law stipulates that there has to be consensus between Laender and federation, the agreement of the Bundesrat has to be obtained; yet at times the opposition controls the Bundesrat. Thus party government can function fully only when the same majority controls both chambers. The need for Bundesrat concurrence has resulted in blockages which have been described by an author as a decision-making 'trap' (Scharpf).

However, the relative stagnation which characterises 'normal politics' may be overcome in some situations and result in a somewhat abnormal form of policy-making. This has been the case for example with the unification process: normal mechanisms of party-government relationships were set aside and the government succeeded in overcoming the entrenched procedures and the resistance of the 'decision-making-trap', although innovative policies were also facilitated by the fact that the same majority controlled both chambers of parliament at the end of 1989 and at the beginning of 1990.

Thus the domination of parties on governments is limited, especially when there are different majorities in the two houses; but more generally the federal government has also been able to achieve a degree of autonomy vis-à-vis their supporting parties and even to dominate the parties of the coalition with respect to policy decisions. The government may then have had to compensate parties not only by means of political patronage but by building the administrative and institutional base necessary to implement their programmes. The dependence of parties on governments is thus strengthened not only as a result of the volume of public resources available and of prevailing recruitment patterns, but by the special circumstances in which some decisions happen to take place.

We shall examine these questions mainly in the context of the 1980s. As was indicated in Chapter 1, we will analyse the distribution of power between government and supporting parties at three levels, those of appointments, policy-making, and patronage. In conclusion, we will attempt to assess the relationships between these three levels and to classify the German case within the space of autonomy and dependence among governments and supporting parties.

## APPOINTMENTS

### Constitutional and juridical constraints

What constitutes a party in the Federal Republic is somewhat unclear. This is in part because, at any rate formally, parliamentary parties are distinct from the parties in the country. Parliamentary parties are juridically independent from the rest of their party given that, in Germany as in many other countries, MPs are not bound by any 'imperative mandate', as this is declared void by the Basic Law. Links between the two elements of the parties are close, however. In general, regional and district organs nominate parliamentary candidates on *Land*-lists; indeed, national party leaders have occasionally complained about their limited influence with respect to the composition of their parliamentary group (Wildenmann, 1989: 106).

The rights of party members to participate in the selection of party leaders are defined by a law of 1967 which regulates parties: these rights are therefore identical for all parties. The statute also stipulates that democratic rules are to be applied, such as secret ballots and the entitlement of members to attend party meetings. There are none the less some differences among the parties with respect to the implementation of these rules. For instance, decision-making within the CSU is highly centralised and is dominated by a homogeneous party elite, whereas the CDU has sometimes known competing leadership groups. In the SPD, Helmut Schmidt still insisted on unity as a traditional socialist principle at the beginning of the 1980s; the SPD has expanded the participation rights of the membership up to 1993.

## Links between government and party elites

The extent of overlap between governmental and party elites can be measured by comparing the composition of the cabinet and of party executives. The cabinet increased in size during the period under study from 17 members (13 SPD and 4 FDP in 1980–2) to 19 members (10 CDU, 5 CSU and 4 FDP in 1987–90); 5 further members were added after unification in October 1990. The executive committee of the SPD had 11 members in 1980–2, 10 of whom had been elected by the Party Congress in 1980. The FDP executive committee had 13 members in the early part of the period; it increased to 15 members in 1987 and to 18 members in 1990. The CDU executive committee had 15 members up to 1987, 11 of whom were elected by the Party Congress, and 16 members afterwards. Finally, the CSU executive had continuously 18 members.

Overall, except for the Liberals, cabinet members were replaced more often than the members of their party executives. After the breakdown of the SPD/FDP-coalition, the FDP had the highest turnover of top party positions. On the other hand, the CSU replaced 90 per cent of its governmental personnel during the 11th legislative term. No uniform picture emerges about the linkage between governmental and party positions, although since 1983 most governmental posts were occupied by persons who had previously belonged to the party leadership. In general, the distribution of cabinet posts is fixed in the coalition agreement, the appointments themselves being controlled by the party elite. It remains, however, that most cabinet members were drawn from the executive committee of their party or were at least party insiders.

There has therefore been a high degree of party influence on appointments in the Federal Republic, with little difference among the supporting parties, except that the smaller parties (the FDP and the CSU) tend to appoint more party leaders than cabinet ministers. Cabinet ministers are therefore selected from within their parties and are responsible to the people through their parties: in the 1980s, all government members were selected by the parties concerned, even though they were appointed and dismissed formally by the chancellor. The relatively high personnel overlap between government and party leadership also indicates the extent to which cabinet members are responsible to their electorate through their parties. Differences among supporting parties have been marginal to this respect, at least during the 1980s; moreover, variations over time appear largely due to increases in the size of the cabinet.

## POLICY-MAKING

### The relative role of government and supporting parties

With respect to policy-making, the autonomy of both governments and supporting parties is markedly limited. Governments need the votes of the supporting parties in parliament; parties need governments to implement policy decisions. There are none the less appreciable variations with respect to the reciprocal influence of one over the other.

Governments have the upper hand in terms of broad output. Overall, respectively 57, 46, and 47 per cent of bills originated from the government in the three parliaments of the 1980s, as against respectively 9, 8, and 12 per cent which were introduced by the government parties during the same period. Moreover, while between 67 and 83 per cent of the government bills were passed, the corresponding proportion for bills introduced by parliamentarians ranged between one-third and slightly under three-quarters. Finally, bills initiated by the supporting parties are generally relatively unimportant and they tend to be single-issue measures. Governments therefore dominate the legislative process: only exceptionally do parties supporting the government initiate legislation which has the support of the administration.

One needs to go beyond these general indicators, however: three specific cases have therefore been considered in somewhat greater detail in order to assess the relative inputs of government and parties. These cases include both policies in which the government was particularly successful and dominated the supporting parties and cases in which the government failed to solve the problem in the context of a serious conflict.

The cases studied include, in the budgetary field, the rapidly and successfully ratified Budgetary Reform Act of 1984 of the Conservative-Liberal coalition under Helmut Kohl, in the labour market field and under the same cabinet, the less successful Employment Assistance Act of 1985, and, in the foreign policy field, the policy of unification which the Kohl government carried out under conditions of considerable pressure and which led to the State Treaty and to the Unification Treaty negotiated and signed by the two German governments in 1990.

### Case I: The 1984 Budget Reform

The budgetary reform was one of the most important activities of the Kohl government in 1984; it was designed to reduce the budget deficit.[1] The bill was successfully enacted despite attacks emanating primarily from the trade unions and the powerful social insurance and welfare organisations. In contrast with the unsuccessful attempts of the government to balance the budget after unification, the budget reform of 1984 provides a good example of the extent to which the situation can determine the way in which government and supporting parties, as well as interest groups, relate to each other. As a result of the change in the nature of the coalition in 1982, the government was able to dominate the legislative process. The FDP and CDU/CSU negotiators were not constrained by party standpoints and could agree on a short coalition compact of four pages. As the question of the budget deficit had played an important part in the 1980 election campaign, there had been no detailed party recommendations for the social aspects of the budget. The cabinet could formulate its reform plans autonomously and the proposals were accepted by the parliamentary parties without major change. Those which required the consent of the Bundesrat were presented to that body in July 1983 and referred to the Bundestag two months later. After only five months of deliberations, in December 1983, the bill had passed three plenary sessions and two hearings[2] and had been signed by the President. In contrast to the lobbying made by some private groups, the supporting parties were not very active. The only party organisation interested in the reform was the Christian Employee organisation (CDA): it supported the bill. The middle-class employer organisation MIT of the CDU and the executive committee of the CDU were not involved; the executive committee of the FDP agreed with the governmental proposal; while the Christian trade union, an employee organisation ideologically close to the Christian Democrats had mixed feelings, it did not display a wholy negative attitude towards the budgetary reform.

On the other hand, nine other trade unions struggled against the reform. They mobilised their members, used formal and informal contacts with party officials and publicised their opposition to the reform in the mass media. Many social welfare organisations also objected to the bill, as they were directly affected by the fact that social benefits were to be cut: they mobilised their resources to fight against the budgetary reform. Meanwhile, the budget reform did not lead to conflict between employee and employer organisations: most employer bodies observed its development cautiously. Overall, the activities of private groups did not succeed in slowing down the decision-making process.

The fact that the bill was quickly passed with only minor amendments is less due to institutional factors such as the bicameral system than to the sudden and unexpected change in the coalition structure. This case is a clear example of governmental dominance over the supporting parties.

## Case II: The 1985 Employment Assistance Act

In 1984, the minister of Labour and Social Affairs, the Christian Democrat Norbert Blüm, was asked to prepare the draft of an Employment Assistance bill designed to deregulate labour law, as the governmental partners, CDU, CSU, and FDP wished to introduce a neo-liberal labour market policy.[3]

The governmental proposal aimed at facilitating employment contracts of limited duration and part-time work, as well as to modify traditional rules such as those giving a monopoly of vocational training to the Federal Labour Agency or those providing social benefits in cases of plant closure. In contrast to the budget reform most of these items were not only specified in the 1983 coalition compact, but they were also published in strategic papers drafted by Messrs Lambsdorff, George and Albrecht.

The supporting parties of the coalition were at first not fully prepared to follow the new strategy. The Left of the FDP was critical. There were differences of opinion between CDU and CSU. Party proposals on social policy had been formulated by the chairman of a working group on labour and social policy of the CDU/CSU parliamentary party in July 1983 and by the former prime minister of Lower Saxony, the Christian Democrat Ernst Albrecht, on the unemployment problem. Yet, in 1984, the CDU drafted its proposals, known as *Stuttgarter Thesen* 'for a modern and human industrialised nation', calling for more flexibility. The governmental proposals embedded in the Employment Assistance bill corresponded to these views.

The bill needed the approval of the Bundesrat. It was sent to that chamber in March 1983 and declared urgent on the grounds that the law had to be implemented by January 1st 1985. Yet the Bundesrat took seven months to decide. Although the CDU/CSU and the FDP still had a majority in the Bundesrat, criticisms were made of the provisions relating to part-time work, to the abolition of the monopoly on vocational training, and to the extension of the time-limit for hiring employees. The government rejected the modifications introduced by the Bundesrat and referred the bill to the Bundestag in October 1984. It went to the Labour Committee where it was discussed during fifteen closed and one public session over a period of six months. About forty organisations participated in the public hearings. Most trade unions were against the bill, the Christian trade union and the Association of Public Officers alone being in favour of the proposal. Polarisation was sharp as all employer organisations supported the bill, while welfare organisations had an ambivalent attitude, as did organisations close to the CDU. The CDU and FDP parliamentary parties introduced numerous amendments. The final committee report agreed to the concept of contracts for limited periods of employment as well as the modifications by the Bundesrat. The bill, amended in this way, was approved by the Bundestag and the Bundesrat.

Supporting parties can thus play a major part in the legislative process, as can be seen by the case of Employment Assistance, which was decided primarily on the basis of negotiations within and among the governmental coalition parties, while the Laender also played an important part, as the Christian-Liberal majority of the Laender was able to convince their parliamentary colleagues. This is therefore an example of interaction and interdependence between government and supporting parties.

## Case III: The 1990 Unification Treaty

German unification resulted from the extraordinary events which started in 1989: policy-making was placed under severe external stress.[4] Within a very short time, major treaties among both German governments were elaborated, negotiated and, by September 1990, approved by all three chambers (the East German People's Chamber, the Bundesrat and the Bundestag). With regard to the institutional and political framework, to timing and to the type of legislation involved, the unification treaty was an example of both pronounced executive dominance and of supporting parties' influence. The time constraints under which the treaty with its 45 articles, comprising 360 pages, was negotiated, resulted in the government having the upper hand. Supporting parties did not have the time to develop alternative proposals; moreover, as the treaty had to be approved in parliament without amendments because of its international law character, the room for manoeuvre of the supporting parties was limited.

The cabinet had a majority in both chambers of parliament up to June 1990. It could therefore initiate and pass its policies on monetary, economic and social unification without delay and without substantial modifications. As the SPD won a majority in the Bundesrat following two Laender victories, the parliamentary parties and the parliamentary arena in general became more important after June 1990; on the other hand, the position of the governmental parties improved as the election of December 1990 grew nearer. Finally, on matters on which the cabinet was not able to come to an agreed position, the supporting parties did play a part: this occurred for instance with respect to some property rights on the territory of the former GDR. The finance ministers of the Federal Republic and of the GDR had not been able to settle their differences on this issue: the matter was therefore excluded from the first treaty. A common governmental declaration was drafted in June 1990 which stated that decisions on possible financial and non-financial compensation were to be postponed and transferred to a future common German parliament. This led to controversies within the coalition, within the parliamentary committee on German unity, and within the CDU/CSU parliamentary party. After three readings, the Bundestag approved in August 1990 the treaty of unification with a number of modifications introduced as a result of the SPD majority in the Bundesrat, the question of property reform remaining unsettled. The Constitutional Court declared constitutional the provision which decided that the land reform of the period 1945–9 would remain unchanged. The issue of compensation versus restitution of property nationalised after 1949 was settled only four years later, in September 1994.

Whereas the State treaty of May 1990 was an instance in which the cabinet dominated the supporting parties, the unification treaty was characterised by a more complex interaction between the two sides. The issue of land reform which was postponed from both treaties revealed a pattern in which the government was, on the contrary, highly dependent on the supporting parties as well as on interest groups.

The pattern of policy-making in the Federal Republic differs therefore substantially from patterns of appointment. Whereas appointments to the government depend, admittedly to a varying degree, on the supporting parties, the government can control aspects of policy-making under specific conditions and in specific domains. This means that, contrary to the view that incremental policy-making is typical of German politics, the obstacles built into the federal system as well as into the 'party state' can be overcome and a more innovative policy style can emerge. This interpretation is corroborated by policy studies in other fields, such as the health policy adopted in 1992 by the Kohl government, a policy which was designed to reduce costs in the health system and which was entirely elaborated by the minister concerned, this being another case of government success.

## POLITICAL PATRONAGE

Patronage in German politics relates to areas in which 'preferential recruitment and promotion of personnel affiliated with the governing parties' is possible and has indeed taken place. Patronage in national enterprises is not very widespread, especially by comparison with Italy, in large part because the size of the public sector is appreciably smaller. At the local level, on the other hand, patronage has been found to exist in savings banks, in gas and water undertakings or in public transport companies. Opportunities for patronage also exist at the *Land* level in the educational field, though not in universities. The most substantial extent of 'colonisation' of the society by the 'party state' occurs in the civil service and in the public mass media (von Beyme, 1993: 58ff.): in this case, patronage on the model of the Treuhand takes the form of a proportional representation of seats on executive boards of public radio-television companies among parties and interest associations; privatisation is currently reducing opportunities in this sector, however.

There are about seven million public servants in Germany, more than anywhere else in Western Europe. While the occupation forces had prohibited party activities among public servants in 1945, politicisation returned first in order to 'defend democracy'. The coming of the SPD to office in 1966 and the return of the CDU/CSU in 1982 provided further occasions for politicisation of the civil service. First, at the top level, about 110 positions are regarded as political: somewhat under half the officials occupying these positions were dismissed in 1982–3 (von Beyme, 1993: 66). Second, politicisation appears to have increased in the last quarter of the century. Whereas in 1970, still nearly three-quarters of civil servants interviewed (72 per cent) declared not to belong to any party, the proportion fell to slightly over two-fifths in 1987 (43 per cent) (Mayntz/Derlien, 1989: 388). The movement is even more marked among top civil servants: only 18 per cent of the state secretaries in office between 1949 and 1969 were members of a political party; by 1987 an increase of party membership among civil servants is observed, '... but those with a strong influence on personnel policy are a bit more reluctant to admit it' (Mayntz/Derlien, 1989: 386).

Among the parties, SPD and FDP members predominated in the 1970s while CDU, CSU, and FDP members dominated in the 1980s. Thus members of the ruling parties are generally in a majority. When the SPD-FDP coalition was in power in the 1970s and early 1980s, the percentage of SPD members grew from 18 per cent to 42 per cent. On the other hand, by 1987 about 45 per cent of state secretaries, division heads and subdivision heads belonged to the governing coalition of CDU/CSU/FDP, while only 12 per cent belonged to the SPD. Party membership within the top bureaucracy changed markedly twice as the governing majority moved first to the SPD and later back to the CDU/CSU.

Who controls these developments is somewhat unclear. In the case of the SPD governments, the Chancellor's office clearly played a large part. As a matter of fact, the problem was not very salient in the first twenty years of the Federal Republic as loyalty to the CDU/CSU governments was largely secured by 'sympathisers' without any formal party membership. When the SPD controlled the chancellorship from 1969, a new personnel policy was initiated. However, as the party itself could not provide enough civil servants, outsiders or candidates without party membership were also recruited (von

Beyme, 1993: 65). The SPD thus did not succeed in wholly replacing the previous administrative elite.

The German public service was traditionally described as being a- or even anti-political: this is no longer the case. At the beginning of the 1970s already, German civil servants were more politicised than their British colleagues (Putnam, 1976: 113ff.). In effect parties have become central recruiting agencies, almost as the ENA in France, admittedly rendering policy implementation somewhat smoother as a result (von Beyme, 1993: 74). Patronage did even increase with unification: thus, while the Liberal-Conservative program of the CDU/FDP coalition was designed to deregulate and 'slim' the German state administration, the opposite occurred since the late 1980s, as the 'superbureaucracy' of Treuhand replaced the state centralism of the former GDR (ibid.: 201).

## CONCLUSION

Government-supporting party relationships in the Federal Republic have a two-fold character. On the one hand, the federal government shares legislative and executive powers with the Laender and to an extent with international organisations; on the other hand, governments have to be involved to an extent in complex legislative bargaining.

There are two ways in which this bargaining tends to occur. First, an important condition for the government to be able to dominate is the existence of the same majority in the Bundestag and Bundesrat. This did occur between 1982 and 1990; on the contrary, the SPD/FDP governments of the 1970s were confronted with a Christian majority in the Bundesrat, as were the CDU/CSU/FDP governments of the 1990s. When the majority is the same in both chambers, policies can be decided primarily within or among the coalition parties. As most legislation needs the consent of the Bundesrat, bargaining with the Laender parties is a mechanism leading to consensus: the parties supporting the government are thus in a brokerage position between Laender and federal government. The Employment Assistance Law is an example of such a development.

Second, unexpected situations increase government dominance. The breakdown of the Social-Liberal coalition in 1982 was an instance of this kind, as was the fall of the Wall in 1989. Policies (may) have to be adopted quickly: the governmental machinery can in such a context draft and pilot 'extraordinary' legislation. More generally, one can also state that most (relatively minor) legislation is prepared by individual ministerial departments and by the government rather than by the parties.

Meanwhile, however, there is some compensation for, as well as influence of, the supporting parties. Since governments seek to maintain their majority in parliament, supporting parties can push for the policies which they (or the interest groups connected with them) tend to prefer, especially when the election is near. Finally, the supporting parties tend to press for distributive policies which are relatively less controversial. Yet, in many cases, the government can act autonomously and succeed in avoiding amendments from the supporting parties which might alter the character of the bill.

Three variables play a major part in this context, the nature of the majorities in both chambers, the timing of the policy, and the type of internal parliamentary organisation. The Bundestag is not an 'entrepreneur-type' parliament, as the US Congress or, to an extent, the Italian parliament, but it is not either of the pure majoritarian-type, based exclusively on parliamentary parties and not on specialised committees, as was traditionally the case in the British House of Commons. In the Bundestag, committee work has the effect of enhancing the dominance of the executive, as a result of the fact that committees follow to a large extent what the ministries suggest, although the parliamentary parties also sometimes intervene and exercise some influence.

Appointment patterns and patronage provide a greater scope for the supporting parties. There is little difference between the parties in this respect: the CDU/CSU, the FDP, and the SPD have all been involved to about the same extent. Overall, the relationship between government and supporting parties in the Federal Republic is rather mixed: governmental influence is exercised primarily in the policy context while this influence is at least in part compensated by party influence in the appointment process and to an extent at least with respect to patronage.

## NOTES

1.  In the process, social benefits were cut by modifying 26 laws and by reducing, among others, maternity subsidies, incomes in the public sector, additional programmes against unemployment, vocational training, and government aid to the disabled.
2.  More than 30 private organisations were invited to the public hearing and more than 85 relevant organisations were interested in the budget reform.
3.  The breakdown of the Socialist-Liberal coalition in 1982 was provoked by the minister of Economic Affairs, the liberal Lambsdorff: the neo-liberal ideas of

Lambsdorff subsequently shaped the government declaration of the new Christian-Liberal coalition.

4.  The massive influx of refugees from East Germany into the Federal Republic, reinforced by the fall of the Berlin wall in November 1989, was the major catalyst of this process; the catastrophic disruption of the East German economy was also an important factor.

# 6. Austria: Party Government Within Limits

## W.C. Müller, W. Philipp and B. Steininger

### INTRODUCTION

Two types of government, the grand coalition and the single-party cabinet, have shaped Austrian politics during the post-war period, except for two years of all-party government in the immediate post-war period (1945–7) and for three years of Social Democrat-Liberal government between 1983 and 1986. There have been grand coalitions between 1945 and 1966 and after 1987; they were led, during the first period by the People's Party (ÖVP), and during the second by the Social Democratic Party (SPÖ). There were two kinds of single-party government, an ÖVP government which replaced the grand coalition in 1966 and was defeated in 1970 and an SPÖ cabinet formed first as a minority government and subsequently gaining majority status in 1971, a status which it maintained until 1983. This chapter relates to the characteristics of the grand coalition of SPÖ and ÖVP which took place after 1987.

The SPÖ and ÖVP have distinct party structures. The SPÖ is relatively centralised and this gives its chairman much leeway. Factionalism is low and party discipline is usually high. In contrast, the ÖVP is an indirect party. It is based on three socio-economic leagues (*Bünde*) which organise farmers (ÖBB), businessmen (ÖWB) and blue and white-collar workers (ÖAAB) respectively. The leagues not only command important resources but also have an independent power base through the system of state-licenced interest groups, known as 'chambers'. Power distribution in the ÖVP is also dispersed territorially, with *Land* party organisations playing a major part.

Corporatist policy making, under the name of 'social partnership', is a major feature of Austrian politics, with the main interest groups taking important decisions among themselves or in cooperation with the government. Corporatism has been in decline since the late 1970s, however (Gerlich et al., 1988; Tálos, 1993). The major interest groups are linked in various ways to the major parties, with the Social Democratic Trade Unionists (FSG) dominating the Trade Union Congress (ÖGB) and the Chamber of Labour (AK), the Business League of the ÖVP dominating the Chamber of Commerce and the ÖVP's Farmers' League dominating the

Chambers of Agriculture. We shall consider these groupings as party factions in the context of this chapter.

## APPOINTMENTS

According to the constitution, the Federal President appoints the Federal Chancellor and, on the latter's proposal, all other cabinet members. In practice the President only ratifies and the Chancellor only proposes what emerges out of electoral and coalition politics. Cabinet composition is thus determined by party politics. In the case of coalition governments, the government departments and positions are distributed among the parties and they are free to choose whom they nominate. Mutual non-interference between parties has been respected in all cases but one: this concerned the position of a secretary of state in 1990, the SPÖ having rejected a ÖVP nominee.

Intra-party decision processes on appointments to cabinet reflect the general character of each party. In the SPÖ these processes have changed markedly during the post-war period. What once, formally at least, was a collective decision of the party executive, has become very much a prerogative of the party leader. Since the SPÖ places much value on (formal) intra-party democracy, the Chancellor interpreted this as a prerogative of his state position rather than as a consequence of being party chairman. According to reports about the 1994 cabinet formation, the SPÖ leader did not even report his decisions to the party executive. However, even a strong leader has to take into account internal party reality. In the ÖVP the party leader is less powerful. The permanent factions, the *Bünde*, and the *Land* party organisations demand cabinet representation. Not all ambitions can be satisfied and the party leader has some leeway; it is part of his task to build and maintain intra-party coalitions. However, there are some unwritten rules, in particular that the Department of Economic Affairs has to go to the party's Business League and that the Department of Agriculture and Forestry has to go the Farmers' League, both of which *de facto* nominate the minister. Formally, it is still the party executive which decides on cabinet appointments.

In selecting cabinet members political parties draw almost exclusively from their own ranks. In the whole post-war period and up to 1994, only 13 persons were not party members. If one looks at the matter from the perspective of the parties, the norm is for the chairmen of the governing parties to occupy the highest cabinet position available to their respective party (i.e. Chancellor or Vice-Chancellor, since Austria has experienced only two-party coalitions since 1947). There have been only temporary deviations from this rule. A change in party leadership has always been followed by a change at the level of government with the new party chairman taking over the highest cabinet position of his party, the only exception is that of Vranitzky who became Chancellor in 1986 without having been elected to a leading position in his party, the SPÖ. The resignation of his predecessor, Fred Sinowatz, from the chancellorship, turned out to be only the first step of the latter's withdrawal from active politics. When Sinowatz also stepped down as party chairman, Vranitzky was well placed to take over the party leadership as well and thereby bring to an end the uncommon separation of the functions of party chairman and Chancellor.

Let us consider the link between parties and government in a broader perspective, focusing on the cabinet and party executive bodies. Between 1945 and 1987 27 per cent of the cabinet members were recruited from the executive of their party. The cabinet with the strongest party profile was the SPÖ-FPÖ government of 1983–6, with 59 per cent of the cabinet members also holding party executive positions. In the first grand coalition of 1945–66, 38 per cent of the ministers were members of the executive of their party; this figure dropped to 15 per cent in the ÖVP single-party government (1966–70) and climbed again to 19 per cent in the SPÖ single-party government (Müller and Philipp, 1987). These figures allow us to see the post-1987 grand coalition government in perspective. In the two cabinets of this coalition altogether 51 cabinet appointments (ministers and secretaries of state) were made, 24 from the SPÖ, 25 from the ÖVP, with two appointments being non-partisan. According to Table 6.1 the overall 'partyness of government' (Katz, 1986) in the two Vranitzky cabinets was lower than any time before, with a mere 17.4 per cent and 10.7 per cent respectively of the cabinet members having served on the party executive before being appointed to the cabinet. The case of the SPÖ in the cabinet Vranitzky III is of particular interest: none of the SPÖ representatives could look back to a true party career. The ÖVP clearly outranks the SPÖ in terms of the 'partyness' of cabinet appointments. This is probably due to some extent to the fact that it was previously in opposition.

Once appointed to a cabinet position, ministers become automatically major party figures. A government position is so prominent that it leads to a quick rise in the party, even if the appointee did not previously belong to the party leadership or was even an active member. Cabinet members are invited to all important party events and inevitably have frequent contacts with many party leaders. They are coopted to the larger party bodies and they are invited to the smaller ones whenever their department figures prominently in the political debate. If the appointee has political flair, he or she will be viewed by party leaders as 'one of them' (rather than merely occupying one of 'their' cabinet positions) and formal recognition by election to a leadership position in the party organisation will soon follow. This, in turn, may lead cabinet members to become in the long run true party members. Table 6.1 therefore also looks at the subsequent career of ministers in two cabinets. In both parties appointment to cabinet indeed constituted a stepping stone for a party career. Altogether about a fifth of the people appointed to the cabinet Vranitzky II were selected to the party executive after (and probably because of) appointment to cabinet.

Table 6.1: *Party executive and cabinet membership in Austria, 1987–1994*

| | Party executive membership (in % of cabinet appointments) before first appointment to any cabinet | | Party executive membership (in % of cabinet appointments) before appointment to | | Selection to party executive after having been appointed to cabinet (in % of appointments) to (a) | |
|---|---|---|---|---|---|---|
| | Vranitzky II | Vranitzky III | Vranitzky II | Vranitzky III | Vranitzky II | Vranitzky III |
| SPÖ | 10.0 | 0.0 | 10.0 | 21.4 | 30.0 | 0.0 |
| ÖVP | 25.0 | 23.1 | 33.3 | 30.7 | 16.7 | 0.0 |
| Total | 17.4 | 10.7 | 21.7 | 25.0 | 21.7 | 0.0 |

(a) Numbers are subject to change since cabinet members may still be selected to the party executive.

Appointments to grand coalition cabinets are not based as precisely on a party career, with ÖVP ministers being more party-based than SPÖ ministers: in the case of the SPÖ the link between party and government is mainly based, on the contrary, on the party recruiting cabinet members to high party office.

## POLICIES

The analysis of policy-making processes is based here on interviews with party and government officials and on such sources as party documents, newspaper reports, parliamentary papers, and so on. Of the cases specifically studied, two relate to taxation, the tax reforms of 1988 and 1993, which became effective in 1989 and 1994 respectively; economic policy is represented by a case study of the privatisation programme of the grand coalition government: this programme includes three key decisions taken between 1987 and 1993; social policy is covered by the study of the introduction of a second year of maternity leave by the grand coalition in 1989–90; housing policy is studied in the context of the reform of the Rent Restriction

Act in 1993; finally, Austria's decision to apply for membership in the EC, which was made in 1988 constitutes a foreign policy case.

All these matters occupied for some time a prominent place on the political agenda; they were also party commitments for a long time. They are therefore examples of policies in which the impact of parties is likely to have been large, while the involvement of political parties is likely to be more limited in other cases.

It is worth recalling the political and social context in which these decisions were taken. The parties which formed the grand coalition in 1987 had faced each other as government and opposition for more than 20 years, the SPÖ having been in government for the last 17 of these years while the ÖVP was in opposition. Policy differences had increased during that period and conflicts over policy had become more intense, with the ÖVP giving itself a sharper policy profile. The SPÖ's position, in particular regarding economic policy, gradually lost favour among the electorate. The SPÖ responded to the decline of its electoral fortunes (in *Land* and presidential elections as well as in opinion polls): in 1986 party chairman Fred Sinowatz stepped down as Chancellor, giving way to the Minister of Finance, Franz Vranitzky. The new Chancellor was an outsider in the SPÖ but popular among electors. He indicated that a policy change would occur under his leadership which was intended to take the wind out of the sails of the ÖVP; this move also corresponded to a rethinking of the SPÖ's economic policy, albeit more by government members than within the party at large. The financial difficulties of nationalised industries in late 1985 and the increasing budgetary problems had changed the perception of social democratic ministers; but members of the SPÖ in general continued to consider the Kreisky period of 1970–83 with its spendthrift budgetary policy and frequent government intervention at a micro-economic level as a kind of golden age.

The policy cases analysed here can be divided into three categories according to the government or opposition status of the parties at the time of policy initiation. Initiation can go back to the time when SPÖ and ÖVP faced each other as government and opposition; it can be a product of the coalition negotiations in 1986–7; or it can fall within the period of grand coalition government after the successful completion of these negotiations.

*Pre-1987 initiation*
The first group includes cases in which important initiatives took place before the formation of the grand coalition. These are the first phases of privatisation and of the tax reform. The ÖVP's economic policy programme of 1985 and its 1986 electoral manifesto are the most elaborate and explicit initiatives. These proposals demanded a substantial policy change, in particular

a turn to privatisation, a simpler tax system and lower income taxes. The ÖVP was in opposition when these proposals were put forward: they must therefore be considered as having a party origin. They were followed by rather vague and indirect statements in the SPÖ electoral manifesto hinting in the same direction: although this electoral manifesto was formally accepted by the party, it bore the imprint of Chancellor Vranitzky and was indeed labelled 'Vranitzky Programme'. Moreover, members of the SPÖ's government team, in particular Chancellor Vranitzky himself, indicated in interviews a greater willingness to introduce a major policy change concerning the nationalised sector and taxation. As far as the SPÖ is concerned, therefore, the initiative was with the government rather than with the party: the party was generally sceptical about these policies but by and large it remained rather passive, in part because of the traditional discipline of the party and in part because of a desire not to undermine the SPÖ's electoral fortunes when no strong commitment had yet been made to these policies.

Coalition negotiations of 1986–7 constituted the breakthrough for privatisation, although in an indirect manner, namely by excluding other forms of raising the capital which the nationalised industries required urgently in order to avoid bankruptcy. Specific proposals for privatisation were elaborated by the Minister of Public Economy and Transport (SPÖ), the Minister of Finance (SPÖ) and the Minister of Economic Affairs (ÖVP). These kept in touch with and were checked by representatives of the other government party. The resulting privatisation programme of the government was hard to accept for SPÖ trade unionists; they protested through the trade union congress ÖGB which they dominated. The government negotiated with the ÖGB and eventually a compromise was found which limited privatisation to 49 per cent of the shares (the government had not proposed to go beyond this for the time being anyway) and to inform the ÖGB in advance about each privatisation (Müller, 1988: 110–11). The implementation of the privatisation programme largely remained a matter for the government. Non-cabinet politicians of the parties which did not occupy the departments in charge of privatisation were involved, however: these politicians were entrusted to check the policies of the departments from a party perspective.

The coalition agreement of 1987 outlined the principles of the first tax reform. Details were to be negotiated by an eight person committee, which included the Minister of Finance (SPÖ) and the Secretary of State in the Department of Finance (ÖVP); the six other members were the finance spokesmen of the two parties, representatives of the SPÖ trade unionists and representatives of both the business and employees' wings of the ÖVP. During these negotiations, both sides had to go beyond what had been considered politically acceptable to each of the parties when the coalition agreement had been adopted. The main contents of the reform were a reduction of the income tax (including a reduction of the top rate from 62 to 50 per cent) and a reduction of corporate taxation from 55 to 30 per cent. The SPÖ was unenthusiastic about the drastic reduction of tax for top earners and for firms as this was regarded as violating the party's long-standing perceptions of social justice. The Minister of Finance was able to win public support for his proposal, with the help of the Chancellor, however. Difficulties were more severe in the ÖVP. Negotiators had agreed to the introduction of a tax on interest on bank savings (this kind of income was already subject to income tax, but tax evasion had prevented the government from obtaining a sizable revenue from this source). A similar tax had been strongly rejected by the ÖVP when it was introduced by the SPÖ-FPÖ government (it was subsequently invalidated by the constitutional court): consequently party chairman and Vice-Chancellor Mock emphatically rejected the idea of introducing this tax; the ÖVP negotiators returned to their SPÖ counterparts but they were not able to obtain agreement on the package without an effective taxation of interest from bank savings. Dissent within the ÖVP grew during this phase of negotiations. The business wing was in favour of accepting the reform package since it offered considerable advantages to them; several ÖVP politicians were concerned with the negative image effects resulting from open fighting within the coalition. Internal party conflict in the ÖVP culminated when party chairman Mock forced the resignation of his party's Secretary of State in the Department of Finance, who had been one of his critics. The ÖVP did extract minor concessions from the SPÖ, but it eventually did have to agree to the tax reform package. The fact that Mock was party chairman and simultaneously held the highest cabinet office available to his party makes it difficult to distinguish between party and government in this case. However, it may be stated that Mock behaved as a party politician rather than as a leading member of the government. His goals were to extract policy concessions from the SPÖ and, more importantly, to make clear which party was responsible for the new tax which he considered to be unpopular; the ÖVP's Secretary of State, in contrast, had behaved as a member of government.

Thus the proposal for the first tax reform had been worked out by the government, with the participation of party representatives, while both parties constituted a hurdle for their respective government members. This hurdle was undoubtedly more difficult to overcome in the case of the ÖVP as is shown by the resignation of the Secretary of State.

*Coalition agreement initiatives*
The second group relates to cases in which the policy was initiated during the process of government formation (Müller, 1988a). Only one example is

analysed here, that of Austria's (possible) membership of the EC. Although both parties had long taken a stand on this issue, the ÖVP being more in favour than the SPÖ of Austria's participation in European integration, this matter did not figure in the 1986 electoral manifestos and campaign. It emerged during the coalition negotiations. The negotiation team of the SPÖ consisted of cabinet members and of party leaders, the ÖVP's team of party leaders, the majority of whom were soon to become cabinet ministers. On the SPÖ side, the Chancellor and on the ÖVP side the party chairman Mock, who was to become the new Foreign Minister, were those who were mostly concerned with this question. The process is similar to that which characterises the first group of cases, except that there were no pre-negotiation proposals. Admittedly, there was a direct involvement of party representatives without government office on the SPÖ's side and there was also some feedback from the party executives; yet the move to bring Austria into the EC is clearly more a government than a party initiative.

During the coalition negotiations the parties had only placed on the agenda the question of bringing Austria closer to the EC with the goal of full participation in the single European market. In December 1987 the cabinet declared EC membership as one of the feasible options. From this position both government parties developed their policy proposals, with the ÖVP opting for full membership in the EC within a month. Policy development within the SPÖ took markedly longer. Without sharing the enthusiasm for full EC membership shown by Foreign Minister Mock, the SPÖ government team had a similar perception of the situation, namely that full membership was the only viable strategy for achieving full participation in the single European market. However, having to accommodate a party in which a substantial part was lukewarm to EC integration, the Chancellor decided to move slowly. His strategy was to induce important sections of the party to commit themselves to EC membership in a context other than that of the party. Thus major interest groups, including trade unions, and the *Land* governments, including three led by the SPÖ, opted for EC membership for economic reasons before the party executive dealt with the question in April 1989. The Chancellor's commitment to opt if necessary for neutrality rather than for EC membership succeeded in accommodating the party. The executive agreed to EC membership, but under conditions, including neutrality, social policy standards, an active environmental policy and the solution of the problem of heavy vehicle transit through Austria. Intense negotiations followed within the cabinet to decide whether qualifications should be included in Austria's membership application: the discussion centred in particular on the question as to whether the application should make reference to permanent neutrality: the SPÖ team demanded such a reference while the ÖVP team argued against it on the grounds that it might delay the processing of the application by the EC. There was also discussion as to who should be in charge of the negotiations with the EC, with the ÖVP proposing the Foreign Minister and the SPÖ the Chancellor. Eventually the SPÖ succeeded in including a qualification concerning neutrality, while the whole cabinet was declared to be in charge of the negotiations. This outcome was the result of inter-party agreement rather than of a cabinet decision; it was even explicitly stated that it would not be bound by the term of the current cabinet. The agreement also covered the whole field where the SPÖ had expressed reservations in its party executive resolution. Meanwhile, parliament examined the question of Austria's strategy for European integration; these deliberations lasted as long as there was no consensus in cabinet. When the consensus was reached, parliament passed a resolution, empowering the government to apply for membership in the EC, this resolution being in a sense a ratification of the agreement made at the cabinet and party level. In July 1989 Austria presented its membership application to the EC (Khol, 1989; Kiesenhofer, 1994).

Policy development was clearly dominated by the government in this case. The SPÖ leadership had none the less to take into account the reactions of the party in determining the pace and content of the policy. The party thus exercised some influence.

*Initiatives taking place during the lifetime of the government*
Third, some policies were initiated during the term of the grand coalition government. One case makes it possible to separate neatly party from government, that of the reform of the Rent Restriction Act. Both government parties had long-standing commitments in this field. The SPÖ 1986 electoral manifesto had contained a few lines on this issue and the 1987 coalition agreement had contained the outline of a policy. The first bill, however, was drafted out in the Department of Justice, which was headed by a non-partisan minister: it was published in 1989, but was not accepted by the government parties. No agreement was reached before the end of the term of the government. The 1990 electoral manifesto of the SPÖ took the issue up again and the coalition negotiations contained more detailed outlines for a new law, both in terms of substance and of procedure. This led directly to the Rent Restriction Act. This must therefore be regarded as an example of party initiation.

Taking the 1990 coalition agreement as a point of departure, the government parties started negotiating such a Rent Restriction Law. The parties were represented by three MPs and a member of the Vienna *Land* government, the Department of Justice being excluded from the talks. When the negotiations were completed, the Ministry was handed over a party agreement, which, however, neither exhausted all potential questions nor provided unambiguous answers. This agreement then served as a starting point for a more technical phase which involved both representatives of the government parties and officials of the Department of Justice. A government draft bill (*Ministerialentwurf*) was published; this started the regular consultation process (*Begutachtungsverfahren*) which led to a large number of mainly negative comments from a variety of interest groups and *Land* governments. A revised version of the draft bill was then sent to parliament, but as a private members' bill rather than as a government bill: it was presented as a joint proposal of the parties' chief negotiators. Negotiations continued in the parliamentary committee and subcommittee. Eventually a text which had been modified by joint amendments of the government parties was adopted. Although the Department of Justice had been heard again in the parliamentary committee, it hardly exercised more than technical influence. Moreover, none of the party representatives in the negotiations held executive office at the national level (one did at the sub-national level). Thus the Rent Restriction Act can be classified as a case which comes very close to the 'dominant party' model.

The introduction of a second year of paid maternity leave was initiated by the Minister of Youth, Family and Environment (ÖVP), who, in early 1989 in a joint press-conference with the ÖVP's parliamentary speaker for family matters, suggested that maternity leave ought to be expanded from one to three years. This issue had not been contained in any of the parties' electoral manifestos or the coalition agreement; moreover, it was not even agreed upon by the ÖVP before this press conference. To be sure, ÖVP programmes of the 1980s had included demands for the introduction of a monthly allowance for all mothers who did not take up or gave up a job in order to bring up their children (the so-called *Erziehungsgeld*): this did bear some similarity with the proposed increase of maternity leave. Moreover, the Minister was also the chairperson of the party's women's organisation. This policy can therefore best be seen as an initiative from a minister who had ensured herself of some intra-party support (the 'family lobby') and could draw on previous commitments of the party. Although the SPÖ was not happy with the idea of enlarging maternity leave (and its ideological background), it recognised that this would be a popular policy, for which the SPÖ wanted to share credit. Moreover intra-party conflict within the ÖVP was predictable. So the SPÖ kept a low profile and declared the enlargement of paid maternity leave as its long-established policy goal.

Indeed, the idea of enlarging (paid) maternity leave met resistance within the business wing of the ÖVP. The party executive decided none the less to support the proposal, as it was regarded as being an asset for the 1990 election. However, the executive also demanded that a solution be found for small businesses, which would suffer considerably from members of their workforce taking two years' leave. The cabinet did little to render the general consensus between the government parties more specific: the ministers of Women's Affairs (SPÖ) and of Youth, Family and Environment (ÖVP), both women, who were appointed chief negotiators, agreed on the principles of extending maternity leave to two years, on granting it to mothers or fathers, and on the date with which the new law should become effective (July 1, 1991); details were left to the social partners, however, namely the business wing of the ÖVP and to the trade unionists of the SPÖ. Because the former were still opposed to this social policy proposal, negotiations moved slowly and did not result in an agreement. A new approach was made in negotiations which involved the Ministers of Youth, Family and Environment (ÖVP), of Women's Affairs (SPÖ) and of Finance (SPÖ), as well as the Secretary of State in the Ministry of Finance (ÖVP) and the General Secretary of the ÖVP.

The stalemate situation was eventually overcome. The dispute between the ÖVP's business wing and the family lobby, that is to say the women's organisation and the Workers' and Employees' League, was settled by a decision of the party executive; inter-party negotiations were then completed. The bill was introduced by the parliamentary parties of SPÖ and ÖVP and was adopted with the support of both parties. Thus government and parties were involved and the parties and their sub-groups had contributed to substantial changes.

The nature of the government-supporting party relationships in the case of the second tax reform which was adopted in 1993 is complex. The 1987 coalition agreement had announced a second step of tax reform and discussions did indeed continue after the adoption of the first tax reform in 1988 within the Ministry of Finance, in particular between the Minister (SPÖ) and the Secretary of State (ÖVP). While the SPÖ's 1990 electoral manifesto contained only vague statements about the second tax reform, the ÖVP's manifesto included the proposal to cut substantially the taxation of firms, an idea which was to become one of the major aspects of the second tax reform. Other points were elaborated after the 1990 election in the Ministry of Finance, in particular by the Minister and his team of advisers. They included the introduction of a 'negative' tax, based on government refunds of social security contributions to those at the lower end of the income scale who do not pay taxes and therefore would not benefit from a reduction of the income tax rate; they also included a new form of local business taxation (giving local communities a fiscal incentive to develop a positive attitude towards new businesses).

Development and adoption in the case of the second tax reform policy was smoother than in the case of the first. The package was agreed between the Minister and the Secretary of State and presented as a joint proposal. There was continuous consultation with the parties during the process of elaboration of the reform. The executive of the SPÖ and the SPÖ's parliamentary party in particular received several reports from the Minister of Finance. Although no formal directives were given to him, the reactions of the two bodies helped to shape the minister's position in elaborating the tax reform. Thus, while the second tax reform and in particular its innovative elements were primarily a governmental initiative, political parties did exercise influence.

Finally, two aspects of the development of the privatisation programme need to be considered under this rubric. The first is the decision to go beyond minority shareholding and to give up the government's majority in nationalised industries and banks. This move had already been proposed by leading ÖVP politicians soon after the formation of the grand coalition government; it became official policy in the ÖVP's 1990 electoral manifesto. It did not become a major issue in the campaign, however, since the SPÖ cabinet ministers in charge of the firms to be privatised had already indicated that they would not oppose further privatisation providing it did not occur merely for ideological reasons but was justified from an economic standpoint. The SPÖ did not make any official commitment, but did not express reservations either. Thus policy initiation in the case of the ÖVP was a mixed party-government case while it was almost entirely due to the government team in the case of the SPÖ.

The question of majority shareholding was settled in the coalition negotiations which followed the 1990 election. It was not truly controversial. The party executives received reports during the negotiations and accepted the new coalition agreement.

The second key decision in the area was that of privatising individual firms rather than the holding company of the nationalised firms (Meth-Cohn and Müller, 1994). To conduct privatisation at the level of the individual firms had long been an ÖVP idea. However, the Minister of Public Economy and Transport (SPÖ), with the support of the ÖVP's chief negotiator concerned with nationalised industries, had held the view that only a holding company would be large enough to compete in the international market, a point which was considered essential, since Austria is a country of small and medium-sized firms. This view changed when the nationalised holding company suffered massive losses in 1992 and 1993 and needed additional financial support from the government. After discussion within the party, the executive of the ÖVP unanimously adopted a resolution which again demanded that privatisation be at the level of firms. The Minister of Public Economy and Transport (SPÖ) remained reluctant to accept the proposal, however. The issue then moved quickly to the top of the political agenda. The general secretary of the ÖVP and the parliamentary spokesman for industrial policy of the party made far-reaching proposals, but these were not adopted as the ÖVP's official policy. In both parties executive and parliamentary party dealt with the issue of nationalised industries. Yet practical negotiations were carried out within the government, by the Minister of Public Economy and Transport (SPÖ) and the Secretary of State in the Ministry of Finance (ÖVP). They eventually agreed on the restructuring of the nationalised sector and in particular on privatisation at the level of firms. The ÖVP had tied this matter to agreeing to support the granting of a financial guarantee by the government to the nationalised undertakings. This agreement became official for both parties and was signed by the party chairmen. Although the solution was found by means of negotiations within the government, it was also the result of party deliberations. Party politics had pushed the issue of privatisation at the level of firms to the top of the political agenda and the solution worked out by government members was determined by the parties. The government's contribution consisted essentially in elaborating a workable proposal which was acceptable to both political parties.

*Of the eight cases examined here, only one* falls in the dominant party category, the Rent Restriction Act. All others are mixed. They were initiated, processed and decided in ways which involved parties as well as government. It must none the less be remembered, as was pointed out at the outset, that we focused here on 'most likely' examples of party influence: political parties can be expected to exercise less influence in other cases.


PATRONAGE

The government has traditionally exercised patronage in Austria. In the Habsburg Monarchy and during the First Republic (1918–34) patronage was given to members and organisations of the social classes which supported the regime. Since the bourgeois parties had a loose organisation, they did not play a major role in these activities. These were rather conducted by factions and by individuals. The Second Republic (since 1945) differs in two respects: first the Social Democrats gained access to patronage resources on a large scale through their government participation, and second the People's Party and its three main factions have largely replaced the different actors which constituted the bourgeois camp in previous periods.

The heyday of party patronage was without doubt that of the first grand coalition of 1945–66. Politics was then pure party politics. Ministers depended on their party: nothing else counted. Politics was also characterised by strong party cohesion, a sharp distinction between the parties, and the non-recognition of non-partisan elements in politics and society ('those who are not with us are against us'). There were therefore good reasons for cabinet members to engage in patronage activities for their party and as long as the grand coalition existed patronage resources were divided between the parties and the coalition agreements were explicit about this (Müller, 1994b). It seems that implementation was planned to a large extent by the party secretariats which at least kept track of party 'possessions' in the public sector. Bourgeois journalists were often concerned that the party secretariat of the Socialist Party was more effective and long-term-oriented than its counterpart from the People's Party (see, for example, Vodopivec, 1960). Social Democrats in turn used to focus not so much on the pace at which they established themselves in a public sector traditionally largely alien to them but rather on the fact that their members still constituted a rather small minority in this sector.

At the time the Austrian party patronage system included the public bureaucracy at all levels (national, *Land* and local) as well as schools, the police, the armed forces and so on, whose personnel technically enjoy civil service status (*Beamte*). High job security (and occasionally also the image that public sector employees are not forced to work 'too hard') made the public service attractive even at the level of low-ranking and modestly paid jobs. Even where there was no shortage of applicants, party patronage was important; more attractive positions in the public sector, however, were automatically filled according to party-political considerations. In the case of the ÖVP, in contrast to the case of the SPÖ, patronage did not necessarily mean that the appointees were card-carrying party members, but merely that they belonged to the Catholic-Conservative camp centred on the ÖVP. The result was an almost total party political penetration of the bureaucracy. Both major parties had their strongholds in those government departments which were permanently under their control but also had 'bridgeheads' in the others (Müller, 1992: 112–15). In the army there were 'black' and 'red' divisions, as there were 'black' and 'red' schools, meaning that the parties had agreed on a kind of permanent distribution of the respective heads among each other.

Due to post-war nationalisations, Austria had probably the largest nationalised sector in Western Europe, comprising the most important industrial firms and banks. Until 1966, coalition agreements were explicit about the division of management positions between the coalition parties. Due to separate arrangements the central bank was a particularly good example of party-political penetration. Public broadcasting was divided into 'black' radio and 'red' television (which in the 1950s was not considered important). Moreover, most professional and societal activities were divided into 'black' and 'red' voluntary organisations receiving funds and other support from national, *Land* and local government. The national government was involved in these activities in two ways, first by engaging directly in patronage activities and second by providing resources to party-dominated institutions which carried out the patronage activities.

This Austrian type of spoils system provoked increasing criticism in the media and the general public. Consequently, it officially ceased to exist during the period of single-party governments (1966–83): unofficially it was still maintained. In the nationalised firms a law of 1967 established the proportional representation of political parties in the *Aufsichtsrat* of the holding company of the nationalised industries ÖIG (ÖIAG since 1969) and from that point party political appointments continued to spread down to the level of middle management or even below. In the nationalised banks party political penetration was less direct but none the less existed. The governing party pushed for a greater share among the management positions, but it was careful not to appear too greedy and it allowed the major opposition party to maintain some influence. Thus the SPÖ refrained from occupying the general directorship of the largest Austrian Bank, the Creditanstalt, for more than 10 years of its 13 years reign. Similarly, it allowed ÖVP supporters to hold the position of president of the central bank, although holders were chosen by the government rather than the ÖVP. In the bureaucracy the governing party took the lion's share of the appointments, but the other major party was not wholly marginalised: the SPÖ government was especially keen to show that it was not exploiting its power or that it was turning the civil service into an SPÖ apparatus. Therefore ÖVP supporters were still appointed to prestigious positions and some high positions were given to 'blood group O' people (that is, non party members). Since the SPÖ originally had had a weak position in the civil service compared to that of the ÖVP, it would not have had appropriate candidates available for all the vacancies, in particular not in the traditional ÖVP departments. Nevertheless, the overall effect of the SPÖ government and the subsequent SPÖ-FPÖ coalition, was a considerable shift in power in the central administration in favour of the SPÖ.

The second grand coalition which started in 1987 faced from the very beginning the criticism that it would return to the old 'iron' system of patronage, simply because the spoils now again had to be shared between two parties of almost equal strength. Given a background of declining trust in the major parties, the government tried to overcome the criticism by introducing an Appointment bill in 1989 according to which entry in the civil service was to be based entirely on the basis of objective tests. Moreover, appointments for a number of leading positions in public administration were to be made only for a fixed and limited period and according to professional criteria. In practice, however, these reforms did not substantially reduce the capacity of the government to influence personnel decisions within public administration. Indeed the top layer of the civil service is almost entirely appointed on the basis of party affiliation, appointees belonging to or being loyal to the party in charge of the department concerned. This point still holds true for the overwhelming majority of appointments down to the middle level of the civil service, although at that level some positions go to supporters of the government party which is not in charge of the department concerned in order to reduce criticisms within the ministry. There seems also to be sometimes inter-departmental log-rolling on these 'non-mainstream' appointments. Prestigious positions such as ambassadors to foreign countries or international organisations are normally negotiated between the government parties and as a result a minority of the positions go to the SPÖ which is not in charge of the Foreign Ministry. Altogether 'party' is more important for appointments in the civil service since the return to grand coalition government in 1987 than under the more 'liberal' regime of single-party rule (until 1983). Having been out of government for 17 years (from 1970 until 1987) and still having a larger clientele among civil servants (as the elections to personnel representation bodies reveal) it is probably more important for the ÖVP to realise its patronage potential in the grand coalition government.

The administrative reforms of the grand coalition have reduced the functions of the civil service somewhat. There are now private sector organisations which are assumed to be more flexible and to produce better results. In the case of the agency concerned with jobs and training (*Arbeitsmarktverwaltung*) this led to the appointment of two managers (and not one as previously), one from each of the governing parties. ÖVP cabinet members were brave enough to state publicly that this decision aimed at maintaining political control over this sector.

In the nationalised industries the formal representation of political parties in the holding company had already been abolished. Party affiliation seems to have lost much of its importance in appointments to managerial jobs: if anything other than qualification counts, it is personal networks. In a sense privatisation has substantially diminished the number of managerial jobs in the nationalised sector; yet privatisation also opens up opportunities for party patronage as well. Party political considerations seem occasionally to have played a part when the relative merits of different bids were evaluated. Moroever, the nationalised banking sector was not affected by major changes in terms of patronage apart from the second largest nationalised bank, the

(SPÖ dominated) Länderbank, which was sold to the (SPÖ dominated) Zentralsparkasse der Gemeinde Wien. Meanwhile, SPÖ and ÖVP engaged in a public battle lasting several weeks and eventually won by the ÖVP over the general directorship of the Creditanstalt; the result was that the Chancellor's image appeared to be less old-fashioned party politician than that of the Vice-Chancellor. Similarly, government parties engaged in a quarrel about the presidency of the central bank. Eventually the ÖVP succeeded in nominating the new president, thus maintaining the delicate balance of a 'black' President while the first Vice-President and the general director were both 'red'. Nothing changed in the central bank's governing body being dominated by the two major parties and the departments being divided up among them. Even within the departments this division of spoils is replicated with a 'black' department head having a 'red' deputy and *vice versa*.

This seems to suggest that Austria has not changed markedly with respect to party patronage: yet there have been some variations worth noting since the heyday of the 'classical' patronage system. The driving force of these patronage activities is no longer the central party organisation or the Leagues in the case of the ÖVP; these are not even keeping track of their 'possessions' in the civil service. It is rather the civil service representatives who are elected on party lists and the party groups in the civil service trade union which monitor appointments and try to exercise influence upon them. The parties' reluctance to deal with these matters is to some extent due to official norms against patronage which are now supported by an overwhelming majority of the population, while investigative journalism, the audit office and the courts are also willing to deal with these matters. Ministerial patronage is therefore more likely to become both a matter of public debate and harmful to the minister in charge of the patronage decision.

Given this situation, what is the rationale of government ministers to engage in party patronage activities? First, many appointments to civil service positions are made from among members of ministerial *cabinets*. These in turn had often been recruited on the basis of political affiliation, skills and above average activity. Returning them to the permanent bureaucracy means both strengthening the minister's and the party's position in the department. Second, the chance of appointment to an attractive position in the civil service or elsewhere within the ministry's sphere of influence functions as an incentive system for the members of ministerial *cabinets*. Thus in a number of cases patronage is at least as much in the interest of the minister as in the interest of his party. To be sure, each minister will be careful not to frustrate his intra-party supporters if they ask for a favour or if vital interests of the minister's stronghold are at stake. However, patronage goes beyond: although the parties as such do not systematically monitor their ministers, ministers carry inevitably an image of relative 'faithfulness' in terms of patronage. This in turn is likely to influence their standing within the party. A lack of standing in the party may be more dangerous to a minister than being occasionally mentioned as exploiting the office in party political terms, as long as this does not lead to criminal prosecution.

## CONCLUSION

As far as appointments are concerned, the 'partyness of government' is low in Austria; it is of great importance, on the other hand, in policy-making. Admittedly, specific party directives to the ministers hardly occur, as has been shown elsewhere (Müller, 1994a, pp. 23–30): party influence to a large extent consists essentially in determining the policy 'corridor' within which a solution has to be found, mainly by the government. This is due to some extent to the lack of resources of the parties, which do not have a permanent staff able to develop policies or to check their representatives in cabinet. Party patronage remains a major phenomenon in Austria: it increases the standing of ministers within their party, which makes it possible, in turn, for policies to be accepted more easily by the party.

Evidence from the single-party government period (1966–83) and from the SPÖ-FPÖ coalition government (1983–86) suggests that parties are more involved in the business of government under the grand coalition formed in 1987 and on which this chapter has mainly focused. There are reasons for such a development. The Vranitzky cabinets set up since 1987 were based on two parties of almost equal strength. Problems of portfolio distribution among two major parties inevitably result in a number of influential politicians remaining outside the government: the departments to which they might have been appointed are led by members of the other party. These politicians are inclined to participate in policy-making both by their party leader and by their own ambition. They also provide expertise and working capacity which incumbent cabinet ministers cannot as easily provide with respect to issues which do not fall within or close to their portfolios. Thus coalition cabinets (and grand coalitions in particular) tend to involve parties to a larger extent than single-party governments.

Furthermore, in grand coalitions, policies have necessarily a compromise character: the enthusiasm of parties for these policies is consequently low. Almost always long-standing commitments, the claims made in party programmes and manifestos have to be watered down in real policy-making. Parties need to be convinced that a particular policy is good or at least that it is the best deal which the party can make in the circumstances. This also means that the involvement of parties in government policy making is likely to be high.

This involvement is further affected by two factors, namely the bargaining power of each party within the government and the internal structure of the party. The party which has more bargaining power will be able to shape government policy to a greater extent; the closer a policy is to the goals of the party, the easier is the life of that party's team in government. This bargaining power depends in turn on the availability of alternative coalitions, the popularity of the policy options under consideration and on the subject matter of the issue. It is suggested in Chapter 1 that parties of the Left are more likely to intervene in the life of government than parties of the Right, because of the former's desire to achieve 'party democracy': these are indeed the general trends, but, in Austria, other factors are more important. The result is that the ÖVP is more interventionist than the SPÖ. Having a heterogeneous social base and being factionalised and geographically divided, the ÖVP creates difficulties for its cabinet members: whatever they do, there will always be some discomfort within the party. Although ÖVP politicians have learned to live with this situation, important decisions cannot be taken by cabinet members alone as they require the backing of the party. In the case of the SPÖ, on the other hand, the intervention of the party at large has been more often due to an uncomfortable bargaining position during most of the period of the grand coalition than to the pressure of the base wishing to obtain more 'party democracy'.

# 7. Finland: Operational Cabinet Autonomy in a Party-Centred System

Jaakko Nousiainen

## INTRODUCTION

Finnish politics has always been highly fragmented within the framework of a Scandinavian-type multi-party system. Especially since the 1960s new groupings have emerged to compete with the six established parties, namely the Communists, Socialists, Liberals, Agrarians, Conservatives, and the Swedish People's Party, either challenging the old ones, such as left-wing socialists or Christians, or mobilizing voters in terms of new social issues, such as the ecological movement. This situation determines the dominant type of government, which is the coalition type, while single-party governments tend to be regarded as temporary stop-gap solutions.

The Finnish party system is distinctly multi-polar, with one of the largest groups – the Agrarian Centre Party – in the middle of the range. For historical reasons there is a sharp ideological cleavage between the political left and the right, but the Centre acts effectively to reduce the gap in that it can form coalitions in both directions. In contrast to the situation in Sweden, coalition-building in Finland has not been based on the juxtaposition of the two blocs, but both socialists and non-socialists participate in governments on an equal basis. The foremost rival of the Centre, the Social Democratic Party (SDP), is in fact in a weaker position in the sense that it has never been able to search for allies from the left (Communists) without including the Centre in the coalition. Over a period of fifty years, from 1937 until 1987, 'cooperation between workers and farmers' formed a solid basis for majority coalitions.

Policy has always been a major factor in government formation in Finland. Bargaining over the formation of a new cabinet is accordingly a tough process. The end product reveals two characteristics of Finnish politics (cf. Gallagher, Laver and Mair, 1992: 189–96). One is the abundance of minority governments: no less than 14 of the total of 37 cabinets in 1945–94 were of this type. However, minority governments have not been 'normal outcomes of the process of democratic party competition', as hypothesized by Strom (1990), but temporary solutions in the absence of better options when all efforts to create a majority government have failed. At one extreme are the six non-partisan (caretaker) cabinets, which have been appointed by the president when parties have been unable to agree on any parliamentary basis for a new government. Insofar as party relationships have been consolidated, minority governments have disappeared: the country's last minority government so far dates back to 1976–7.

The other characteristic is that more often than in any other Western European country, majority governments in Finland have been oversized, that is included one or more surplus parties over the minimal winning coalition (Lane and Ersson, 1991: 242; Laver and Schofield, 1990: 71, 82). Several factors contribute to this phenomenon. One is the peculiar provision, kept in force up to 1992, that one-third of the members of parliament could delay the final adoption of most ordinary laws by one-and-a-half to two years on average. This acted to intensify endeavours to form governments that commanded at least two-thirds of the parliamentary votes. Yet perhaps of even greater importance is the fact that, in large coalitions, the bloc system has been built inside the cabinet. Together, the equally strong Centre and the Swedish People's Party might have commanded over half of the parliamentary seats, but if, as has usually been the case, there is a strong bourgeois majority in parliament, the same relationship has been brought into the government by including small centre groups. In policy terms these have not been particularly costly for the Centre Party, whereas the Social Democrats have really had no other option but to comply. The opposition has typically consisted of both extremes, the Communists and the Conservatives.

The formally appointed 37 cabinets of 1945–94 can be grouped into the following types:

| | |
|---|---|
| Non-partisan caretaker | 6 |
| Single-party or dominated | 8 |
| 2–3 parties | 3 |
| 4 parties or more | 17 |
| Grand coalition | 3 |
| Total | 37 |

Over half of all governments have been more or less heterogeneous surplus majority coalitions; in extreme cases, their parliamentary basis has exceeded 80 per cent. The Centre participated in 27 and the SDP in 21 governments. The coalition was stretched towards the left to take in the Communists in 11 governments in 1945–8, 1966–71 and 1975–83. The most frequent supplementary partner has been the Swedish People's Party, which has occupied 1–2 portfolios in 24 cabinets. The conservative National Coalition Party remained in opposition almost permanently until 1987. Since the late 1970s the situation has changed dramatically. First, Finnish governments have moved from being among the most unstable to being among the most stable in Western Europe. For sixty years the average duration of governments in Finland was about 12 months; since 1977 cabinets have resigned after presidential or parliamentary elections only and stayed in office for the whole of the four-year legislature. This is probably due to the transformation of political parties from ideological fortresses to being catch-all type electoral organizations. In a fragmented system parties have naturally retained their peculiar profiles, but, as they have broadened their support fields, their ideological fervour has been dampened down and policy conflicts have been pragmatically settled within the cabinet.

Second, the party system and the dominant coalition pattern have been reorganized. The number of small splinter parties has not been reduced, but the effective nucleus has been shaped within the frame of a three-party model: Conservatives-Agrarian Centre-Social Democrats. All two-party combinations are possible and have been tried. The Sorsa cabinets in 1983–7 formed the last red-green coalition to date (SDP-Centre). It was succeeded by an 'unholy alliance' of Social Democrats and Conservatives in the Holkeri cabinet in 1987–91, and when this coalition was dissolved after the defeat of the governing parties in the 1991 general elections a bourgeois coalition of Agrarians and Conservatives was constituted.

These governments are loose and disintegrated combinations – marriages of reason, if not marriages of necessity. Governmental policy-making in these circumstances means an incessant search for consensus and bridge-building over ideological cleavages. One must also remember that in relation to a single party the word 'government' does not mean the whole body of ministers but only a cohesive partisan group of ministers in the cabinet.

## APPOINTMENTS

As their counterparts in Scandinavian countries, Finnish parties are unitary and tightly organized mass movements. They are built bottom-up on the representative principle, and the profile of personified leadership has remained relatively low. The parliamentary party forms a dependent annex in the national organization, and ministerial groups are advanced posts defending in large coalitions vital partisan interests. Hence, the cabinet is not a unitary actor but an arena of competing forces. This fact determines the overall relationship with respect to both recruitment and policy-making: the party is the representative principal accredited by the electorate, and the party ministerial group is its agent.

The selection of ministers is wholly controlled by the party leadership. To a varying degree parties endeavour to balance the influence of the parliamentary party and the organizational leadership. In everyday reality ministers act primarily as agents of their party organizations, but the participation of MPs in the process is a concession to the formal relationships of the parliamentary system.

In the Social Democratic Party, both the party executive and the parliamentary group elect four members to the committee, chaired by the party president, which carries out the negotiations relating to cabinet formation. The final decision on participation, government programme and ministerial candidates rests with the party council or the executive, but parliamentarians are also entitled to state their opinion on these matters.

In the Centre Party the necessary decisions are made by the party council and the parliamentary group in a joint meeting. The bylaws of the People's Democratic League, which was dissolved in 1990, did not say anything about this matter, and in the Coalition Party it is settled briefly: 'As concerns negotiations about participation in government and other most important political questions, joint meetings of the parliamentary group and the party council must be arranged and decisions made in them.'

Decision-making on the issue of government formation has thus generally been moved from the party executive to a larger representative body, still within the party machinery. That body also has the power to make the basic decision about participation in a coalition, but most probably it will merely ratify ministerial selections made elsewhere. On the bourgeois side, the pivotal position is held by negotiation delegations, the majority of which consist of presidents and vice presidents of party organizations and chairmen of parliamentary groups as well as general secretaries. These comparatively small groups lead and coordinate programme discussions, distribute portfolios to participating parties, while each of them separately selects persons to these posts. The negotiators themselves are always potential ministerial candidates. In left-wing parties the grip of the regular organization is stronger; in the Social Democratic Party, ministers are ultimately selected by the party executive. Competing internal interests are adjusted in the selection process. The organizational leadership prefers its own members, persons who are already experienced in ministerial duties, as well as specialists; the parliamentary party presses for a quota of senior MPs; the largest party districts claim a territorial representation of their own.

Within the framework of this predominant model there have been noticeable variations among the parties. In general, the traditional weakness of the organizational machinery in right-wing parties emphasized in the past the autonomy and influence of parliamentary parties as well as of leading individuals, whereas officials in the left-wing mass parties had a firm grip on the top leadership of the government. Some differences may still remain, despite the fact that there has been a narrowing of the gap from both sides and a standardization of procedures.

Part of the variation comes from personalities and situations. A strong party leader, in the role of formateur, might retain the right to select the ministers of his own party; this is how the Centre's Urho Kekkonen proceeded in the 1950s. In single-party cabinets the party assumes full responsibility and possibly authorizes the prime minister to nominate members to the team. This was the case when Rafael Paasio formed his Social Democratic government in 1972 (Nousiainen, 1992: 32). Otherwise party leadership and government are combined in the nominator only when ministers are reshuffled or when a new minister is appointed to a sitting cabinet. During the period under investigation President Koivisto nominated one prime minister, the Conservative Harri Holkeri, irrespective of his party. Presidential consent is always required for the selection of the foreign minister. The president has seldom been the effective nominator, but he has an indisputable right of veto with respect to the candidates presented to him.

The governmental party groups of even the largest parties are small and variable and do not possess authority to steer organizational life. The selection of persons to leading bodies is firmly in the hands of provincial cadres. Party executives are composed of representatives of district organizations – district chairmen in the Coalition Party – and the election of the party president is a purely organizational decision taken at the party convention. The ministerial group is involved in the selection of the leader of the parliamentary party and occasionally tries to determine the decision; MPs, for their part, defend the autonomy of the parliamentary party. In 1994 Prime Minister Aho managed to prevent his rival Paavo Väyrynen from becoming group leader and thus to supervise ministerial behaviour.

In this study appointments to government and party leadership were analysed during four majority coalitions.

| Government | Formation date | Tenure months | Cabinet type |
| --- | --- | --- | --- |
| Sorsa IV | 19.02.82 | 11 | 'Red-green' + Communists |
| Sorsa V | 31.12.82 | 3 | 'Red-green' |
| Sorsa VI | 06.05.83 | 48 | 'Red-green' |
| Holkeri | 30.04.87 | 48 | Conservatives + SDP |

44 per cent of all appointed ministers were recruited from among formal party leaderships, defined as presidents and vice presidents, secretary generals and presiding officers of parliamentary groups. Over one third or 36 per cent could be regarded as 'insiders' and only 20 per cent as 'outsiders'. It is considered important in Finland that effective party leaders should enter the government; as partisan groups in cabinets are small it is understandable that they should account for a significant share. In small parties almost all ministers were party leaders, whereas among Agrarians and in the Social Democratic Party only one-fourth of the ministers belonged to the party leadership. Except for leaders of parliamentary parties, the nominees remained in the party leadership after their appointment to the cabinet. The overlap of different roles has increased in step with the consolidation of governmental policies. The Karjalainen five-party cabinet in 1970–1 is the last not to have included any party president or secretary general.

Party leadership in the institutional sense comprises the national executives of the parties which are in the government and are 10 to 30 strong. An examination of 159 cases of appointment showed that only 18 (11 per cent) were ministers of the cabinet of the day while a further 4 per cent had previous experience in government. In no case the government (the ministerial group) had been the formal or effective nominator.

The picture is therefore clear and consistent: as far as personnel recruitment is concerned, the flow of authority runs from parties to government. Furthermore, there are hardly any variations among parties and governments. The selection of ministers is controlled by party leaderships; a large majority among the ministerial nominees belong either to the top leadership or the group of party 'insiders' and individual ministers – excluding a few leaders at the topmost level – are under partisan control with respect to their recall, reshuffle and reappointment.

Yet is this control real and effective since ministerial groups are mostly composed of the respective parties' top elite who maintain their position in the party machinery? These politicians nominate themselves in effect to the cabinet and Finnish cabinet–party relationships display a high degree of integration. Yet this is not a fusion of party and government. The government is not composed of a single party leadership, but of a number of ministerial groups. At its best party policy only translates into governmental policy in the fields that the party has managed to colonize in terms of portfolio occupancy. Thus some tension is maintained between government and party, and ministerial behaviour is scrutinized by members of the party at large and by members of parliament. The party leadership in government is influential: it is not autocratic.

## POLICY MAKING: A TWO-STAGE PROCEDURE

In broad, consociational coalitions, agenda formation and policy-making have
a number of basic characteristics. Two phases need to be distinguished in
this respect, the strategic or programmatic level and the operative level. In
the first phase the agenda is settled during the negotiations over the formation
of the government and it is confirmed in the coalition agreement. In the second
phase the broad goals are made specific and operationalized, while policy
solutions on a number of new questions are formulated. Such a process
continues throughout the life of the cabinet. The relationship between the
government and supporting parties can be very different during these
two phases.

Participation in government has its disadvantages, but, given the amount
of distributive policies in which benefits are concentrated but costs are
diffused (La Spina, 1990), so has non-participation in broad coalitions. Party
leaders enjoy therefore a wide 'area of tolerance' during the cabinet negotiations. The leaders are willing to make compromises on their objectives
and to limit their demands with respect to the principles which are dear to
their party (Luebbert, 1986: 44–53). This spirit sets the tone for the coalition
agreement: it is not a detailed listing of steps to be taken but a collection of
mutually agreed-upon principles. These principles are later specified, but in
a different arena of the coalition system, the cabinet.

Yet the agenda of the cabinet cannot be fully pre-determined: new problems,
goals and solutions are continuously introduced, as only exceptionally can
modern cabinets anticipate most social problems; they normally tend primarily
to react to changes in the environment.

The dependence of the whole cabinet on the parties must be distinguished
from the dependence of the ministerial group of each party. The whole
cabinet is dependent if decisions are taken by party summits, for instance,
and if it receives ready-made, packaged solutions to be formally ratified. The
cabinet is autonomous if it discusses and decides on conflicting demands.
On the other hand, ministers and partisan groups are autonomous to the extent
that they are able to set the initial demands themselves and accept compromises that have been reached. The combination of the two variables produces
the following figure (Figure 7.1).

At one extreme the cabinet has only an implementation role, as the detailed
coalition agreement determines basic policies in detail and new problems
are settled at the party level and solutions are passed on to the cabinet. At
the other extreme the cabinet is the real centre of decision-making, with
ministers enjoying considerable latitude in policy determination. The third
type is that of the cabinet acting as a clearing house for policy problems, but

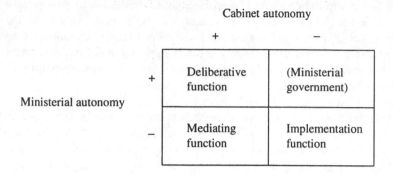

Figure 7.1: *Cabinet autonomy and ministerial autonomy in Finland*

in which ministers are instructed and steered from outside: such a decision-making model is rigid and exposed to repeated deadlocks.

In Finland, the first, programmatic phase of policy-making is dominated by the parties. Programme items are elaborated in working groups composed of parliamentarians and party specialists. At that point the coalition structure is already known, but ministerial nominations have not been made, except for the prime minister-designate, although the negotiators appointed by the parties are close to being sure of a place in the government. In the second half of the 1960s the political climate became less tense and more rational, while increased tax revenues improved the opportunities for innovative policies. Government programmes were formulated more carefully than before: they became detailed and concrete documents striving to outline in comprehensive and authoritative terms public policies for the years to come. A centrally coordinated monitoring system was introduced at the beginning of the 1980s.

Experience showed to politicians that it is difficult to introduce new initiatives once the government has started to work; this is particularly true of policies the benefits of which are reaped by the initiating group but costs fall on other groups or on the whole society. This is why a large number of issues are mentioned in the government programme. Party leaders know that the real settlement of the issues will take place later, but, by including many items in the government declaration they can succeed in having at least a voice in any future settlement. Yet even the most recent coalition agreements remain general, reading as mixtures of action programmes and of declarations. These documents, which are typically about 20 pages long, give something to everyone; they do not include implementation schedules, cost

estimates, or draft bills. With respect to major reforms the most likely pattern
is one in which broad intent is expressed with the general direction for the
project being mentioned in one sentence only. Party leaders are satisfied with
these general formulations; time and effort in the cabinet formation phase
are being saved, while costly and politically sensitive issues inevitably will
have to be processed at the collective cabinet level.

Eight policies were selected for specific analysis from the period 1977–91.
The fields covered were foreign affairs and Europe (2), financial and economic
policies (2), social and labour questions (3), and justice (1). All four cabinets
in power were large coalitions cutting across the left-right ideological divide.

Of these eight policy cases, seven had been placed on the governmental
agenda by a brief mention in the governmental declaration. Only two of them
originated directly in the electoral programmes of parties; yet even these cannot
be regarded as pure party initiatives because the issues which they covered
only gained relevance in the context of agreements between the parties of
the coalition and received their final shape as specific projects in complicated negotiations within the government. In six cases the project itself
began during these governmental discussions; in one case initiation was shared
between party and government and only one foreign policy measure was raised
inside the cabinet after the government had been formed.

Thus parties, through the agreements which they reach, are influential
agenda-setters in the first phase of governmental policy-making, economic
and welfare policy issues being typically placed in this way on the agenda,
while questions of foreign policy hardly ever are: thus even such an important
question as the unilateral alteration of the 1947 Paris Peace Treaty was initiated
in 1990 in the foreign ministry and elaborated there, the president, the prime
minister and the foreign minister being the only political participants.

If one moves from major reforms to middle-level issues, bureaucratic
initiation increases. The minister is rarely the initiator, as a survey of the drafting
of laws and regulations showed: in this respect, initiatives normally come
from officials, from semi-independent public agencies, and from the 'clients'
of departments and interest groups. When an emergency occurs, however,
the cabinet itself reacts, as was the case in 1985 when the People's Front
coalition warded off acute economic difficulties without any elaborated
programme.

A policy can hardly be said to be initiated when it is referred to in a
governmental agreement: it is merely an idea without a firm shape. Initiation
proper involves a long and cumbersome elaboration process and the inclusion
of the items concerned on the effective government agenda. The programme
of the first Conservative-Socialist coalition, formed in April 1987, contained
among other things two important new items, a tax reform and an industrial

relations reform. The parties had little difficulty in reaching a general agreement, but the following year saw endless heated debates on specific aims as well as on implementation mechanisms. Similarly, the establishment of a centrally coordinated and controlled system of occupational health care took ten years from 1968 to 1978: a variety of models were considered during the lifetime of ten cabinets. In the programme of the Aho cabinet set up in April 1991, full membership of the European Union was one option among others, and only a six-month popular debate induced the government to take a positive initiative. The issue was settled in the governmental declaration by noting that 'the Government will assess the internal development of the EC and its potential expansion from the Finnish point of view, and will strive to make decisions which will secure our national interests in the best possible way'.

At this phase of policy initiation and formulation, the concepts of cabinet autonomy and dependence and of ministerial autonomy and dependence become important. In general cabinet and ministerial autonomy have tended to increase. The cabinet hardly ever was merely implementing, but it has become an arena where coalition policies receive their final formulation; case studies did show that policy-making is cabinet-centred. General secretaries of government parties may have occasional meetings, but there are no institutionalized arenas for negotiation outside the cabinet for deliberation and mediation, while an arena for discussion and policy elaboration has been set up within the cabinet. It is established practice for the leaders of the coalition to sit on the three most important cabinet committees, namely the Economic Committee, the Finance Committee and the Foreign Affairs Committee. The first of these in particular has become a general preparatory committee for the cabinet. Moreover, a major part of the publicized conflicts are resolved inside the cabinet system, while the parties are involved in a small number of cases only (Blondel and Müller-Rommel, 1993: 275).

Long collective experience has led to the rule that far-reaching, high-cost and politically hot issues must be brought from ministries to the party-political arena for discussion and arbitration as early as possible: taking others by surprise is the surest way to ruin a good initiative: it creates suspicion and leads to rigidity, while the credibility of the minister concerned is adversely affected.

Thus *ad hoc* working groups consisting of the relevant ministers or of representatives of all government parties are the standard mechanisms aimed at steering the elaboration of policies as well as at resolving conflicts. Party representatives on these groups receive some guidance from their ministerial groups, but they still enjoy discretion to agree to compromises; when there is complete deadlock, however, the prime minister and other party leaders of the coalition may be involved. The agreement is then ratified at an unofficial policy meeting of the whole cabinet, but the question has to go back to the ministry concerned for further technical drafting.

Ministers could be given binding instructions by their parties and be mere messengers of the party executives at the coalition meetings, but this does not seem to occur. Case studies and interviews of secretary generals of the largest parties showed that detailed policy determination is essentially in the hands of the ministerial groups and that the link to the party executive is rather loose.

On the Right, party executives meet once a month only on average. At these meetings, internal party business is settled and a general discussion about the political situation takes place, based on ministerial statements. In effect, the practice is for ministers to report the development of governmental policies, on their own actions and on likely outcomes: real debates rarely occur. Both the low frequency of these meetings and the scarcity of advance information given to provincial delegates make it impossible for members to discuss seriously on-going policy measures.

Effective policy determination takes place instead at the weekly meetings of smaller groups, called working or leading committees. These inner circles consist normally of the party's ministerial group strengthened with the ministers' private secretaries, the chairman and vice chairmen of the parliamentary party, and the secretary general of the party. The group is led by the party president, who in his/her capacity as prime minister or as one of the key ministers identifies more with pragmatic coalition problems than with rigid partisan attitudes. 'High policy' issues which must be brought to the parliamentary party or to wider party arenas for discussion are also examined at these meetings.

Ministers are in principle obliged to take part in the weekly meetings of their parliamentary party. The latter may often be critical of the government and the party's ministers, but its position remains subordinate to the party leaders in the cabinet.

The smaller Social Democratic party executive used to meet regularly on a weekly basis and thus provide an opportunity for effective policy steering. Party influence was also strengthened by the fact that the secretary general was a powerful figure in policy-making and by the fact that the matters presented to the executive were prepared in the party bureaucracy. Since the early 1990s these meetings have become less frequent, however, while the secretary general has tended to concentrate on organizational activities and the policy division at party headquarters has been closed down. The ministerial group has acquired more autonomy as a result.

The experience of 1979–81 and of 1987–8 showed how isolated the party executive can be if the top leaders remain outside the cabinet. A newspaper report on an exchange of words between the newly elected Party Chairman Pertti Paasio (who at that time was still outside the government) and the Minister of Finance, Erkki Liikanen, in the Social Democratic party council was revealing: 'Paasio made it quite clear that the party sets the pace. Liikanen repeated what he had said earlier, insisting that the party should concentrate on drawing the general policy line. Matters are rolling and falling down in the government, and there is not always time to debate them with the party leadership' (Helsingin Sanomat 19 November 1987, p. 9). In his statement Liikanen summarized the nature of the decision-making process: party machines may set programmatic goals, but in a system of consensual competition efficiency requires that a wide policy space be left to ministerial groups and to individual ministers.

The policy style was summarized as follows in one policy case: 'The reform project (of industrial relations in 1987–8) highlighted the cabinet's power vis-à-vis the governing parties. Some models predict that ideologically divided coalition cabinets, such as the one in power in Finland after the 1987 elections, should be heavily dependent on guidelines and principles set by the parties. However, reality points in the opposite direction. The cabinet was very autonomous in its handling of the reform. Ministers had extensive leeway and took many decisions in a pragmatic, compromising manner, free from binding ideological commitments. The dynamics within the Social Democratic Party are an example. Although Party Chairman Paasio had claimed in the fall of 1987 that the party organization should provide the final leadership in the preparation of the reforms, Finance Minister Liikanen's conception of relative governmental autonomy did prevail. Minister Puhakka settled the reform points one by one in a closed session with three other ministers, without interference from either the party organization or from interest groups.'

Corporatism gives a variety of groups access to policy-making. Interest groups can exercise vetoes in many respects, but corporatist decision-making also requires consensus, as the industrial relations reform process showed. 'Once that consensus disappears and strong conflicts emerge on a variety of fronts, as was the case with this proposal, corporatist institutions seem to lose much of their strength. The main winner appears to be the cabinet, which sees its own power position revitalized in a conflictual situation which calls for politically directed mediation and guidance.'

Yet there are cases in which the interests at stake are so clearly outside the party political battlefield that the cabinet will not take the risk of endangering its position by pushing the project through. This occurred in the case of the establishment of the occupational health care system in the 1970s. Even though the issue was incorporated in the cabinet working agenda, majority governments made no effort to push the reform through the parliamentary machinery; they kept waiting until relevant social interests had reached an agreement not only on the general outlines of the project but on its smallest details. The final substantial solution was reached in tripartite negotiations between the Central Organization of Finnish Trade Unions, the Finnish Employers' Federation and officials from the Ministry of Social Affairs and Health.

The nature of coalitions being what it is, the issue could be labelled in four of the cases studied as being highly controversial and in two cases as somewhat controversial between coalition parties. In these controversial cases, the process lasted much longer than would have been needed for preparation and parliamentary procedure. One way to avoid clashes among government parties and with the opposition is to divide the project and proceed step by step: this increases the coordinating role of the minister and ministry concerned. This method was used successfully in the context of constitutional reforms after the failure of a complete revision in the 1970s; the government also resorted to this method from the late 1980s with respect to privatization, which has remained a highly sensitive issue. The cabinet did not formulate a comprehensive privatization programme, but handled the matter quietly by requesting in each case an authorization from parliament to reduce state ownership in an enterprise or to privatize it altogether.

Thus policy-making in Finnish coalition governments is clearly a two-phase procedure. In the first, the interests of participating parties are mediated through negotiations, in which differences are diminished and turned into consensual national goals: the party machine exercises considerable influence at this point. In the subsequent process of detailed operationalization, the ministerial group in the cabinet enjoys increased autonomy: in relation to their parties ministers are trustees rather than delegates.

Rarely, if ever, have Finnish governments been reduced to merely implementing policies dictated to them. Even when party battles were heated, the government was a broker; with policy-making having become pragmatic, the deliberative function and the operational autonomy of the government have been increased.

The nature of the coalition does not seem to play a major part: Agrarian-Socialist, Conservative-Socialist, and Agrarian-Conservative majority coalitions have all managed to fit their policy-making within the same framework. Admittedly, three of the four most conflictual measures were settled in 'red-green' coalitions, but this was probably more because of the nature of the issues than because of the type of coalition. Minority coalitions dominated by one party and the very few single-party governments have acted differently: there has been in these cases a direct link between party preferences, government declaration, and cabinet agenda; operations can then be led by either the party or the government. A minister who served in Rafael Paasio's Social Democratic government in 1972 gave a concise description of the atmosphere of that cabinet (Nousiainen, 1991: 52): 'The government declaration was put together hurriedly and summarily. The starting point was that it is always possible to agree within the cabinet or in the party about what would be done and how it would be done. This was the great advantage of a single-party government. If someone asked something about the government programme, we could say: which Social Democratic platform do you want to see?' Policy-making was thus highly party-centred.

Although it is not possible to be definite, it seems that in consociational coalitions parties will fight hardest for policies whose benefits and/or costs are concentrated in specific groups in the society, whereas general policies, for which benefits and costs are more diffused, are willingly left for cabinet ministers to elaborate and settle. The issues which have been most conflictual and took longest to decide on were indeed in the social and economic fields.

## PATRONAGE

In multi-party systems, the borderline between macropatronage and policy is rather vague: political actors are directly linked to particularistic interests. In a large and sparsely populated country such as Finland, geographical distinctions also apply: thus, if the Centre Party in the cabinet asks for special support for farmers in Northern Finland – the party is by far the largest in that part of the country – is this an example of party policy or of party patronage? Similarly, the constant endeavour of Swedish People's Party ministers in the government is to improve the living conditions of the Swedish-speaking population in the islands off the Western coast of the country: this is regarded as being an integral part of the policy objectives of the party.

Even if defined in narrow terms, patronage is not unknown, although it is clearly not a core element of the political system or a major factor in the relationships between government and supporting parties. The political culture is legalistic; the spoils system has never been applied and administrative formalism sets its limits to partisan profit-seeking. Yet, without giving precise figures, a number of specific points can be made.

### Jobs

The allocation of jobs, both at the national and provincial levels, on party-political grounds is the most visible form of patronage. The partisan tone is clear in the highest offices of the ministries, the central public agencies, and in the highest offices of provincial administration. In earlier years Social Democrats and Agrarians used to conclude major appointment packages to preserve a mutual balance; this task was assigned to one of the ministers of the party. The partisan use of appointing power is regarded by the public as a form of corruption, but even though President Kekkonen once threatened to open the packages and the most recent governments have promised to drop the practice, it still exists.

*Public works*
There has been some patronage in relation to the building of roads, bridges, ferry connections, schools, airfields, in the more remote parts of the country; decisions are based on party-political relations and not on administrative criteria. One of the ministers put it openly in an interview: 'I thought that the achievements of every minister should include the building of one road in his or her home province. The cost was only five million. A provincial party influential had entrusted it to me' (Nousiainen, 1992: 99).

*Subsidies and grants*
Parts of the budget are allocated to parties and other political organizations which are not technically part of the party, as well as to party-bound enterprises which run rehabilitation centres, spas, and holiday hotels. Government and opposition often make behind-the-scene deals about these grants. Party financing as a whole is a multifaceted and complex network (see Wiberg, 1991).

It is difficult to state definitely whether the party or the government (ministerial group) requests the patronage. Ministers act in the name of their parties and the allocation is made by individual ministers or by the cabinet collectively. Meanwhile, provincial and local patronage is clearly a reward for deserving party work and an incentive to further endeavour and it largely satisfies demands from both party officials and mass supporters. Party activists expect it from their MPs and ministers: they are disappointed if these 'trustees' confine their activities to the national level only. Yet it remains ultimately difficult, even there, to differentiate patronage from policy.

CONCLUSION

We have examined party-government relationships in Finland on the basis of an analysis of the role of cabinets and ministers in appointments, policy-making, and patronage. Yet Finland obviously differs from other Western

European countries, except France, in that it is regarded as being 'semi-presidential': does this difference in regime structure influence the relationship between government and supporting parties?

The answer is clearly negative. The combination of parliamentarism and presidentialism in Finland is based essentially on a clear division of duties. As Lijphart (1994: 15–16) stated: 'although the directly elected Finnish president has special authority in foreign policy, Finland operates like a parliamentary system in most other respects'. Foreign policy is an exception because it has been taken away from the party-political decision-making arena: typically parties did not make any inroads into foreign policy and governmental initiatives were supported by the presidential authority in this respect. The situation changed with the decision to apply for membership of the European Community in 1992, in part because this went beyond the bounds of conventional foreign policy; both parties and interest groups were very active in this respect, with the cabinet assuming the role of a clearing house for differing views and with the president remaining in the background.

The president supports every government he has appointed. Ministers feel loyal towards the formal 'nominator' and in conflict situations cabinets are occasionally tempted to hide behind the president. Foreign policy may also serve to an extent as a compensating device for the government vis-à-vis the supporting parties. Yet the tone of politics is not altered as a result.

Overall patronage distribution plays only a marginal part in the overall pattern of relationships. By satisfying some of the particularistic needs of supporting parties – including by agreement with the opposition – the government can buy itself time to work in the general policy field and calm down party officials who are uneasy about the perpetual compromises which have to be made in coalition governments.

The critical factors are the appointment procedures and style of policy-making. The primary actors are the party organizations, with respect to which parliamentarians and ministers are 'agents'. Most parties were born as 'extra-parliamentary' and 'extra-governmental' organizations in the country: they are the 'principals' of the parliamentary system, a point which is not denied even today.

The system is thus heavily party-centred and government-dependent. Yet its everyday appearance is influenced by the fact that both appointments and policy-making contain strong compensatory factors which modify the balance in favour of the government. It is not that ministerial groups have access to the selection of the leadership of the parties, but that they can be released from their dependence, to an extent with respect to ministerial appointments and to a greater extent in the policy process. Compensations occur both within each element and as an exchange between the two elements.

In appointments to the cabinet there is a transfer of leadership. Personalized leadership increased markedly since the 1970s while greater governmental stability led to the conclusion that policies are made in the cabinet. Ministerial groups are composed of their parties' top elite and are led by the party president. Party presidents have no formal powers to appoint members of their team, but the effective choices are largely made in the parliamentary party and among a small group of negotiators.

In policy-making, the following interrelated factors play a part: (1) mutually agreed broad programmatic goals to specific policy measures have to be elaborated; (2) the collective cabinet is the arena for this elaboration; and (3) ministerial groups constitute partisan policy-making committees and have wide discretion. Such a state of affairs may be the result of the centralized and representative structure of the parties. Once leaders have been selected, they are entrusted with the task of representing the party in the policy-making complex on the assumption that they do what is best for the party and the country.

The cabinet is a central clearing house for public policies, but the economic and social policy area is largely corporatist. The cabinet is the only body with enough resources and information to keep the corporatist conglomerate together. Meanwhile, MPs are not steered by party headquarters but by the cabinet.

There is thus interdependence of the government and its supporting parties. The constitutive principle is the dependence of the ministerial groups on party organizations, but there is scope for cabinet autonomy in the policy-making area as parties do not have the resources needed to be informed about day-to-day operations, nor the means to supervise ministerial behaviour.

The autonomy of ministers has increased since the 1970s, in part because of changes in the nature of coalition politics in the country. With governments lasting 12 months, governmental cooperation was characterized by rigid attitudes among partners and a tendency to draw ministers back after even minor misfortunes. The coalition agreement was not able to direct effectively cabinet decision-making and coalitions had little room for manoeuvre: the policy elasticity of governments was low but coalition elasticity was high (Nousiainen, 1991: 55–7).

Since the 1970s, strong consensual pluralism has prevailed. Participation in the government has acquired a different meaning: parties enter the cabinet to pursue long-term national policies and not to fight on narrow group interests. Party leaders cannot afford to stay outside; both political visibility and the desire to exercise major influence forces them to take the important portfolios. Governmental stability presupposes functional flexibility; changes of government result directly from a major shift in the electoral support of the parties. Policy elasticity as a means of coping with stress presupposes an adaptation to changing circumstances as well as a slow bargaining process in order to reach decisions: party leaders in government play a key part in this process. Indeed, in extreme cases the relationship is reversed: the government appears as the principal, the parliamentary party and the party in the country being the agents, as the former ratifies policies accepted by the cabinet and the latter explains the policy to supporters and secures the continuing support to the government.

Ministerial autonomy also tends to be strengthened with the increased duration of governments. Ministers begin to identify with the cabinet team: in the past, this was a problem, in particular for the Communist Party which was involved in seven governments between 1966 and 1982. The ministers were also drawn back from two governments in the middle of the term.

The relationship between policy-making and government autonomy is not linear. During the period of prosperity of the late 1970s and 1980s, much could be distributed and the parties could therefore give their ministers a free rein. As the effective policy space became smaller, party officials were mobilized to defend the interest of their supporters. The experience of the Aho government of the early 1990s indicated that in times of deep recession perceived alternatives are few and programmes drawn up in advance are meaningless. The government struggled by means of emergency measures from one month to another in order to relieve the acute effects of the economic crisis.

# 8. The Netherlands: Parties Between Power and Principle
## Rudy B. Andeweg

### INTRODUCTION

At first sight, the relationship between Dutch governments and their supporting parties during the post-World War II period is characterized by a great many constants. The institutional context in which parties and government interact has not changed: throughout this period the Dutch political system has been a constitutional monarchy, equipped with a bicameral parliament and with probably the most proportional electoral system in the democratic world. It was and still is a highly centralized political system, in the sense that local and regional governments enjoy very little autonomy, while also being fragmented in two other ways. Policy-making is fragmented because more or less neo-corporatist networks of interest groups, quangos and advisory councils, specialized agencies or departmental officials, as well as specialized MPs and even ministers, assume a highly autonomous position. Because policy-making of this type crosses party lines and divides the government, we shall not dwell on this otherwise important source of fragmentation of the Dutch political system in this analysis of the relationship between governments and parties in the governing majority. The second and equally constant source of fragmentation is the party system. On average, more than 21 parties have contested post-war parliamentary elections, and more than 10 have been represented in the Second Chamber, the Dutch Parliament's most important house. Even if we count only 'relevant' parties according to Sartori's criteria of having participated in government or of having blackmail potential, there are still between five and seven parties in the decades since World War II. Within this multi-party system there have been changes, such as the decline of the three main Christian Democratic parties, their subsequent merger into the CDA, and the ascendancy of the Conservative Liberal VVD and Progressive Liberal D66; yet what is of greater significance is what remained constant, namely that no political party ever obtained a majority in votes or seats; indeed, no party is sufficiently close to the 50 per cent mark to even dream of majority status.

A country of minorities can either be governed by a minority single-party cabinet or by a majority coalition. For reasons that still await elucidation, the former option has never crossed the minds of Dutch political elite, although three out of 21 post-war cabinets have been minority coalitions, always as interim solutions after some governmental crisis. More strikingly, ten cabinets were oversized coalitions, that is they were supported by more parties than was necessary to obtain a parliamentary majority. Eight of these oversized coalitions date back to before 1966, and since then minimum winning coalitions have been the rule. Lijphart interprets this as an important change, and the only movement away from a consensus democracy in the Netherlands (Lijphart, 1989: 147–9). To a large extent it is an artifact, however: without the merger of the three Christian-Democratic parties into one, most coalitions would probably still be oversized.

Finally, the primary ideological dimensions on which the parties align themselves, and on which governing coalitions are formed, have also remained unchanged. There is the common socio-economic Left-Right dimension, with the Social-Democratic PvdA on the Left, the Progressive-Liberal D66 on centre-left, the Christian Democratic CDA on centre-right, and the Conservative-Liberal VVD on the right. In addition, there is a religious-secular dimension with the CDA on the religious side and all other major parties in more or less the same position on the secular side. There are indications of other ideological dimensions growing in importance, such as ethnocentrism (with the arrival of the extreme right-wing CD) or post-materialism (with a Green Left party, and deep divisions within the PvdA), but these have yet to surpass class or religion as the main cleavage lines.

Until 1994, all coalitions have been formed along the socio-economic dimension, and have included the Christian-Democrats.[1] This is important for an analysis of the relationship between government and governing parties, because the secular governing parties have always been restrained in their pursuit of liberalization of abortion, euthanasia, and similar topics, by their participation in governments with the Christian-Democrats.

In terms of institutions, party system, ideological cleavages, and type of government, the stage on which governments and supporting parties play their respective roles has thus remained relatively unchanged throughout the post-war period. Yet these roles have undergone a marked development. To follow the distinction made in Chapter 1, there has been a movement away from the relative autonomy of government and parties to something approaching a merger. In the Dutch literature this is often described as a move away from 'dualism' between government and parliament, towards 'monism' of government and governmental majority in parliament, although the implication is wider than merely about executive-legislative relations. This change can be noticed with respect to the recruitment of ministers, policy-making, and patronage, as we shall see in the course of this chapter. Interestingly, the relationship has been criticized as undemocratic, both in the past when there was near-autonomy, and at present when there is near-merger.

There are several possible explanations for the fact that in the past, although governments have always been supported by a parliamentary majority of parties, these governments and these parties used to maintain a considerable degree of autonomy. First, despite the fact that the Dutch constitution clearly establishes a parliamentary system of government, it also stipulates that ministers cannot be members of parliament. Ministers can participate in parliamentary debates, but they sit on separate benches, facing MPs. Such an arrangement gives to Dutch politics a flavour of separation of powers: this contributes strongly to the autonomy of government and of supporting parties, as can be seen in Chapter 1. Second, the Queen still initiates and formally supervises the formation of cabinets, appoints the ministers, and keeps in regular contact with them. Clearly, the Queen's role belongs to what Bagehot called the dignified, not the effective, part of the constitution, but the result is none the less that ministers still see themselves as being to some extent representatives of the Crown. As one of them remarked in the 1950s: 'The closer to the throne, the less partisan'. Finally, consociational democracy has not left its mark on this aspect of Dutch politics, as it did on most others. Lijphart observed that, in order to maintain their politics of accommodation, the leaders of the various pillarized segments in society, observed a set of 'rules of the game'. One of these rules was the government's right to govern (Lijphart, 1975: 134–8). For the government to be legitimate to all pillars, it had to be raised above the daily political squabbles and to assume a relatively non-partisan, technocratic posture.

The resulting relative autonomy of government and supporting parties has been severely criticized as undemocratic, especially during the wave of neo-democratic fervour of the late 1960s and early 1970s. It was argued that the political parties, as the political arms of the pillars, mobilized the voters with ideologically worded manifestos and campaigns, after which a government was formed almost regardless of the election outcome, which then governed in a pragmatic, depoliticized manner. Some of the criticisms were shared by well-known advocates of consociational democracy. Daalder started his career criticizing the patrician style of Dutch politics (Daalder, 1964). Lijphart was sympathetic to D66, a party founded in 1966 to democratize the system by introducing 'majoritarian' reforms such as direct elections for prime minister (Lijphart, 1970). Later, he seemed to regret his earlier critique: '(...) if I could write *The Politics of Accommodation* over again, I would be much less apologetic about the democratic quality of consociational democracy' (Lijphart, 1984: 14).

The renewed international interest in democratization coincided with the erosion of pillarization in the Netherlands. When the loyalty of subcultural electorates was no longer automatic, election campaigns became heated battles for the undecided voters. This resulted in increased polarization between the parties and in the politicization of issues hitherto left unpoliticized. The newly- rediscovered democratic ethos demanded that this should also affect the composition and policies of the government. In general, all efforts to establish a direct link between a party's electoral fortunes and its influence in government have foundered on the unchanged reality that all parties remain minorities and coalitions are therefore a necessity. As a consequence, despite the continued decline of pillarization, consociational practices were resumed in the 1980s (Andeweg and Irwin, 1993: 44–9). However, the remaining effect has been that the political parties have more or less colonized the government in terms of its personnel, programme, and policies. It is precisely this result of past attempts at democratization that is currently decried as undemocratic. The new role of the government programme as a negotiated coalition agreement, binding all ministers and MPs within the governing coalition, is seen as stifling democratic debate in parliament, rendering ministers immune from parliamentary sanctions, making all opposition proposals fruitless, and reducing elected representatives to lobby fodder. Some go further, and accuse the parties of moderating their manifestos in order to enhance their attractiveness as coalition partners to such an extent that, in the words of one critic, Holland has become a one-party state (Oerlemans, 1990). It is, in fact, a Dutch version of the international lament of the end of ideology.

This critique is reinforced by the circumstance that Dutch politics has not proven immune to the general malaise of political parties. Dutch parties have been weakened in terms of voter loyalty, membership, the role of the party press, and so on. At the same time, they have colonized the government, and are making increasing demands on the government for the direct funding of their activities. In the Netherlands, as elsewhere, one can simultaneously detect fear of 'a decline of parties' and anger about 'partitocrazia'. According to Mair, these are simply different sides of the same coin, 'for despite the apparent decline in the "partyness" of European society (…), there has certainly been no decline in the "partyness" of the European state' (Mair, 1994: 18): the political elite have moved the parties more and more towards the state and have weakened the parties' roots in civil society.

Even if we leave aside the question as to whether this situation is the result of voluntary actions by the political class, the Dutch case may thus highlight a more general phenomenon with regard to the relationship between governments and supporting parties. As intermediaries between state and civil society, parties are caught between the devil of 'autonomy' and the deep sea of 'merger'. When there is autonomy of government and parties, parties are criticized as being irrelevant; when there is merger of government and parties, parties are accused of losing their proper role and of becoming 'para-statal' organizations. In the Netherlands the parties have been in both positions, and have suffered both types of criticism.


## APPOINTMENTS

Truly non-partisan ministers have been rare in the post-war period. The last cabinet minister without party affiliation left the government in 1956 and the last junior minister to be in the same condition did so in 1967. Although formally appointed by the Queen upon nomination by the *formateur*, ministers are in reality recruited by the leaders of their party, subject to only the rarest of vetoes by another party in the coalition. However, it was not uncommon in the past for ministers to become party members between nomination and appointment only. In 1971 the VVD leadership was unable to find a party member able and willing to take responsibility for the Economic Affairs portfolio which had been assigned to the VVD in the cabinet formation. The *formateur* then suggested a non-partisan professor of economics who had voted for his own party, the (subsequently defunct) protestant ARP. The professor was invited, recruited into the VVD, and sworn in as government minister. In 1982 a junior minister for Defence was forced to resign after only three days in office, when it was revealed that he had lied about his party membership, army commission, and academic title. The last two lies contributed most to his downfall, however. Such anecdotes testify to a measure of autonomy in the relation between governments and governing parties.

The constitutional incompatibility of ministerial office and membership of parliament has contributed to this autonomy.[2] Had a seat in parliament been a prerequisite for ministerial appointment, the 'partyness' of the government would have been much higher, as entry into parliament is through a party slate of candidates. From the introduction of ministerial responsibility in 1848 to 1990, only 35 per cent of all cabinet ministers were recruited from parliament, and an additional 7 per cent had some prior parliamentary experience. This is now changing, however. For cabinets between 1946 and 1967 the figures were still similar to the averages mentioned above, but of the ministers appointed between 1967 and 1990, 53 per cent came directly from parliament, and another 15 per cent had been an MP before

(Secker, 1991: 198, Table 12.1). In subsequent cabinets, ministers without prior parliamentary experience have become exceptional.

A similar development has taken place with regard to the position of the prime minister. In the past it was not uncommon for the party leader of the largest party in the coalition to stay in parliament, while a representative from a smaller coalition party, or even an outside recruit, became prime minister. As late as 1973, a former Catholic Party leader could still assert that 'being the parliamentary leader of the largest governing party is a much more influential, powerful, and creative function than being Prime Minister.' (Schmelzer, quoted in Ammerlaan, 1973: 241). Four postwar cabinets have been led by prime ministers from minor governing parties, but all four were pre-1973. Between 1945 and 1994, out of 12 prime ministers, only five have been leaders of their party, but four among these five cover the 1971–94 period (Andeweg, 1991: 123–5). There are thus symptoms of a gradual move away from autonomy towards merger, but the move is not complete nor is it irreversible,[3] as a more detailed examination of the three most recent cabinets in the period under consideration (Lubbers I–III, 1982–86; 1986–9; 1989–94) shows.

In these cabinets the CDA was the leading party. Indeed, throughout the postwar period until August 1994, Christian-Democrats have been included in all governments. As one of its MPs became famous for remarking: 'We run this country'. It is with regard to this party that the shift away from autonomy is most evident. Dutch political parties do not have a formal leader (Hillebrand, Irwin and Zielonka-Goei, 1989); the most important positions are those of chairman of the parliamentary party in the Second Chamber, president of the party executive, and – when in government – of (deputy) prime minister. The constitution and party by-laws preclude holding these positions jointly. Yet it is generally possible to identify one of the three office-holders as the true party leader. Before 1977, with few exceptions, the leaders of the three Christian-Democratic parties that were to form the CDA were the chairmen of the parliamentary parties. Since the merger of the three parties, the party leader is the prime minister. However, as the three Lubbers cabinets show, there can be three different situations: (a) a new party leader is not part of the outgoing cabinet, but becomes the new prime minister, nominates the other ministers from his party, and has a decisive voice in their future reappointment (Lubbers I); (b) the prime minister cum party leader continues in a new cabinet, appoints or reappoints his party's ministers, and decides over their future reappointment (Lubbers II); and (c) the prime minister cum party leader continues in a new cabinet, but announces his coming retirement, and thereby loses the power to appoint his party's ministers in the future (Lubbers III). The nomination process comes closest to 'fusion' in the apppointments to the Lubbers II cabinet, whereas the nomination process in the Lubbers I cabinet shows signs of 'government dependence on party', the Lubbers III cabinet being intermediate.

From the point of view of the nominees, in all three Lubbers cabinets the informal party leader was also the leader of the government ('fusion'), although the early designation of a successor as party leader during the Lubbers III cabinet resulted in more intra-party conflicts, especially between the party's MPs (led by the crown prince) and its ministers (led by the leader himself). It is characteristic of the CDA as a long-term governing party that many of its nominees belonged to a previous government. Although Lubbers was a new party leader in 1982, when he made his seven appointments (excluding that of himself), he kept three cabinet ministers from the outgoing government, promoted a junior minister to cabinet rank, and appointed a senior civil servant, Brinkman, his later crown prince, as minister. Of the remaining appointees, one was a complete outsider (a banker and personal friend), and only one can be regarded as a party insider. In his second cabinet, Lubbers retained seven incumbent cabinet ministers and reappointed someone with previous ministerial experience. The appointment to a ministerial post by the chairman of the party executive constituted the only input from the party leadership. In the third and last Lubbers cabinet, the proportion of incumbents was reduced, but only one incumbent was not replaced by a party leader, but by an outsider.

The two other parties which have participated in these cabinets, the Conservative-Liberal VVD (Lubbers I and II), and the Social-Democratic PvdA (Lubbers III), regularly alternate between government and opposition; the two parties approach their role of supporting party from very different perspectives, however. The PvdA has always advocated the 'government dependent on party' position, whereas the VVD is reluctant to abandon 'autonomy'.

When the VVD entered the Lubbers I cabinet in 1982 after a brief spell in opposition, its new leader, Nijpels, returned to the previous practice according to which the party leader stays out of the cabinet. His predecessor had broken with that tradition by combining the party leadership with the deputy premiership, with his replacement being merely an interim parliamentary party chairman. Although Nijpels did not enter the cabinet in 1982, he claimed to have the power of recall over his party's ministers, a suggestion roundly rejected by the ministers concerned. Despite Nijpels' efforts to direct the VVD's ministers, the party had in fact returned to 'autonomy'. This was reaffirmed in 1986, after the VVD had suffered heavy losses. During a stormy meeting of the parliamentary party, it was decided that Nijpels would be allowed to stay on as leader only for the duration of the formation of the new cabinet. He would then nominate himself as one of his party's ministers, on condition that he would not become deputy prime minister. When the subsequent struggle for his succession for the leadership was unresolved, it was further decided that the VVD would be led by a duumvirate: De Korte, as deputy prime minister, and Voorhoeve, as parliamentary party chairman. That it was the latter who was soon recognized as the true party leader testifies to the Liberal preference for the autonomy of government and supporting party.[4]

This might suggest that ministerial appointments in the VVD would be 'outsiders': yet this is not the case. Only two of the seven VVD ministers in the Lubbers I cabinet were outsiders and none among the six appointments to the Lubbers II cabinet were outsiders.[5]

Although the PvdA twice had unhappy experiences with its leader in the role not of prime minister, but of deputy prime minister, there was little discussion in 1989 when Kok decided to join the cabinet in that capacity. He also became minister of Finance, and doubts were raised, and later proven justified, about the combination of such a demanding portfolio with the party leadership. Although he could have nominated several party members who had been in government before, Kok invited only one experienced cabinet minister and two with previous experience as junior minister. The fact that he appointed one outsider is probably the exception that proves the rule that the PvdA nominates party leaders and insiders to government positions.[6]

With respect to appointments to the government, therefore, one can conclude that there has been a long-term trend away from autonomy, with the CDA closest to 'fusion', the PvdA to 'party dependent', while the VVD was little affected. On the other hand, autonomy still seems the rule when nominations to positions of party leadership are concerned. It is difficult to determine what constitutes party leadership in Dutch political parties. In some parties regional party leaders sometimes play an important role, but in general it seems safe to say that the party organization's executive, and the executive of the parliamentary party, together with the (deputy) prime minister, constitute the party leadership. In general, the emphasis in all parties is on the chairman of the parliamentary party or, when in government, on the (deputy) prime minister, but not on the party organization chairman: during the Lubbers III cabinet the chairpersons of both PvdA and CDA acted as scapegoats and resigned because of blunders committed by others in the party leadership. There is only limited overlap between party organization leadership, parliamentary party leadership and governmental party leadership. The chairman of the parliamentary party, for example, is usually an *ex officio* member of the party executive. However, in all parties positions in the government are incompatible with positions in these bodies. Formally, the parliamentary party elects its own chairman and executive, while the party conference elects the party chairman and executive; in practice, the party leader, regardless of his formal position, is involved in the recruitment to leadership positions. This is certainly the case for the selection of the party chairman in CDA and VVD (but not in the PvdA) and for the selection of the parliamentary party chairman in the CDA and the PvdA when the leader is in government. These are also the most important positions. Interestingly, few are appointed from the government to the party leadership; cabinet

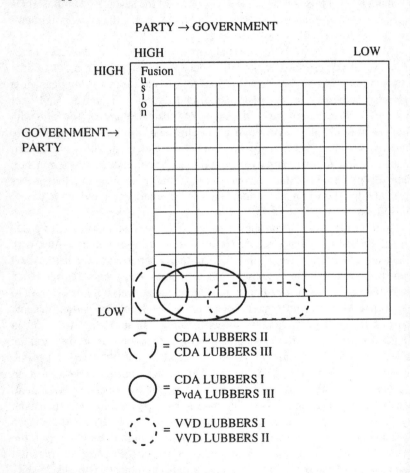

Figure 8.1: *Recruitment and the relation between government and supporting parties*

ministers are sometimes 'parachuted' in the chairmanship of the CDA parliamentary party, but not so much to control the party's MPs, as to provide an opportunity for the leader's 'crown prince' to assume a more public profile and as an apprenticeship to gain leadership experience. Former ministers can be found from time to time in the party executive, but they tend to fall into the category of 'men in grey suits' rather than in that of representatives of the government.

Thus because of the relative autonomy of the party to recruit its own leaders, the development towards more 'partyness' of ministerial appointments does not result in complete 'fusion'. Only as a result of its long and uninterrupted participation in government, the CDA approaches a situation of 'fusion'. For the other parties, and especially the PvdA, the government is more dependent on the party.

POLICY

The formation of a new government is important not only because of the nomination of ministers, but also as an arena for policy formulation (Petersen et al, 1983). Dutch governing coalitions have comprised up to five different political parties: there is therefore not one election manifesto transforming into a government programme on election night.

As with ministerial appointments, this transformation used to be characterized by a considerable degree of autonomy of parties and government. Since the 1920s, the leaders of the parliamentary parties have negotiated a policy package known as *'regeeraccoord'* (coalition agreement), but only fairly recently has this coalition agreement come to dominate the policy relationship between governments and governmental parties. Originally, the agreement dealt with broad outlines of government policy only and was binding on the ministers only. During the first meeting of the new government, ministers would elaborate the coalition agreement, adding projects which were not mentioned, in order to produce a government programme to be presented to parliament in an official declaration. Since 1963, however, parties extended their grip on the government programme by negotiating increasingly elaborate and detailed coalition agreements, leaving less and less leeway for newly appointed ministers to amend or add. The government programme has now come to be almost identical to the coalition agreement. Moreover, also since 1963, the agreement came to bind not only ministers, but MPs of the governing majority as well.[7] Within the PvdA the coalition agreement needs the consent of a special party conference before the party formally accepts to become part of the government. In other parties the party outside parliament is bound to the agreement only informally through the approval given by the party chairperson or executive. In this way the coalition agreement has become a kind of contract or treaty between the government and its supporting parties. This development is reinforced by the evolution of a system of consultations within the governing majority. Every Thursday evening, ministers of each governing party meet the chairman of their parliamentary party in the Second Chamber (and in the VVD and the CDA the chairman of the parliamentary party in the First Chamber as well; in the PvdA this occurs only on an ad hoc basis) and the party organization chairman. Sometimes others, primarily MPs who are experts on whatever is on the agenda that week, will be present. This meeting serves to discuss the party's strategy for the weekly cabinet meeting on Friday.[8] Before that meeting, on Wednesday, the prime minister meets with his deputy prime minister(s) and with the chairmen of the parliamentary parties which support the government. The coalition agreement is an important document in both these intra- and inter-party meetings, especially in the first months in office. Later, the agreement may be rendered out of date by new economic trends and international events, but it would be a mistake to underestimate the importance of the coalition agreement for this reason.

The greater importance assigned to the government agreement was intended to strengthen the governing parties' grip on government policy, but the fact that the agreement is now also binding on the parties or at least on the parliamentary parties, may also have the opposite effect. The negotiations on the coalition agreement are conducted by the party leaders. Indeed, when they are likely to become ministers themselves, anticipatory socialization will make them see the agreement from the government's perspective. In the published diaries of Jan Terlouw, D66-leader and deputy prime minister from 1981–3, the author mentions a meeting, during the negotiations with his future department's permanent secretary, advising him on what should be put into the coalition agreement (Terlouw, 1983: 75–6). A minister for development cooperation recalled in an interview how he had written the relevant paragraph of his party's election manifesto, and how he had assisted his party leader by writing a draft on development cooperation for the coalition agreement: 'I was carrying out my own policies' (interview by the author). During the 1982 cabinet formation, teams of MPs from the prospective governing parties were formed to negotiate the most important chapters of the coalition agreement. Some of these MPs later became ministers, but the teams were also assisted by civil servants. Whole parts of that coalition agreement on socio-economic policy were written by two senior Treasury officials. The government's input into the coalition agreement is strongest when incumbent ministers who expect to belong to the next government are directly involved in the negotiations or are indirectly involved by proposing amendments to the first draft of the agreement as members of the parliamentary party.[9] There are many indications that such influence was especially marked in the 1986 cabinet formation, when the CDA and the VVD both continued to be in government, but it can be traced before as well, in particular in the CDA. In this respect, too, that party's long tenure of office resulted in something approaching 'fusion'.

However, the fact that the Christian-Democrats never governed alone, but were always joined in government by, alternately, the PvdA and the VVD (as well as occasionally by minor parties) prevented the development towards fusion from affecting the whole government and governmental majority. A change of coalition partner clearly does have policy effects. These effects are not visible on the total level of government spending, admittedly, as in the Netherlands, for example, coalitions including Social-Democrats did not increase government spending more than other coalitions (Cameron, 1978: 1255, Fig.1); but the policy impact of the government's party composition makes itself felt in other ways. Such an impact is notoriously difficult to ascertain, as we never encounter the ideal experimental situation with different coalitions governing the same country at the same time. Fortunately, Dutch cabinet-making provides us with the next best solution. In 1977, an attempt to form a coalition including the CDA, the PvdA and D66 failed at the last moment and a coalition of the CDA and the VVD was formed. Both rounds of negotiations resulted in a coalition agreement. As we shall see below, the text on abortion was identical in both documents: this suggests that the PvdA and the VVD, being both secular parties, have a similar impact in this policy area. On housing, however, there is an emphasis on rent protection in the centre-left agreement, and on stimulating home ownership in the centre right agreement. The centre-left agreement provided for compensation for expropriations to be based on the real estate's user value, the centre-right agreement provided for similar compensation based on market value. The centre-left agreement continued the development of comprehensive education; the centre-right agreement planned to stimulate experiments with alternatives to comprehensive education and added measures to protect small schools in less densely populated areas. The centre-left agreement allowed for trade union participation in the implementation of a profit-sharing law; the centre-right agreement contained no such provision. The centre-right agreement was also more firm in its commitment to defence.

Whether the coalition agreement serves as a mechanism to commit the supporting parties to government policies or to commit the government to its supporting parties' policies varies not only from party to party, but also from policy area to policy area, as becomes evident when some of the same policy areas are analysed. It is to these that we now turn by considering privatization, welfare, foreign policy, constitutional reform, and abortion.

**Privatization**[10]

As elsewhere, privatization came to epitomize in the Netherlands the 'retreat of the state'; at least, this was the intention. Privatization was one of the 'Great Operations' launched by the Lubbers I cabinet (CDA and VVD). Because the 1982 elections were held shortly after the regular 1981 parliamentary elections, the parties relied on their 1981 manifestos in the campaign and subsequent negotiations to form a new government. None of these manifestos contained any reference to privatization; the VVD manifesto referred in general terms only to a strengthening of the market. The origins of privatization policy are to be found neither in the parties, nor in the government. In 1980 a Royal Commission on Administrative Reform, the Vonhoff Commission, consisting of outside experts, had recommended, inter alia, 'decentralisation to the private sector' (the term 'privatization' itself was not used then), as a means of reducing administrative overload. In 1981 a committee of civil servants had been allowed to 'reconsider' a range of government programmes without interference from ministers. It recommended privatization as an instrument to reduce government spending. Meanwhile, the Wagner commission (an ad hoc tripartite commission headed by the former president of Royal Dutch Shell) advocated privatization as a means of strengthening the market economy. These three recommendations – administrative, budgetary, and macro-economic – can be regarded as the official motivation for the privatization programme launched in May 1983, half a year after the formation of the cabinet. It was only in the subsequent elections, in 1986, that CDA and VVD mentioned privatization in their manifestos. The policy was thus initiated by outside experts and interest groups, it was put on the political agenda by the government, and was only then adopted by the parties. As a consequence, privatization never achieved the status of and ideological dogma so visible in other countries.

The coalition agreement of the Lubbers II cabinet (a continuation of the coalition of CDA and VVD), embraced the recommendations for the specific privatization proposals prepared by a committee of civil servants. It was at this stage that many advocates of privatization began to be disappointed. The programme consisted primarily in contracting out of cleaning, catering, accounting, and so on, and in converting erstwhile state enterprises such as the PTT into limited liability companies of which all the shares were owned by the government. Selling of shares also took place, but on a relatively limited scale. These disappointing results are not due to conflicts between or within the government and its supporting parties: it turned out that there was not much to privatize because in the past little had been nationalized. In 1989 a new coalition took office, including CDA and PvdA (Lubbers III). The Social-Democrats had never adopted privatization in their manifesto. The 1989 coalition agreement no longer mentioned privatization, and the leader of the PvdA, finance minister Kok, admitted that 'he was not as burning for privatization as his predecessor'. This seemingly party-inspired change of direction was also largely at the level of rhetoric: no renationalization took place; the projects agreed upon by the previous government were implemented; some large scale selling of shares took place. The Social Democratic minister of finance even authorized the Dutch Central Bank to sell some of its gold reserves.

## Welfare[11]

Partly because of the lack of success of privatization and of related programmes, attention turned to transfer payments as an area where the (welfare) state should or could retreat. In their 1986 manifestos, the parties that were to form the Lubbers II cabinet (CDA and VVD) did not announce anything more drastic than efforts to reduce fraud in social insurance. Disability benefits soon became the focus of concerns about the affordability of social insurance. When the law on disability benefits was passed in 1967, it was estimated that at most 200 000 people would be eligible for benefits. By 1988, the number had already exceeded 800 000 and was still rising. All parties became aware of the skyrocketing costs. Within the PvdA, for example, a secret report was prepared by members of the party leadership, but it was shelved. In 1987, relatively quietly, disability benefits were lowered from 80 to 70 per cent of last wages earned.

Perhaps because the parties thought this reform sufficient, or because they did not dare to enter the election campaign with an attack on transfer payments, no plans for drastic reforms were offered in the 1989 manifestos of the parties which were to form the Lubbers III cabinet. The 1989 coalition agreement between CDA and PvdA did not announce such plans either. In the autumn of 1990, however, the government took the initiative. It presented a bill which introduced fines to employers for each employee declared disabled, and a compensation to be paid to the employer for each disabled employee kept employed. The government also formally asked the advice of the tripartite Socio-Economic Council (SER) about possible further reforms. In 1991 the SER offered a majority advice (without the support of the unions), and it was expected that the government would sit on it and eventually introduce a watered down version of these recommendations. Unexpectedly, however, the government suddenly announced even more radical proposals on 14 July 1991: the level of the benefits was to be reduced, the duration was to be restricted, and all those on disability benefits were to be re-examined by doctors. They would have to accept any job they could physically do, even if it paid less than their previous. If necessary, re-training would become compulsory.

Immediately after the announcement of these plans, the PvdA leadership went on vacation. The party organization chairperson did not leave an address and could not be reached. Meanwhile, however, urged by the unions, other elements in the party were up in arms. Members resigned by their thousands. Eventually, the PvdA parliamentary party took the criticisms on board and demanded changes in the proposals. The critique soon centred on exemptions for 'irreversible cases', that is those who already were on disability benefits and for whom there was no hope of gainful employment. The press began to comment on a leadership crisis within the PvdA and the party organization chairperson resigned. In August party leader and deputy prime minister Kok promised to try to renegotiate the plans in cabinet. At a special PvdA party congress Kok received a 80:20 majority for reform, but only after he had threatened to resign if defeated, and after he had promised that the PvdA would exhaust every possibility to protect the 'irreversible cases'. Inside the CDA similar criticisms of the plans were heard, but without creating such a furore.

So far, the conflict was primarily within the PvdA, or between PvdA and cabinet. A year later, at a 1 May meeting, the deputy chairman of the PvdA parliamentary party unexpectedly announced that it would be impossible to separate the 'irreversible cases' from other 'existing cases' and that the PvdA therefore sought protection from the reforms for all those already receiving disability benefits. The PvdA ministers were not told in advance of this change in party position, but grudgingly fell in line. The CDA reacted strongly: tension within the ruling coalition mounted. In September 1992, the cabinet promised to be open to alternative solutions, as long as the financial targets of the reform would be met. PvdA and CDA started negotiations, but to no avail. In January 1993 Prime Minister Lubbers (CDA) suggested a compromise solution which was rejected by the PvdA parliamentary party. The leader of the CDA parliamentary party had been threatening for some time to start negotiations with the opposition Liberals (VVD). In early 1993, it was announced that MPs from CDA and VVD had reached an agreement. PvdA-leader Kok threatened to bring down the cabinet if the CDA-VVD agreement were to be implemented. During a hectic weekend, the prime minister, the deputy prime minister, the leaders of both parliamentary parties met at the home of the minister of social affairs who came up with a proposal acceptable to the PvdA. Lubbers then forced his own party's parliamentary leader to agree to it as well and to break his promise to the VVD. Under the terms of the compromise a disabled person would get 70 per cent of the previous wages earned for a period between 1 and 3 years (depending on years employed), after which that person would get 70 per cent of the minimum wage plus an amount determined by age and last wages earned. If the government's objectives had been both to achieve budgetary savings and to make disability less attractive, they met the first objective, but not the second: in negotiations between employers and unions the 'disability gap' was filled by additional (private) insurance. Social insurance premiums went up, although they were partly paid to private insurance companies.

There are thus similarities with privatization: the policy did not originate in the parties, but in the government. A phase of conflict between one of the supporting parties and the government then followed, however. The final phase was one of conflict between supporting parties, eventually solved by the government. Considerable delays and amendments did occur in the process. Whether the amendments changed the proposals significantly is open to question. Although the PvdA may feel it scored a symbolic victory, it only won material improvements for existing cases.

## Foreign policy[12]

As in many other countries, foreign policy is to a large extent the 'domaine réservé' of the government and its diplomats, conducted in a largely bi-partisan atmosphere. The days that coalitions fell apart over such issues as sending an ambassador to the Holy See are long past. Membership of NATO and the European Union have never been seriously contested. Parties differ only marginally on defence spending and on the selection of countries for development aid. Occasionally, however, foreign policy issues come to dominate the political agenda: this has been the case for instance with decolonization, the Vietnam war and economic sanctions against South Africa. The most recent case revolved around NATO's 1979 so-called dual track decision, namely simultaneously to modernize the nuclear arsenal and negotiate arms reductions. As part of this decision, the Netherlands was to agree to the stationing of 48 cruise and Pershing II missiles on Dutch territory. Domestic opposition to the cruise missiles was fierce. A few years earlier, the proposal to deploy the so-called neutron bomb had mobilized large groups of Dutch society in a successful attempt to influence parliament to vote against this 'bomb that kills people but saves property'. The result was a well organized 'peace movement', composed of a coalition of Left-wing parties, trade unions, fringe groups and individuals, dominated by church-related organizations. In 1981 about 400000 people demonstrated against the missiles in Amsterdam; in 1982, 550000 people marched through The Hague in a similar demonstration; and in 1983, 3.2 million Dutch citizens petitioned the government to reject the NATO proposal.

The involvement of the churches made the situation particularly awkward for the ruling Christian-Democrats, whose supporters were evenly divided on the issue. The PvdA was adamantly opposed to the missiles; the VVD as adamantly in favour of the missiles. Unable to reach a decision, in 1979 the Dutch government raised formal objections to these plans in what became known as 'the Dutch footnote' to the protocol of the NATO meeting. Despite these objections, the government narrowly escaped defeat in a vote of no confidence in the parliamentary debate that followed. In each of the subsequent years the government announced a further postponement of its decision.

This was the situation when the Lubbers I cabinet came to office in 1982. The election manifestos of PvdA and VVD clearly formulated each party's position; the CDA manifesto was equivocal: a decision was now not opportune. The issue had played a prominent role in the campaign. The then leader of the CDA had suggested that the government leave the decision to parliament, a proposal quickly rejected by the PvdA. After the elections it did not take long for CDA and VVD to agree to form a governing coalition. The 1982 coalition agreement contained a compromise on missiles: preparations for the stationing of these weapons were to start, but the final decision to accept them would only be taken with the consent of a parliamentary majority. In 1984 the Dutch delays became untenable within NATO. The government then proposed an ingenious compromise: a final decision on the missiles was to be postponed by one more year. If, during that year, the Soviet Union had not increased the number of its SS-20 missiles, the Dutch would refuse to accept the cruise missiles, whereas an increase in the number of Soviet missiles would lead to automatic acceptance of the cruise missiles. In practice, this proposal shifted responsibility for Dutch foreign policy to the Kremlin, but it did prevent a rift between the two parties supporting the coalition. After a year the Soviet Union appeared to have added to its number of missiles and without any significant protest it was decided to accept the American weapons. They were never installed because an arms reduction agreement had been reached by then.

The policy thus originated in an international organization and was reluctantly put on the domestic agenda by the government. As the government's supporting parties were divided on the issue, non-decision making resulted in long delays until the cabinet offered a compromise that was acceptable to both parties.

**Constitutional reform**[13]

It is widely agreed that the Achilles heel of Dutch democracy is the absence of a direct relationship between the outcome of the elections and the composition of the government. The period between 1963 and 1967, when three different coalitions governed on the basis of a single election has come to epitomize the lack of influence of the electorate. It was during these years that a party, Democrats 1966 (D66), was formed with the explicit aim to democratize the Dutch political system. Direct elections of mayors and of the prime minister, the introduction of territorial representation in the electoral system, and, more recently, a corrective referendum, are among this party's most important proposals for constitutional reform. More by accident than for ideological reasons, D66 found more support for its proposals on the Left, than on the Right. Independently, the PvdA had come to similar conclusions. The CDA has been generally opposed, with temporary exceptions with respect to territorial representation or the referendum, while none of the proposed constitutional reforms is supported by the VVD. The routine reaction of most governments has been to appoint a Royal Commission to study the problem and the proposals. Whenever a Commission has recommended reforms, such as the direct election of the *formateur* in the late 1960s or a corrective referendum in the early 1980s, the recommendations have been ignored or rejected. Only the 1973–7 Den Uyl cabinet did put the proposals before parliament, but in a free vote the Christian-Democratic parties joined the opposition to defeat them. When the proposals were introduced in the form of a private member bill, they met a similar fate. Gradually, the PvdA lost interest in the issue.

After the end of the Cold War the debate was rekindled amidst generally unfounded assertions of a 'confidence gap' between the people and the politicians, frequent references to events in Italy, and fears of right-wing extremism. The issue finally reached the coalition agreement of the Lubbers III cabinet in 1989, but not because D66, the only party still demanding reform, was included in the coalition. On the contrary, for reasons still not entirely clear, the CDA was only willing to accept D66 in a centre-right coalition, but not in the centre-left coalition that eventually was formed. As a consolation price, or to steal the opposition D66's thunder, the CDA and the PvdA agreed to give new impetus to the campaign for constitutional reform. A commission was yet again set up, this time composed of all parliamentary party leaders, headed by the Speaker of the Second Chamber, Deetman. The Commission made an inventory of more than a hundred political and administrative reforms. A first parliamentary debate weeded out the proposals with no chance of success, and subcommittees further elaborated on the reforms. Some of these were eventually accepted by the majority of parliament (rationalization of the system of advisory councils, a single, unified, civil service and so on), but the most far-reaching among them (introduction of a German-type electoral system, of referendums) were not.

The 1994 elections resulted in a landslide and in the subsequent cabinet formation the key part was played, not by the CDA, but by D66. The coalition agreement of the first cabinet without Christian-Democrats again mentioned constitutional reform as a priority and a cabinet committee was appointed to prepare legislation. Constitutional reform is thus an area in which proposals originate within a political party and not within the government. Moreover, 'supporting party' status is not necessary (although certainly helpful) to place a party initiative on the governmental agenda.

## Abortion[14]

Abortion is one of a number of ethical and religious issues (euthanasia, homosexuality and so on) on which the left-right dimension does not apply, as in the cases discussed so far.[15] Until 1994, governing coalitions had been formed according to that dimension; on the ethical and religious dimension, however, the positions of the parties are different: D66, PvdA and VVD are on the secular side (in that order), the CDA on the religious side.

Up to 1967 abortion was primarily regarded as a medical-ethical issue; it became redefined when a feminist movement developed in the 1960s. In 1967 the minister of justice still had the support of all political parties when he announced his intention to wait for the judiciary to develop guidelines on abortion; in 1969 the party executive of the the the PvdA urged the PvdA parliamentary party to demand a liberalization of abortion. In a parliamentary debate later that year, the PvdA and the VVD (as well as communists and pacifists) were in favour of liberalization, while D66 took an intermediate position and the other parties were opposed. The junior minister in the public health department promised to appoint a committee to study the issue, but it was set up over a year later. The PvdA did not want to wait and, in 1970, introduced a private-member bill designed to liberalize abortion.

Because of the PvdA initiative, as well as because of the opening of the first clinics, abortion became an important issue in the 1971 election and the subsequent government formation process. The Biesheuvel cabinet included the VVD and left the PvdA in opposition: to prevent the Liberals from lending support (and a majority) to the PvdA initiative, the coalition agreement stipulated that the government would introduce legislation itself. Two Catholic ministers did draft a proposal, but the cabinet fell on an internal budgetary disagreement before the abortion bill could be debated in parliament. In 1972, after a long and difficult process, the Den Uyl cabinet was sworn in: it was a coalition of three 'progressive' parties (PvdA, D66, PPR) and two Christian-Democratic parties (KVP and ARP). The progressive parties did not want to introduce the previous cabinet's abortion bill. It was agreed that the old bill would be withdrawn as soon as the Catholic KVP had introduced its own private member bill on abortion. Parliament would then be left to decide between the PvdA proposal and the KVP proposal. The Christian Democrats were in no particular hurry to introduce their private member bill. When the Catholic minister of justice, without the cabinet's knowledge, tried to close down an abortion clinic, the issue resurfaced on the agenda and the Christian Democrats could no longer procrastinate. They introduced their proposal in January 1975. The Liberals did not fully support the 1970 PvdA proposal; they introduced their own private member bill, which was less radical than that of the PvdA. This would have split the pro-liberalization camp and the PvdA parliamentary party started negotiations with the VVD parliamentary party to search for a compromise: by the end of 1975 they had reached agreement.

In September 1976 the Second Chamber adopted the PvdA-VVD proposal by 83 votes to 53; in December 1976, however, the First Chamber rejected that proposal by 41 votes to 34. Many Liberal senators did not support the proposal because it did not contain a 12-week limit after which abortion would remain illegal. The VVD moved quickly to close its ranks by drafting a clause on abortion for its 1977 election manifesto. It also approached the PvdA to organize a second attempt, but the PvdA campaign committee refused.

The 1977 cabinet formation process started by an attempt to maintain the ruling coalition. Negotiations between 'progressives' and Christian Democrats proved arduous, however, and abortion was one of the stumbling blocks. The negotiations faltered and the Queen appointed a new *informateur* to find a procedural solution. It was a combination of the 1971 and 1972 compromises: the cabinet was to try to introduce legislation on abortion: if, by 1979, the cabinet had still not done so, the coalition parties would be free to introduce or support private member bills. Later, the negotiations broke down on an unrelated issue; the cabinet formation process had to start again, this time the CDA and the VVD being the prospective partners. The attempt succeeded relatively quickly, partly because the parties literally copied the PvdA-CDA procedural agreement on abortion in their coalition programme (Van Agt I cabinet).

Within the cabinet the issue was left entirely to the minister of public health (VVD) and the minister of justice (CDA), both relatively moderate technocrats. They produced a compromise bill, which, taken literally, was a victory for the CDA, as, in effect, it kept intact the previous practice. In 1980, with tight party discipline and the support of one maverick party, the government proposal won with a 76–74 majority. In early 1981, again with tight party discipline, the proposal won a 38–37 majority in the Senate. However, a large number of related Executive Orders had to be drafted before the bill became law in November 1984: by then there was a CDA-PvdA-D66 cabinet (Van Agt II), but, significantly, no attempt was made to renegotiate the abortion bill. The issue had disappeared from the political agenda.

Thus large issues of an ethical-religious nature are not initiated by a Christian-Democratic/secular governing coalition. Instead, the government procrastinates in order to avoid conflict. Eventually, however, the cabinet does solve the matter by forcing a compromise through parliament.

These five examples of party-government relations in different policy areas (privatization, welfare, foreign policy, constitutional reform, abortion) are not representative of all possible modes of interaction between the government and its supporting parties. Nevertheless, they do provide us with some general contours. It is not surprising that the government should take the initiative in cases of a real or imagined crisis (such as the uncontrolled increase of persons on disability benefits): centralization of decision-making is a well-known consequence of crises. It is more interesting to note that the initiative for new policies often originates neither in the government, nor in its supporting parties, but in neo-corporatist networks (privatization) or international organizations (foreign policy). In such cases it is always the government which tables the issue, often hiding behind 'the social partners' or 'Brussels' in defending the proposal. As long as the supporting parties are not divided on the issue the government does not face serious difficulties. If they are not in agreement, the cabinet may still win, but only at the cost of substantial delay and of concessions or threats of crisis (cruise missiles, disability benefits). The cases in which parties were shown to have initiated a proposal involve policy areas considered of secondary importance (constitutional reform) or which relate to the secondary secular-religious ideological dimension of Dutch politics. The case of constitutional reform indicates that Dutch governments do not automatically ignore proposals coming from opposition parties. The point is more general: government bills are often altered by opposition amendments which are either adopted by the executive or passed by a parliamentary majority including MPs from supporting parties (Visscher, 1994).

## PATRONAGE

It is difficult to assess the extent of political patronage in the Dutch political system. The absence of any form of territorial representation and the lingering

effect of Calvinism on the political culture seem to have limited the opportunities for and the social acceptance of patronage. The only clear cases of
patronage publicly admitted concern the appointments of mayors and
provincial governors. Such appointments are made by the minister of the
interior, who needs cabinet confirmation for appointments to the provinces
and to towns of more than 50 000 inhabitants. All major parties have
designated one of their MPs as the official 'party lobbyist'. Vacancies are
advertised and potential candidates are well advised to consult their party's
lobbyist before formally applying. The minister and the cabinet will not appoint
someone who is opposed by his own party. However, the government does
not only appoint mayors and governors from the ranks of its supporting parties;
the opposition parties are expected to receive a proportional share of the
appointments. A study of mayoral appointments has shown that these expectations are borne out by the actual appointments made (Andeweg and
Derksen, 1978). Nothing is expected in return for such an appointment: it is
regarded as the 'right' of each major party to obtain its fair share; mayors
and governors are expected to act as their city's or region's ambassador in
The Hague, rather than as the governments 'prefect' at the subnational level.
Moreover, as far as mayors are concerned, criticisms of the unique Dutch
practice of appointment by the central government have gradually forced the
central government to pay more attention to local preference.

Patterns of appointments to advisory councils, quangos and high-level
positions in the civil service resemble those of mayors and governors. A party
connection is a virtual necessity for a successful application, but it is not
necessary to belong to one of the government's supporting parties. As exact
figures for these appointments are less easily available than for mayoral
appointments, however, it is less clear whether the appointments are pro-
portionally distributed over all major parties: during the first two Lubbers
cabinets in particular, there have been complaints of a 'Christian
Democratization' of the higher echelons of the civil service, for example.

For all such appointments the government does not expect anything in return.
They do serve a function for the parties, however, as party membership and
party activity are more attractive to careerists in the public sector and old
party 'elephants' can be easied in this way.

Despite the highly centralized nature of the Dutch political system, there
is very little evidence of patronage in the form of government contracts or
pork barrel legislation. The electoral system treats the whole country as a
single electoral district, so that MPs have no particular constituency to look
after. This in turn removes any temptation for the government to favour a
particular region in order to secure its MP's support, or to influence voting
behaviour in marginal constituencies. As an exception to this rule, there are

persistent rumours that the (primarily Catholic) South of the country, and especially the province of Limburg, has benefited from the prominent role of Catholic politicians in successive Dutch governments when it came to decisions such as the location of a new medical school.

There is or was probably more patronage to be found at the local level. One of the consequences of pillarization in the Netherlands was that some services (health care, housing, education) were distributed not by governmental agencies, but by local subcultural organizations (albeit financed by the government). Being part of the relevant subculture was a prerequisite for obtaining those services. In contrast to Belgian parties, Dutch parties have not used this potential for patronage to shore up their organizational networks, but have allowed these organizations to become independent and professionalized. Hence, since the 1960s, the Dutch pillars have eroded markedly more quickly than their Belgian counterparts.


CONCLUSION

The pattern which emerges from the examination of the relationship between governments and their supporting parties in the Netherlands is not clear. There is considerable variation across time, across parties, and along the three planes of analysis of recruitment, policy, and patronage. All major governing parties started from a position of 'autonomy', although the PvdA has always had a preference for the 'government dependence on party' position. In the 1960s government-party relations gradually developed in this direction when the CDA, and (reluctantly and to a lesser extent) the VVD moved towards the PvdA's posture. The CDA's long tenure in government shifted the party's centre of gravity towards its ministers, moving government-party relations further towards 'fusion' or 'party dependence on government'. It seems not unreasonable to attribute at least part of the CDA's landslide losses in the 1994 elections (from 35 to 22 per cent) to voter alienation from this 'governmentalized' party.

This move away from 'autonomy' has not affected recruitment, policy-making and patronage to the same extent, however. The impact on recruitment is most visible, not only because it is easier to measure. As far as policy-making is concerned, parties have attempted to strengthen their grip on the government, but have not been fully successful. This is partly because all Dutch governments are coalitions, and a governing party is wise to insulate itself from the electoral effects of unpopular policies by not identifying itself too much with the government; it is also because a governing coalition is formed along only one of the ideological dimensions which define the Dutch party system.

Finally, the development of political patronage seems to go in the opposite direction: the potential for patronage in mayoral appointments or 'pillarized' services is declining. Despite complaints in this respect, the move away from the autonomy of governments and supporting parties is still limited: it remains a far cry from the 'partitocrazia' of some other European countries.

## NOTES

1. In 1994, a 'purple' coalition of the PvdA (red) and the VVD (blue) was formed, together with D66; the CDA was left in the opposition.
2. The incompatibility between a seat in parliament and a ministerial portfolio was written in the constitution in 1938 only, but it had been a customary practice for much longer: between 1848 and 1938 only ten MPs who joined the cabinet did not resign their seats in parliament.
3. The Kok cabinet of 1994 aimed to put an end to the move from 'dualism' to 'monism' in executive-legislative relationships: half its ministers had never been elected to parliament.
4. In 1994, Voorhoeve's successor as party leader, Bolkestein, reaffirmed his party's tradition of 'autonomy' by also staying in parliament when the VVD entered the government.
5. In the 1994 cabinet, two of the five VVD ministers can be considered as outsiders.
6. Similarly, in 1994, when the PvdA remained in the government as the largest party, despite heavy losses, there was no doubt that its leader, Kok, would become prime minister. Only one of the party's nominees to cabinet posts was not a party insider, which probably resulted from the need to give representation to women in cabinet.
7. That is to say the party's MPs in the Second Chamber. The members of the less powerful First Chamber are not committed: this leads to markedly less predictable support for the government in that House.
8. According to most PvdA ministers, during the Lubbers III cabinet, the Thursday evening meetings generally failed in this respect, because of acrimonious conflicts over budget cutbacks between the party's departmental ministers and its leader, the minister of finance (Rehwinkel and Nekkers, 1994).
9. For the duration of the interregnum between governments, the constitution makes exception to the rule that combining a parliamentary seat with ministerial office is not allowed.
10. For a more extensive discussion of privatization in the Netherlands, see Andeweg, 1988, 1994.
11. For Dutch socio-economic policy-making in general, see Andeweg and Irwin, 1993, 187–211.

12.    For Dutch foreign policy-making in general, see Andeweg and Irwin, 1993, 212–28.
13.    For a more detailed discussion of attempts at constitutional reform, see Andeweg, 1989.
14.    For a more detailed discussion of the abortion issue, see Outshoorn, 1986.
15.    The case of euthanasia is more recent, but the story has not ended yet. The process has tended to be on the same lines as that which the abortion issue followed.

# 9. Belgium: Still the Age of Party Government?

Lieven De Winter, André-Paul Frognier
and Benoit Rihoux

## INTRODUCTION

In terms of party-government relationship, as a political system which is often labelled a partocracy, Belgium represents, together with pre-Berlusconian Italy, one of the most 'advanced' cases of party government in Europe. This is still accentuated, compared with Italy, by its consociational character (Lijphart, 1981), even if this feature can be discussed (Huyse, 1981, 1987). In addition, variations occur within the Belgian case, as will be shown later.

Table 9.1: *Belgian cabinets, 1981–1995*

| Period | Name | Parties |
|--------|------|---------|
| 17 Dec.81–28 Nov.85 | Martens V | CVP-PSC-PVV-PRL |
| 28 Nov.85–21 Oct.87 | Martens VI | (same) |
| 21 Oct.87– 09 May 88 | Martens VII | (same) |
| 09 May 88–06 Mar.92 | Martens VIII | CVP-PSC-SP-PS-VU |
| 06 Mar.92–April 1995 | Dehaene I | CVP-PSC-SP-PS |

Party labels: PSC: French-speaking Christian-Democrats; CVP: Flemish-speaking Christian-Democrats; PS: French-speaking Socialists; SP: Flemish-speaking Socialists; PRL: French-speaking Liberals; PVV: Flemish-speaking Liberals (became the VLD in 1992); RW: Walloon Regionalists; FDF: Brussels French-speaking Regionalists; VU: Flemish Regionalists; ECOLO: French-speaking Greens; AGALEV: Flemish-speaking Greens.

The two main interconnected features of Belgian governments since World War II are their coalition character and their relative instability. Out of the 32 governments between 1946 and 1993, only 5 (usually short-lived) were single party; since 1958, all governments have been coalitions. In the 1970s, following the split of the three 'traditional' national parties (Christian-Democrats, Socialists, Liberals) and the need to secure two-thirds majorities in parliament for institutional reforms, the coalition size grew up to a maximum of six parties in 1977–9. The minimum number of coalition parties is four since the late 1970s. This instability is however counterbalanced by the stability of the individual ministers (Frognier, 1988) and by the continuous presence in government of the Christian-Democrats, the largest political family, both centrist and pivotal (De Winter, 1989b).

We shall focus on the 1981–93 period which is far less complex than the 1977–91 period in terms of number of cabinets, coalitions, prime ministers, and party chairmen.[1] Given this stability, empirical indicators concerning the dimensions of party-government relationships studied are more available as well as reliable.

## APPOINTMENTS

The analysis is restricted to the selection of cabinet ministers as far as the governmental positions are concerned, and to the party presidents for the party positions.[2] The highest and most powerful leadership position within the Belgian parties is that of party president, who is the head of the general party organisation and whose position is clearly differentiated – because of rules of incompatibility – from the position of the leader of the parliamentary party and from governmental positions (De Winter, 1993).

With respect to governmental positions, secretaries of state are excluded, as they are less important governmental actors than ministers and normally do not attend the cabinet meetings. Among the regular ministers, one finds basically three categories: the PM, who is sometimes also in charge of a small policy department, the vice-PMs – one from each supporting party (except from the PM's party) – who are usually in charge of at least one large department and who serve as the *chef de file* of their party's ministers, and finally the regular ministers, who head a specific department. The PM and the vice-PMs constitute the *Kerncabinet*, an inner cabinet in which major decisions are reached between the coalition parties on conflictual matters, whereby the final decision is later only formally approved by the full cabinet.

### Appointment of ministers: formal and informal processes
The appointment of ministers is the final stage of a lengthy and intricate process of cabinet formation, where parties – and more particularly the party presidents – are the main actors. Indeed, party presidents defend their party's claims during the talks, defend the governmental coalition agreement to their party executive and party conference, negotiate over the departments their party wants to obtain[3] and, finally, appoint the future cabinet members.

Yet party presidents are evidently not entirely free to appoint those whom they personally prefer. Former ministers will ask to be appointed again, ministers representing strong constituency parties or intraparty factions will ask for ministerial representation, ministerial appointments have to be spread in a fair way over the provinces and constituency parties, the sexes, and between representatives and senators. In addition, the degree of freedom of a party president depends strongly on his position of power within his party. This position depends on party culture, as well as on his personal resources and background. Finally, they have to take into account the complex equilibria (linguistic ones, not the least) between the coalition parties in the distribution of ministerial portfolios.

Let us examine the impact of party and government actors on the selection of ministers of the three cabinets under consideration.[4] The unit of analysis is the party as a whole.

In the CVP, two positional actors have played a central role in the selection process: the outgoing PM (especially in 1981) and the party president. The third actor, Dehaene, has probably been the most influential, independently from his formal position (Martens' *chef de cabinet*, vice-PM, PM after 1992). For example, it was he who reached the government agreement in 1988, and then presented it to the future (and outgoing) PM. Besides, at each government formation, a significant element lies in the balance of power between the party's three factions or *standen* (estates). The role of the factions' leaders is predominant, since each one of the factions submits a list of its ministrables in preference order to the government formateur. Indeed, both Martens and Dehaene stem from the trade unions' faction, the strongest one.

In the PSC, the picture is less clear in 1981, when the nomination process of ministers was controlled by at least three actors: the newly-elected party president (Deprez) and one outgoing senior minister, both 'estateless', as well as another outgoing minister and first trustee of the trade union faction. In 1987, however – and even more so in 1992 when he was at the peak of his power – the party president was the main nominator. He nonetheless needed to preserve a careful balance between the intraparty factions and to satisfy the party heavyweights.

Both in 1987 and 1992, the nomination of SP ministers was in the hands of a troika. In 1987, it consisted of the former chairman, former vice-PM and the party's most prominent ministrable (Claes), the leader of the parliamentary party (Tobback) and the party president (Van Miert, in office since 1977). In 1992, the impact of the latter's younger and less influential successor (Vandenbroucke) was less clear, whereas the former two heavyweights, by then respectively outgoing vice-PM and minister, kept their influence.

In the PS, the nomination process was clearly a one-man job in 1988, as is usually the case in that party. The party president (Spitaels) was not only the main nominator, but also the main negotiator, and PS negotiators or potential ministrables who did not stick to the presidential line were replaced by *spitaelsiens*. The 1992 picture appears less clear, as the newly elected party president (Busquin) was more constrained in his choice than his predecessor, since he had to take into account the balance of power within the most conflictual party federations and between Wallonia and Brussels federations.

The nomination of PRL ministers in 1981 appears as unambiguous as was the case of the PS in 1988. Indeed, the party president (Gol), who had in the previous years consolidated his full grip on the party and just won the elections, was obviously the most prominent nominator. Indeed, he nominated himself to the vice-PM position, whereas the other ministers were not chosen among the party heavyweights.

In the PVV, the party president's (Declercq) freedom of action was assuredly smaller than that of his PRL counterpart in 1981. He was still the main man behind the nominations and managed to push one of his proteges onto a ministerial seat, but he was forced to include a high-profile and influential leader within the party and a potential challenger for the party presidency as well (Decroo).

In the VU, the two ministerial kingmakers in 1988 were clearly the former chairman – and still informal leader – (Schiltz) and the acting chairman (Gabriels). The self-nomination of Schiltz was self-evident, given his status of main formation negotiator, former minister in the Flemish executive and most influential man of the party. The second appointee (Geens) was a loyal follower of both Schiltz and Gabriels.

Three common features emerge in these nomination processes. Firstly, except for a few cases, the party presidents clearly play a dominant role; in some cases it is a one-man job. However, in most cases, they have to come to terms with their party's heavyweights, who sometimes gain access to the nomination process and/or are nominated themselves as ministers. Thirdly, although the formal positions of the party heavyweights (former minister or vice-PM, head of parliamentary party) do determine their access to the selection process, key men with little formal status (such as Dehaene in 1985 and 1988) can also play an important role.

*The nomination of party presidents: formal and informal processes*
There is wide variation in the procedures under which Belgian parties select their president, and a wide gap between the democratic prescriptions contained in the party statutes and actual practice.[5] In most parties under consideration, the party president is formally selected by the national party congress, composed of delegates of the constituency parties, who in a secret ballot select the candidate for office. In practice, in most cases (22 cases out of 27 from

1981 to 1993), there is only one candidate, the one upon which the party oligarchy has reached a consensus, who is either acclaimed or elected with overwhelming majorities at the national party conference. Only in the PSC (from 1969 on) is the party president elected by a secret vote in which all due-paying party members can participate.

Let us consider, party by party, the selection processes of party presidents when the relevant parties were in the government.[6] Governmental actors do exercise influence on the selection of party presidents, but in an informal and usually invisible way.

In the PS, out of the 35 nominations and renominations in the 1944–92 period, apart from the 1981 election (Spitaels), not one case featured more than one candidate (De Winter, 1993: 237),[7] as an elite-chosen, consensus candidate is always legitimated *ex post* by a vote in congress or by acclamation. The 1992 nomination (Busquin) is no exception to the rule. As Spitaels' resignation occurred in the delicate coalition formation period, the party urgently needed a decision on the succession question. Although Busquin (a spitaelsien in a strongly anti-spitaelsien constituency party) must have been fully supported by Spitaels and by most ministrables (some of whom were outgoing ministers), there are no clear signs of interference of any of those actors in the nomination process. Busquin finally was elected with near-unanimity, which shows that he had full support of the party organisation.

Similarly, the SP congress has until 1993 always nominated a single candidate by acclamation. The SP has always tried hard to solve intraparty and interpersonal conflicts as far as the presidency was concerned before these conflicts could reach the congress stage. The party elite – and particularly the troika which had led the party since the late 1970s – have always been able to put forward a consensus candidate. Vandenbroucke's nomination (1989) is a case in point. Several succession scenarios had already been prepared in 1988 but, after several months in government, the main présidentiable chose to keep his cabinet seat instead. From then on, the main decision-makers were the departing president, the acting vice-PM and the minister of Interior (that is, the troika). Their own choice was easily confirmed by the party bureau, by the parliamentary groups, and finally by the party congress by acclamation.

In the period considered, the case of the CVP is probably the most complex, since the party is factionalised, as each estate (*stand*) intervenes in the process, since the PM has always been a CVP member (this adds one more actor), and since the CVP has remained uninterruptedly in power. As in the case of the socialist parties, and both before and after the split of the national Catholic party in two autonomous linguistic wings in 1969, there had very rarely been more than one candidate for the party presidency (De Winter, 1993: 239). In 1981, the CVP elite[8] had already decided on the president's successor (Swaelen). The formal nomination itself went very fast: the choice was confirmed by the party bureau, by the council, and by the subsequent party congress. In 1985, as Swaelen wanted to become a member of the cabinet after the general election, the CVP troika (himself, Martens and Dehaene) agreed on a candidate. However, as the latter represented the farmers' union faction, some leaders within the two other *standen* reacted negatively and put forward other candidates. This created some confusion, and Swaelen had to stay on another term; his mandate was renewed by the congress without competition. In 1988, after Swaelen had expressed his intention to become president of the senate, several competing canditates were presented by the different factions. The party elite feared a devastating intraparty competition and installed an ad hoc committee, but it could not come to a conclusion due to unresolvable conflicts between the *standen*.

This lead the troika to launch a new candidate (Van Rompuy), whose candidacy was first sounded out at an informal meeting with most members of the bureau, some ministers, the leaders of the *standen* and the parliamentary group leaders. Only then did the party council formally designate Van Rompuy as the only candidate with a large majority, and he was elected unopposed by the party congress. Finally, when Van Rompuy joined the government in 1993, the former head of the party youth and leader of the parliamentary group (Van Hecke) was picked by the acting PM and by the departing president and his choice was easily confirmed by the party bureau and party council. Van Hecke was elected (for the first time by the party members, through a general secret poll), as the only candidate. Thus decisions on the nomination of the CVP party presidents were taken by a small number of actors, which usually included the PM, the departing party president, and Dehaene, the top trustee of the trade union faction of the party in the cabinet, while the leaders of the *standen* were the main veto players in the process. All things considered, the CVP leading cabinet members have had a strong say, especially if one considers the fact that, both in 1981 and 1993, the outgoing presidents directly joined the government.

Unlike the CVP, the PSC broke with the tradition of elite-chosen single candidate elections in 1969 and introduced a direct secret vote by all party members. As a result, in most nominations, there was more than one final candidate and, in that case, competition was real. Moreover, incumbent presidents have been more often challenged, and candidates have had to campaign in order to capture internal party support. This selection procedure does not allow for direct control or monitoring by the current party and governmental leaders, although they naturally attempt to promote their candidate behind the scenes. However, in spite of this more competitive nomination system and after a high turnover of presidents in the 1970s, the presidency has not changed hands since 1981 (Deprez). Deprez's nomination occurred in rather chaotic circumstances, as the party had just suffered an electoral defeat, and as the outgoing president (and former PM) had lost much support in his party. He was rapidly replaced ad interim by Deprez, the national party secretary. This decision was taken by the party bureau, which then unanimously decided to back him up for the presidency. Hence, no direct and decisive interference from ministers seems to have occurred. At the presidential elections of January 1982, Deprez won easily despite the presence of two challengers. He was re-elected in 1985, 1988 and 1991, only once facing a challenger. Thus this obviously more democratic nomination process drastically reduces the opportunities of the party leadership and the PSC ministers to control the process. In spite of its inherent threat to stability of the office, Deprez has successfully managed to accommodate the demands of the party in government and that of the party organisation.

In the PVV, as more generally in the Liberal parties, there never was in practice more than one final candidate in the period under consideration, which is not to say that the party and governmental elite entirely control the selection process. The case of the succession of Declercq by his dauphin Verhofstadt in 1982 illustrates this ambiguity. After an ad interim presidency by one of the most senior party leaders, Verhofstadt was elected as only candidate with a large majority. As leader of the Young Liberals, he had already managed in the previous years to radicalise the party's ideology towards neo-liberalism. Hence, his selection was not the result of a process strictly monitored by party and ministerial elite, but rather the result of a grass-root intraparty renovation movement. Indeed, once in power, he rapidly managed to bring some of his fellow party youth leaders into top party positions and to reduce the influence of some of the older leaders who had joined the government in 1981. In 1985, as he chose to join the government himself, the party bureau unanimously nominated an ad interim president (Mrs Neyts), in a procedure which violated the statutory rights of the party vice-presidents. Her nomination was not only facilitated by the fact that she was Verhofstadt's personal first choice; she also had a personal following within the party, came from the 'neglected' Brussels constituency and represented the humanist social-liberal wing of the party. She was rapidly confirmed by the party congress.

In the PRL, the real leader since 1979 has been Gol, independently from his position of party chairman or vice-PM. He joined the party in 1977, became the party president in 1979 and was in complete control by 1981 when he became vice-PM. He then put forward Michel (national party secretary since 1980) as ad interim successor, with whom he had a smooth and long-lasting cooperation. As in the case of Neyts in the PVV, this nomination violated the statutory rights of the vice-presidents. Michel was however easily confirmed by the party congress, as the only candidate. Hence, like Declercq in 1981, Gol managed to have his protege and first choice elected as successor. However, contrary to Verhofstadt, Gol's successor Michel remained a low profile president, mainly a conciliator of internal party conflicts. Gol, as vice-PM, continued to control the party, more than his successor. Hence, in the PVV since 1985 and the PRL since 1979, the question on whether governmental or party leaders exert most influence is irrelevant, as influence is clearly associated with the two leading figures, Gol and Verhofstadt, regardless of the formal positions which they occupy (party or government).

Three conclusions can therefore be drawn. First, the selection of ministers and party leaders is a complex and multi-layered process, as many types of actors interfere, with different degrees and types of impact (formal power, informal influence, veto and blackmail power). Moreover, the desiderata of an even wider set of actors are anticipated and taken into account, without them having interfered directly in the process: these are the factions, the parliamentary party, the rank-and-file and the voters.

Second, leaders strive to maximise their personal utility in terms of power and status, by trying to conquer the position which they view as 'the highest attainable one' in a given opportunity structure. For instance, in the PS, the position of party president is clearly considered as the highest attainable one (higher than that of minister or vice-PM) at all times. For the liberals (PVV and PRL), on the contrary, the office of vice-PM is considered as the highest attainable position when the party is in power; then, when the party returns into opposition, the leaders jump back to the party presidency.

Third, in terms of nomination power, the positions of power can be basically characterised by two dimensions: on one hand their institutional locus (party versus government) and, on the other hand, their leadership basis (positional or personal).[9] Figure 9.1 charts the positions of the main supporting parties along these two dimensions.

The two 'purest' cases are, on one hand, the PS and, on the other hand, the two Liberal parties (PRL and PVV). In the PS, power is concentrated in the hands of the party president, namely in those of an undisputed positional leader who dictates the moves of his ministers. This is not so surprising if one considers that the PS is a highly structured mass party. In the PVV and PRL, the power centres on the vice-PMs, the former party presidents who are self-appointed, who remain the real party bosses even when they hold a governmental position. Their leadership is thus mainly personal; it is not directly linked to the formal position they hold. This situation is also due to the fact that the Liberal parties are still largely cadre parties.

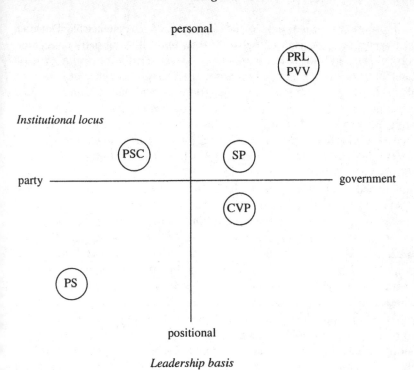

personal

Institutional locus

party ————————————————— government

positional

*Leadership basis*

Figure 9.1: *Positions of power in terms of nomination*

The other cases are intermediate. In the SP, the leadership basis is slightly more personal, while the nomination power is shared by the party president and two prominent ministers, with a slight dominance from the latter. In the PSC, the most powerful member of the leading troika is the party president. Finally, one observes a slight governmental predominance in the CVP, this time more linked to formal positions: it is a mass party built around highly institutionalised factions whose support is essential for nomination procedures.

## POLICY MAKING

### Modes of party control

(1) Governmental agreements. In Belgium, the most important interaction does not occur during a cabinet's term, but beforehand, during the period of formation of the new government: the supporting parties formulate their policy preferences, come to a policy compromise, and adopt an agreement which will strongly determine the future governmental policies.

There are several indicators of the importance of governmental agreements. First and foremost, nearly all governments fall following party policy disagreements, and not before parliament. Moreover, the formation process usually takes a very long time: an average of 78 days between 1968 and 1994, that is the longest duration in any Western European country. Third, the final governmental agreements tend to be ponderous documents in which the supporting parties define in detail the future governmental policies.[10] Finally, as the coalition agreement has to be confirmed by a national party conference before the government is sworn in,[11] this formal investiture vote binds the entire party to the agreement and any violation by party actors can be sanctioned as a breach of party discipline.

Once a government is launched, ministers and party presidents often refer to the governmental agreement, either in order to defend a specific policy measure or to attack a measure taken by a minister of another party. Indeed, breaches of the governmental agreement are also at the heart of intracoalition conflicts and often lead to the resignation of the cabinet. Specific institutional arrangements facilitate this reciprocal control on the implementation of the agreement. First, Belgian governments are truly collective, in the sense that most decisions made by individual ministers have to receive the approval of the cabinet as a whole (Frognier, 1988). Moreover, vice-PMs are equipped with a special ministerial staff (the *cabinet*) whose main task is to follow the decision-making of the other ministers in the government and safeguard the party's interest. In addition, special 'watchdog cells' are sometimes installed within a given ministerial *cabinet* whose sole task is to scrutinise the policy-making in a politically delicate ministry run by a minister from another party.

(2) The intraparty mode. During a cabinet's term, Belgian parties exercise a direct influence through different mechanisms. The intraparty mode, which refers to direct contacts between cabinet members and members of the party organisation outside the cabinet (De Winter, 1993), is clearly the predominant mode.

The first and most binding form of intraparty interaction between party and governmental elite occurs during the informal meetings between ministers, the party president and some other party leaders. These meetings take place before the full cabinet meeting: the agenda of the cabinet is carefully scrutinised, and the positions to be defended by the ministers are defined. These meetings exercise more influence on the positions of ministers than the meetings with the party executive. However, the importance of these meetings depends on the power of party president vis-à-vis the party's ministers. In the Socialist parties, cabinet ministers operate more often like delegates: in the case of the PS, the president has always been the main decision-maker with regard to cabinet affairs; in the case of the SP, ministers are steered by their party president and the top party leadership. The influence of the Liberal and Christian-Democrat party presidents is more limited and there are variations over time: the turnover of party presidents is relatively high, since the real political heavyweights of the party decide to join the cabinet, and thus are sometimes replaced by low-profile figures or political newcomers. This was particularly the case in the centre-right governments of the 1982–7 period. In these cases, supporting parties were de facto dominated by prominent cabinet members, who acted as the trustees of their party. Yet some of these relatively unknown party presidents gradually managed to become quite influential, as Verhofstadt in the PVV and even more Deprez in the PSC. Finally, apart from these regular and formal types of contacts, informal and ad hoc contacts are important as well. For instance, when major issues or new facts are unexpectedly raised during the cabinet meeting, the meeting is sometimes suspended in order to allow ministers to phone their party leader for advice.

The second intraparty mechanism lies in the weekly official meetings of the party executive, which nearly all ministers regularly attend. Indeed, in almost all parties, all ministers are members of the party executive. That was the case for all the governmental parties from 1978 to 1991 (CVP, PSC, SP, PS, PRL, VU and FDF), except the PVV. Most ministers were members of the party executive prior to their promotion to governmental ranks: they are thus chosen among the persons who have had a successful party career. This certainly constitutes an element of 'party dominance' on government. According to most party statutory rules, ministers cannot vote in the party executive; however, the level of influence of ministers in the party executive is clearly very high. On the other hand, party executives are usually large: hence the proportion of ministers in the executive is usually small and is at least not sufficient to constitute a majority. Yet this does not exclude a predominant influence of the ministers in qualitative terms. Finally, the impact of the party executive on the decision-making process and on the ministers' behaviour varies among the parties. In the Christian-Democrat and Liberal parties, ministers play a predominant role, as the executive can only exercise a veto on matters crucial to the party. The executives of the Socialist parties have greater influence, as ministers often receive 'marching orders' and for important matters generally have to sound out their views.

The third less direct intraparty mechanism refers to the ministerial *cabinets*. One of the idiosyncrasies of the Belgian cabinet system is the large size of ministerial staffs, which has indeed increased continuously from 1966 to 1988.[12] Most cabinet members are appointed by the party organisation. Ministers have obviously some say, especially in that they can reject some candidates. Yet, they can usually only appoint themselves a small number of collaborators at the highest level, while having more leeway at the lower levels. The party leadership has thus men whom it can trust in the immediate entourage of the ministers and these provide information. This placement provides the parties with a political personnel, paid by the state, which is devoted to party interests and can exercise supervision over the ministers.

(3) The interparty mode.The interparty mode also plays an important part, sometimes at least. It involves meetings between the presidents of the supporting parties and other members such as ministers and leading MPs, usually including the PM (De Winter, 1993, Frognier, 1988). The intensity, the scope and the 'life expectancy' of the policy agreements reached through these mechanisms range between two extremes.

At one end of the spectrum, there are real 'pacts', sometimes involving the main opposition parties, which will affect decision-making in a particular sector for several decades: this is the case of the large consociational 'School pact' of 1958 and of the 'Culture pact' of 1974, both related to the denominational cleavage, which were in force in the 1990s. Such pacts are achieved through large (and usually lengthy) 'party summits'.

At the other extreme, there are smaller agreements which will only temporarily settle a specific conflict within the government. In that case, the coalition parties intervene as 'mothers-in-law', to settle the conflicts between the ministers and to render the governmental agreement more precise.

Finally, between these two extremes, there are implementation meetings, usually related to an entire sector, for instance, to the budget, which take place on a regular basis. Once the issue concerned is settled in this way, the cabinet can resume its work.

## The neo-corporatist mode

Neo-corporatist procedures have been an ongoing feature of the post-war Belgian system (Dewachter, 1992: 127–57). Such procedures have been predominant in some social and economical sectors such as working relations (working status, wages, trade union rights), social security (health care, pensions) and some other economic aspects (energy, price controls). Hundreds of concertation and advisory bodies have been installed; among the most important ones, one finds the Central Economic Council, The Price Index Committee, the Steering Committee for Gas and Electricity.

There are two main types of neo-corporatist interaction. On the one hand, there are direct relationships between interest groups and the government (the PM and/or the minister(s) in charge of the sector), either through regular concertation in consultative and advisory bodies, or through ad hoc negotiations. In the most 'advanced' cases, the government's role is reduced to being merely an observer and a rubberstamp, after the negotiation between the social partners has taken place, for instance between trade unions and employers' organisations. In most cases, however, the government is a full participant. On the other hand, there are direct relationships between parties and interest groups, in three ways at least. First, most interest groups are 'pillarised', and the party which is linked with a particular 'pillar' (or *zuil*) then acts as spokesperson of its pillar for various constituent organisations in the political arena. Second, ministerial *cabinets* are often largely 'permeable' to staff members stemming from the various pressure groups. Third, through the partisan nominations in the public sector, as we shall see in the next section, large sectors of some ministerial departments are literally colonised by one or the other interest group. An example is the relationship between the ministry of agriculture and the powerful farmers' organisation, the Boerenbond.

*The alternative modes*
There are also at least four alternative modes to party-centred and neo-corporatist forms of decision-making. One is the genuinely autonomous parliamentary decision-making. In very rare occasions (as the parliamentary groups are tightly controlled by the political parties), the governing parties decide that parliament, rather than the government, is to be the arena in which a difficult issue should be resolved. In this case, the government explicitly refrains from interfering in the decision-making process, as the matter is usually judged too delicate and hazardous to governmental stability. The final solution found in parliament is often supported by an ad hoc coalition different from the one supporting the government. On the other hand, in a more moderate form of the same arrangement, the government sometimes leaves a matter at one stage of the process to parliament. This then constitutes only a temporary break in the rubberstamping role of the parliament.

Second, at the other extreme, special powers are sometimes granted to the government by the supporting parties. In substance, the parliament gives the government large powers over a broad range of policies, over a sector such as economic affairs, for instance, for a fixed period and decisions taken under this system cannot be altered during that period by parliament.[13]

The third mode is that of 'decision-making under external pressure'. This occurs most often with regard to issues which were not foreseen or foreseeable during the process of formation of the government. They are often brought on the agenda by actors completely out of control of the supporting parties, such as foreign governments, supra-national authorities or new social movements. In this mode, the government is less vulnerable to party interference and more vulnerable to interference from actors external to the polity.

Finally, the fourth mode is the one of a minority government. Although genuine minority governments are exceptional, majority governments will sometimes appeal to the opposition's support, usually in case of constitutional reform proposals that require a two thirds majority in both houses.

We shall illustrate the importance and the modus operandi of these different modes of party-government policy relationship by examining five issues which reached the agenda during the 1981–93 period. The first three are related to the traditional cleavages within the Belgian polity, namely abortion (the main denominational issue after the central issue of education was settled in 1958), budgetary orthodoxy (the 'Maastricht norms'), and the multi-phased process of constitutional reform leading to the transformation of the unitary state into a *sui generis* federal state. We shall then consider two issues related to 'new politics', namely the installation of euromissiles and the introduction of 'ecotaxes'. In each of these policy cases, one tends to find a mixture of decision-modes rather than a single predominant mode.

*Party-government relationship with respect to five policies*
(1) Denominational policies: abortion. The denominational cleavage constitutes the oldest political cleavage in the Belgian polity. Since the main conflicts on this dimension were settled by large consociational 'pacts' (the 'School pact' and the 'Culture pact'), abortion has been the main issue on this conflict dimension to come on to the political agenda since the beginning of the 1970s, an issue on which Christian-Democratic parties have strongly opposed the pro-legalisation views of the Socialists and Liberal parties. The settlement of the abortion issue constitutes an unusual – if not unique – case.

After having been shortly on the governmental agenda in 1973–4, the Christian-Democrats succeeded in removing this issue until 1988 by burying it in parliamentary and other committees. The coalition agreement of the Martens VIII government (1988) delegated the issue of abortion once again to parliament. A private members' bill for depenalisation was then introduced by a Socialist MP (in the coalition) and a Liberal MP (in the opposition). After long and animated debates both inside and outside parliament, a majority voted for the bill in the Senate and in the House (mainly Socialist, Greens and most Liberals against Christian-Democrats and VU). After the monarch refused – for 'reasons of conscience' – to sign the bill so that it could become law, an unprecedented constitutional crisis broke out. It was solved by the government in a peculiar way: the monarch was declared 'temporarily incapable' to govern, then the government unanimously signed and promulgated the bill and, finally, the government called both chambers together in order to have them declare that the monarch was fit to reign again.

This decision-making process was very unusual in two respects. First, the parties supporting the government as well as the opposition parties were divided on the issue, and the 'pro-depenalisation' majority did not correspond to the governmental majority. Usually, issues on which governmental parties strongly oppose are not decided at all, as any attempt towards deciding such matters would be considered as a violation of the trust and solidarity between governmental parties, and therefore threaten the survival of the cabinet. Second, it is a pure case of delegation to parliament, an unprecedented case in post-war Belgium.

(2) Public deficit reduction and the application of the Maastricht treaty convergence criteria. These two connected policies stood high on the agenda from the early 1980s, as Belgium was persistently the EU country with the highest relative level of public debt, and since the Maastricht norms impose stability and reduction of the deficit of the public sector. Indeed, under the Martens V and Martens VI cabinets, efforts were made to improve the country's competitiveness and to reduce such a deficit. After 1992, following the Maastricht treaty, the emphasis was mainly put on the reduction of the deficit, including zero-growth of public expenditure, new taxes and modifications of the social security system.

The policy process has been classical, though with some variations from one cabinet to the other. First, following interparty negotiations, future policy decisions were included in the governmental agreement. Second, once the government was in power, the policies were implemented with both ex ante and ex post concertation mechanisms with the main socio-economic interest groups (employers' organisations and trade unions). The ex post concertation mechanisms have tended to become more important since the Martens V government (1981), thus restricting the interest groups' real influence on the policy decisions. Furthermore, some cabinets resorted to special powers procedures, whereby the parliament allowed the government to decide on some matters without parliamentary debate.[14]

Yet, despite these mechanisms, some crises did occur. In those cases, dramatisation often took place, as when, in 1993, PM Dehaene submitted his resignation to the King and opportunity was given to negotiate again and to allow mutual concessions. When such difficulties occurred, the negotiation process was delegated to party summits, that is to say to the party presidents and to the PM.

(3) Institutional reform. The community/linguistic question has been regularly on the Belgian political agenda since 1963, when the process of the 'reform of the state' was initiated. From 1970 to 1993, Belgium was gradually (and strenuously) transformed from a unitary state into a *sui generis* type of federal state, following four main stages: the creation of

linguistic groups in parliament and of the French-speaking and Flemish-speaking Communities (1970); the creation of the Walloon and Flemish Regions and of the German-speaking Community (1980); the creation of the Brussels Region (1988); and the transformation into a federal state (1993).[15]

Parties have played a central role, but with variations. Moreover, the successive attempts to find a solution to the question of the linguistic communities have given rise to a variety of procedures: this is in itself an indication of the difficulty to find an appropriate procedure. From 1977 to the early 1990s, the relationship between parties and government on the community issue has closed the circle, insofar as the party presidents have held a central position in the decision process both at the beginning and at the end of the period, but not in the middle of the period.

During the 'Egmont' period (1977–8), the procedure centred around the governmental agreement, followed by the formation of extra-parliamentary, that is to say party-controlled, ad hoc committees during the cabinet's term. This period is named after the 'Egmont Pact', which was intended to be the large consociational-type pact designed to bring about a permanent solution to community conflicts. The Pact failed, mainly because of sharp conflicts within PM Tindemans' party, the CVP. In substance, the PM rejected the pact (officially) as a sign of unacceptable 'partitocracy', and also (unofficially) because of personal struggles at the top of the party. The Pact's failure provoked a deep internal and inter-party crisis from 1978 to 1981, the main actors being the coalition party presidents and the PM. Indeed, negotiations began before the formation of a new government and involved the *formateur* and the party presidents of the future coalition. The new government was then expected to send the 'Pact' (which was finalised at the end of this process) to parliament. A 'committee of 22' composed of the PM, the supporting party presidents and some ministers, followed by a 'committee of 15' (with the same composition, but without the ministers) adopted the 'Stuyvenberg Agreement', which rendered the Egmont Pact more concrete. Thus, at every stage of the procedure, there was a primacy of the parties – mainly through the party presidents – over the cabinet.

During the second period, from 1980 to 1991, that is to say throughout the 'Martens era', the political elite tried to elaborate new arrangements after Egmont's failure. The procedure centred once again on the governmental agreement, this time followed by a delegation to parliament through the formation of ad hoc committees. In 1989, for instance, the Martens VIII government appointed a mixed parliamentary committee with members of the majority and of the opposition, but which was reduced after some time to the majority only. Negotiations took place inside the government rather than outside it. This did not mark a decline of the power of parties, however;

it was rather a change of the arena in which party influence is exercised, as the main governmental discussions were held between PM and vice-PMs, that is to say among the parties' political heavyweights who acted as the parties' main representatives in different bodies such as the *Kerncabinet*, cabinet committees, or informal meetings, and in close contact with the party authorities outside the government.[16]

Finally, under the Dehaene cabinet of 1992, the institutional reforms were deepened in order to transform Belgium into a federal state. The strategy consisted in giving the initiative back to the parties and to their presidents, but in closer association with the PM, who was in some way detached from the other ministers. There is once again a direct power of the parties on the cabinet, but with better coordination with the PM, whose personality has also been a factor in establishing a more sensible relationship between parties and government. Moreover, contrary to what had been done in the previous cabinets, the governmental agreement was 'minimalist',[17] as the locus of the negotiation was transferred to an external body. The PM convened both the majority and opposition parties in a 'Community to Community dialogue'[18] in order to examine the constitutional reform. Rapidly, this dialogue was reduced to the majority parties, the Volksunie and the two Green parties. The dialogue failed, however; it was followed by a classical party summit procedure involving the party presidents of the supporting parties and the PM. They discussed and elaborated a plan and then attempted to associate to it the Volksunie and the two Green parties in order to reach the two-thirds majority for the constitutional revision. After some concessions in favour of the the Volksunie and the Greens,[19] a two-thirds majority for passing the new constitutional reform was reached, and this majority proved reliable.

(4) Defence policy: the 'double track' decision and the deployment of the 'cruise' missiles. In both cases, the decision was strongly contested by one of the supporting parties, the SP in 1979 and the CVP in 1984–5, as this party – including its ministers – was split over the issue.

The NATO 'double track' decision (1979), a policy not mentioned in the governmental agreement of the Martens I government, was initially opposed by the SP national executive (including 3 out of 4 of the party's ministers), as well as by the leader of the SP parliamentary party, whereas the SP vice-PM and minister of economic affairs,[20] the CVP and PSC supported the decision. At the following NATO conference (which had to approve unanimously the 'double track' decision), the PS minister of Foreign affairs and the PSC minister of Defence were given a mandate to negotiate a compromise proposal, whereas the SP remained split on the issue. The issue was dramatised on the final day of the NATO conference, as a vote on the 'double track' decision was scheduled to take place in parliament on that same day. Despite last minute attempts by the SP MPs and party president to block the decision, the party executive approved the government's 'compromise' proposal. The cabinet then unanimously approved the government's position which was subsequently endorsed by parliament. On the same day, the NATO summit participants unanimously approved the 'double track' decision without any trace of the Belgian 'compromise' proposals.

The approval of nuclear cruise missiles deployment in 1984–5 under the Martens V government (Christian-Democrats and Liberals) led to internal tensions within the CVP, as the trade union faction (ACW), supported by the party president, wanted to freeze any decision which could lead to missile deployment until the end of the government's term, while both the CVP national council and the party executive also asked for further delays in order to give disarmament talks a chance. Conversely, both the CVP minister of Foreign affairs and the PRL vice-PM advocated immediate deployment. After a CVP top meeting, a compromise proposal was agreed: the CVP was to accept the deployment of all cruise missiles only if disarmament talks fail, and to ask for the first deployment date to be re-negotiated with the allies. In the end, after many internal conflicts within the CVP, only the minister of Social affairs remained opposed to immediate deployment. A last-minute attempt by the minister of Foreign affairs was unsuccessful and all CVP ministers accepted the deployment decision. This was immediately followed by the cabinet meeting. On the very night, an airplane carrying the 'cruise' nuclear warheads took off from the USA. A few days later, in spite of large peace demonstrations in Brussels, parliament passed a vote of confidence in the government.

There are five similar features in the 1979 and 1984-85 cases. First, a conflictual situation arose in one coalition party, along the pre-existing intraparty ideological cleavage lines. Namely, the leaders of the left (or centre left) of these two parties opposed the governmental position. Second, a conflict took place between, on the one hand, the party president and, on the other, the minister of Foreign affairs, although both belonged to the same party (CVP) or ideological family (Socialist). Third, the defence minister did not belong to the rebellious party and apparently did not play a leading part in solving the conflicts. Fourth, in both cases, the minister of Foreign affairs defended the governmental standpoint. Finally, external actors played an important part: these were mainly the US and the NATO allies, who kept a constant pressure on the Belgian government, not the least in terms of imperative timetables. Admittedly, the room for manoeuvre of Belgian ministers in NATO bodies was limited (if not non-existent) in both cases. Hence, pressure was exercised on the rebels within the supporting party by the other governmental actors, on whom pressure had been exercised by external actors.

The government always had the final word when it faced opposition from one factionalised supporting party.[21] The final consensus was reached mostly through intraparty and interparty informal negotiations and cross-pressures between PM, party presidents, vice-PMs, and ministers. The government thus predominates over its individual supporting parties in the field of defence policy:[22] once the stability of the government is at stake, it seems that the ministers' view usually carries more weight than that of a rebel party president, who does not dare to go as far as to make the government fall.[23]

(5) 'Ecotaxes'. This new type of fiscal instruments became a highly controversial issue between April 1992 and July 1993. It is a mixture of both 'new' and 'old' politics: its proponents, the Green parties, are relative newcomers on the political scene, but it has gone through 'traditional' Belgian-style negotiations, with a blend of both consociationalism and neo-corporatism (Rihoux, 1993, 1994a, 1994b, 1994c).

The 'ecotaxes' can be traced back to the electoral programme of the Greens of 1985, but these early proposals remained largely unnoticed. After the November 1991 general election, the new PM convened the opposition parties (Liberals, Regionalists and Greens) to the 'Community to Community Dialogue'. On this occasion, the Greens put forward various 'ecotaxes' as one of their preconditions for their support to the institutional reforms. After the Dialogue's failure, as the government was left with the potential support of only the VU and the Greens, it accepted 'ecotaxes' on some products as part of the future government platform. Negotiations on the concrete modalities of the 'ecotaxes' then took place in an ad hoc interparty committee. After several laborious partial agreements and several dramatisation phases followed by re-negotiations, a global agreement was reached; it was then discussed and adopted in parliament, in parallel with the institutional agreements and with only minor modifications. Eventually, the initial implementation timetable was modified by the government in late 1993. Thus, by mid-1994, only two minor 'ecotaxes' had been implemented, whereas the implementation of the most important ones is still subject to negotiations within a follow-up committee.

The main actors were the PM and a few heavyweights of the negotiating parties, namely the supporting parties and the Greens. The government as a collective actor played little or no part, as the whole negotiation process was steered by the PM himself and his entourage, while the experts of the ad hoc committee refered directly to their respective party presidents and ministers. The last difficulties were settled directly by the PM, the supporting party presidents and the Green negotiators. In addition, one strategy used by the PM and by the leading ministers in order to put the Greens under pressure was to open up the negotiation – in a controlled way – to the social and economic interest groups through the existing channels of the neo-corporatist concertation bodies.


PATRONAGE

Patronage is a widespread and manifold phenomenon in Belgium. It is examined here in analytical rather than descriptive terms in order to determine what is in the hand of parties, what is in the hands of the government, what is shared by party and government, and what is in the hands of other bodies or persons.[24]

*Patronage fields and party-government control*
(1) Jobs and promotion. Through a variety of measures, parties succeeded in circumventing to a substantial extent the normal non-partisan recruitment procedures in the civil service sector, which happens to be among the largest of the OECD countries in terms of the proportion of the working population (De Winter, 1981, 1989b). Moreover, the recruitment and promotion of judges is also almost completely determined by party patronage. In addition, in most other sectors in which parties are influential, such as public media, public education, public, semi-public and quasi-autonomous companies and services, local government, and so on, parties (to some extent together with trade unions) largely interfere with the recruitment and promotion of personnel, at all hierarchical levels.

It is difficult to assess differences in the extent to which patronage in relation to jobs is distributed by the cabinet or by the parties. On the one hand, all the supporting parties participate in such practices. However, as Liberals and Socialists are not always in power (contrary to the Christian-Democrats), they try to set up 'catch-up' operations designed to compensate for the fact that these parties have not been able to appoint their clients when they were in opposition. In coalition talks, parties usually agree on appointment and promotion quotas for each party. Differences between cabinets seem mainly due to the number of jobs governments are able to create.[25] Before 1981, several special employment programmes to fight rising unemployment were launched; between 1981 and 1988, recruitment into the national public service came nearly to a halt, because of budgetary constraints. The return of the Socialists expanded public employment again.

It is also difficult to assess the extent to which this patronage can be used by ministers to curtail the action of the party machine, as many nominators are active at the same time and all contribute to appointments. Theoretically, the final decision on recruitment and promotion is taken by the ministers, but the content of the decision is to a large extent determined by the desiderata of actors in the party organisation. In practice, MPs (De Winter, 1992: 311) and other elected representatives,[26] as well as representatives of the constituency party organisations and of intraparty factions recommend their candidates to the national party president, who tries to aggregate the demands and compose a final preference list of his party to be communicated to the appointing minister or to the interparty conference(s) which decides on the allocation of jobs.

Belgian parties exercise an even stronger influence on promotions in the public sector. Until the end of the 1980s,[27] the promotion of university-trained civil servants was strongly controlled by the majority parties. Two types of interparty concertation govern promotions among governmental parties. First, the distribution of top positions in the civil service is decided by the cabinet itself, where a candidate's support by a coalition party is obviously taken into full consideration. Second, for the lower ranks of university-trained civil servants, an unofficial interparty committee was established in the 1970s, chaired by a collaborator of the PM.[28] For each position, the committee considers the candidates for promotion, and the support each candidate has from a coalition party. In principle, each coalition party can make nominations in proportion to its parliamentary strength. In order to prepare the meetings of this committee, most coalition parties (especially Christian-Democrats and Socialists) have installed intraparty nomination committees, in which the political and professional merits of candidates supported by party leaders, MPs, and other patrons are compared (De Winter, 1981; Hondegem, 1990: 198–203). The composition of these committees suggests that several types of nominators interfere at that level (party president, prominent ministers and their cabinets, factions, constituency parties, MPs and other brokers). It is difficult to assess which actor carries most weight in this internal party appointment process.

(2) Government contracts and pork barrel legislation. Government contracts are to some extent subject to political patronage, as political actors (party leaders, ministers, trade union and employer leaders) can and do lobby for different companies competing for a government contract. It is difficult to assess which actors are most involved in this allocation process, as one clearly enters into the sphere of political corruption and illegal party finance.[29] It is also difficult to determine to what extent the revealed facts are common practice or are exceptional, although some scattered evidence suggests that the impact of political actors is large (Ackaert & De Winter, 1984; Beuls, 1993).

On the other hand, De Winter's (1992) survey of Belgian MPs indicates that they are quite active in distributing collective benefits to their constituency, and therefore that pork barrel legislation constitutes an important patronage commodity in many policy fields.[30] Hence, pork barrel activities represent an important task of Belgian MPs. This is also related to the 'non-rational' way in which public expenditures are allocated: as decisions on the allocation of public investments are largely based on political criteria rather than on socio-economic cost-benefit calculations,[31] Belgian politicians have a larger pork barrel market to manipulate than politicians in many other countries.

Finally,[32] De Winter's (1992) analysis of the content of MPs' constituency service reveals that several other public service products and services are subject to political patronage, in many policy sectors.[33] Furthermore, to the extent that the media are subject to party or governmental control, access to the media and favourable media coverage also fall under patronage commodities (De Winter, 1981).

### The rationale of patronage

MPs have often to rely on the ministerial *cabinets* to receive a favourable treatment in response to their interventions on behalf of constituents. One can therefore assume that some political exchange occurs between MPs (and other party officials seeking benefits for their clients) and the ministers who take the final decisions on these matters. Yet little is known about the ways ministers use governmental patronage resources for controlling their party organisation. Although some extreme cases reveal that manipulation of the party through government patronage does occur, ministers mostly use governmental patronage not as a negative sanction against party rebellion, but rather as a means of raising support within the party for their position, for the party as a whole, and to reward clients outside the party.

### Ministerial cabinets and party-government patronage

All ministerial *cabinet* members do not participate in governmental work. First, many among them, especially those at lower levels, exercise 'clientelist' functions with regard to the minister's electoral district. Second, some higher level collaborators work directly for the party in fields which have nothing to do with the departmental powers of the minister or with his or his party's 'clientelist' network: this is the case for instance for policy fields where the party does not have a minister or secretary of state of its own. Within some ministerial *cabinets*, 'shadow' *cabinets* are set up in order to scrutinise the policies proposed by ministers of other parties. Third, parties also place in the ministerial *cabinets* MPs who were not re-elected or promising young party workers who need to undergo a political or governmental apprenticeship. Finally, members recruited from within the civil service use their passage through a ministerial *cabinet* to ensure their promotion in the civil service, as parties completely control promotion.

It thus seems that the main political function of the ministerial *cabinets* is to provide the party organisation with government-paid personnel used for a variety of purposes, governmental as well as others. At the governmental level, even when the main collaborators help ministers in their ministerial responsibilities, they also supervise these ministers on behalf of the party, as they have to rely on the party for their career. Yet *cabinets* are also means by which ministers can influence the party, at least if the ministers are themselves political heavyweights. *Cabinet* members are then personal followers whom ministers can deploy as loyal troops at the party's congress. In addition, if ministers enjoy some autonomy vis-à-vis their party, they can appoint *cabinet* members from a difficult coalition partner, with or without the consent of the latter and thus incite that party to make fewer demands on the minister.

Patronage is thus a multi-faceted process, in which many actors are involved and all these actors influence the final outcome to an extent. Meanwhile, actors usually attempt to fulfil multiple objectives while fostering patronage; in particular, by satisfying demands they will also probably silence the party and improve their own standing. The reasons why patronage occurs are also likely to vary according to each type, however. Finally, goods and services allocated through patronage by regional and community executives are also controlled by the national actors: hence, patronage commodities below the state level – which tend to become increasingly important – can also be used in a way that affects party-government relationships at the national level.

## CONCLUSION

In spite of the fact that Belgian parties exercise a strong impact on the selection of government personnel, play a large part in the elaboration of government policies, and have large political patronage resources at their disposal, there are substantial variations in government-supporting parties relationships.

First, there are differences among parties. At the one extreme, in the PS, the position of party president is quasi-omnipotent; at the other, in the Liberal parties, power resides in a specific leader and government-party relationships vary according to the party or governmental positions such a leader decides to take up. The Christian-Democrats stand in the middle: the party organisation as such has less impact than in the PS, but internal party factions exercise considerable influence on ministers.

Second, government-party relationships vary over time. In the 1977–8 period, the presidents of all parties involved in the government played a predominant role. The 1982–8 governments wanted to curtail permanent party interference by appointing the parties' strongmen as vice-PMs and by placing low profile figures at the head of the party organisation. The governments of the early 1990s constitute intermediate cases.

Third, government-party relationships vary according to the policy area involved. With regard to defence policy, until 1988, the government managed to force the hand of those parties or factions which defended policy alternatives. In the decision-making process with regard to the reform of the Belgian state, party presidents often played a more important part than ministers and even the PM. Given the institutional involvement of pressure groups in the sector of socio-economic policies, parties have had to compete with these actors for influence on the government.

Fourth, government-party relationships vary with the personality of governmental and party leaders. The influence of the two Liberal strongmen on other Liberal party and governmental actors does not stem from the positions which they held, but from their personal leadership. This is also the case with the PM: lack of prime ministerial leadership invites party interference.[34]

Finally, government-party relationships are affected by the electoral vulnerability of parties. Parties tend to interfere more frequently at the end of a government's term, especially if opinion polls are unfavourable. In order to boost their electoral support, party presidents often make demands upon their ministers which are clearly unacceptable to the other parties. Direct party interference is indeed the main reason why most governments fall.

The relationship between government and supporting parties is thus determined in Belgium at any given moment by the type of parties included in the coalition, their electoral vulnerability, the type of leaders that occupy governmental and party positions, and the policy sectors involved. In spite of a prevailing Zeitgeist which seems to become less favorable to partitocracy, party governance remains the predominant feature of the relationships between governments and supporting parties in the Belgian polity.

NOTES

1. The 1977–91 period covers 11 governments, 4 prime ministers, 8 supporting parties, 6 types of coalition and 22 party chairmen. This makes it impossible to identify 'the' features of a party-government relationship at a particular

moment in time or over short periods. Apart from the Tindemans IV government (1977–8), analyses of the following six governments from 1978 to 1981 are scarce.

2.  Little data is available with respect to other party actors (members of the executive, leaders of the parliamentary party, parliamentary candidates, and so on …) though there are some indications that government members often interfere in the recruitment process.

3.  The distribution of portfolios between parties is operated on the basis of a 'points' system, whereby each position (PM, minister, …) has a specific weight and each party receives 'points' proportional to its electoral strength. Several bargaining rounds are usually required to reach a final solution.

4.  The Martens V, VI and VII governments are considered as one single cabinet, since the Martens VI and VII governments can more or less be considered as a reconduction of the Martens V government.

5.  Data based on De Winter, 1993.

6.  We will only analyse the cases in which a new president was appointed and not those in which an incumbent president is confirmed in office, unless he was challenged. The case of the Volksunie (where, contrary to the traditional parties, presidents have had to deal with serious competition) will not be dealt here: given the party's limited governmental participation, no party leader was selected for the first time in a period when the party was in cabinet.

7.  The unified Belgian Socialist Party (PSB-BSP) split along linguistic lines in 1978, with the creation of the PS and of the SP. The figures correspond to the national presidents from 1944 to 1971, the French-speaking national co-presidents from 1971 to 1978, and the PS presidents after 1978.

8.  Namely Dehaene, PM Martens, the party president and Van Rompuy (head of the large party research centre).

9.  Based on charisma, intelligence and/or coercion.

10. Often including the timetables, but also the policies or problems which should not be tackled due to lack of consensus. This indicates that, in complex coalitions, the supporting parties need an overall and detailed agreement in order to maintain their support, and cannot operate by evaluating on an *ad hoc* basis the policy proposals of the cabinet and individual ministers. The Dehaene government of 1992 broke with this tradition (see institutional reforms).

11. Usually by overwhelming majorities, as most congress participants benefit personally from participation.

12. For all ministers, the number of collaborators at the higher level (university level) grew from 205 in 1966 to 330 in 1973 and 589 in 1988. For each minister, it grew from 9 to 11, with a peak of 13 in 1980. As for *cabinet* personnel at lower levels, the figures grew from 1328 in 1973 to 2037 in 1988, an increase clearly above the increase of the number of ministers. Subsequent governments have attempted to reduce this inflation.

13. During the 1926–86 period, the government ruled with special powers for about 15 per cent of the time (Alen, 1986).

14. During the 1982–4 period, the Martens V government took about 300 special power decisions, concerning a broad range of economic, social and financial policies (Alen, 1986).

15. Many other decisions were of course taken during the period: new parliamentary procedures, new institutions (such as the arbitration Court), new distribution

of prerogatives between the levels of power (Brassinne, 1989, for a detailed analysis from 1970 to 1989; Brassinne, 1994, for the latest developments).

16. Indeed, many heavyweights – including former party presidents – were included in the cabinet.

17. As the future coalition parties could only agree on an emergency programme made out of general principles which could settle the most important points.

18. Named after the French-speaking and Flemish-speaking Communities.

19. Mainly the 'ecotaxes', but also some institutional and budgetary arrangements.

20. Who eventually became Secretary-general of NATO in October 1994.

21. The end result would probably have been different if the whole party had opposed the governmental position.

22. However, the predominance of government in defence policy seems to have vanished since 1988, since the re-entry of the SP into the government has made defence and foreign affairs policy a fully collective matter, which cannot be decided by the ministers of defence or foreign affairs alone.

23. This was once again the case in 1991, under the Martens XIII cabinet, when both the presidents of the Volksunie and of the SP opposed weapon sales to the Middle-East.

24. For these aspects, see De Winter, 1981, Hondegem, 1990, Tegenbos, 1992.

25. In addition, the probably most fertile job patronage fields since 1981 are no longer in the national administrations, but in the regional and community administrations. However, the actors within the party involved in recruitment and promotion patronage have basically not changed.

26. Provincial councillors and deputies, mayors, aldermen and members of local councils, all engage in service activities towards individual citizens. In terms of numbers of clients and jobs involved, patronage at the local and provincial level probably exceeds patronage at the national level.

27. One notices a temporary decline of party patronage in relation to the promotion of civil servants in the late 1980s (Martens VIII government). However, since 1992, the impact of the interparty committee seems to have grown again.

28. Since the federalisation of the national civil service, similar committees have been set up to monitor patronage in the promotion of regional and community level civil servants: this has not declined -- on the contrary.

29. Usually only cases of corruption provide evidence about the extent to which political and other actors have lobbied and have been rewarded for their lobbying. This is the case for instance with respect to the investigation of the assassination of the former Socialist party president (and vice-PM) Cools in 1991.

30. The most often cited fields, in decreasing order of importance are: communication and transport infrastructure; private investments stimulating economic development and employment; infrastructure relating to the educational, health, cultural and sport sectors; urbanisation and housing problems; environment and physical security.

31. Given the ongoing conflicts between the different regions and cultural communities, departmental spending is carefully distributed between the regions and communities: each unit receives public investments according to its size.

32. Although practices such as the granting of decorations or of aristocratic titles and the appointment of ministers of state do occur, they play no significant

part in Belgium. While housing falls within the patronage of the parties, it is distributed at a sub-national and mainly local level.

33. These are, in decreasing order of importance: income problems (mainly social security transfers); army and draftees; education, culture, and leisure (mainly scholarships); taxes; transport and communication (telephone connections, car licence plates, road works and security); family problems; police and justice.

34. For example, in 1988, PM Martens accepted, under strong pressure of the supporting parties and of the monarch, to head a government which was already formed by his vice-PM. As it was not 'his' government, he failed to give leadership and acted as the record-keeper of the decisions taken by his vice-PMs.

# 10. Italy: Sunset of a Partitocracy*

## Maurizio Cotta and Luca Verzichelli

### INTRODUCTION

Between 1992 and 1994 the Italian political system went through a major crisis which directly affected the actors discussed in this book and the relationships between them. Writing in the immediate aftermath of the 'revolution' obviously creates special problems. First, the past looks more 'past', that is to say, less relevant for understanding the present than in other cases. Second, the 'new' is difficult to evaluate accurately and there are still serious doubts as to whether the new rules of the game will be consolidated. On the other hand, the crisis of the 'old regime' exposed to public scrutiny a significant part of the less visible side of politics, thus rendering easier the understanding of some political phenomena. Moreover, the opportunity to compare within the same country (that is other things being equal) different 'regimes' or, more accurately, the 'old regime' in its full strength, the transitional phase of its fall, and the emerging new phase provides a basis for a better understanding of the characteristics of political life. Finally, when the regime of party dominance was in full swing, its strengths were naturally underlined and the control exercised by the parties over all political processes was stressed; the abrupt crisis and breakdown of the regime leads to questions being raised also about its weaknesses.

In this chapter attention will be centred on the period of party dominance before the crisis: the analysis will cover mainly the years 1980–92 when the old regime was still in place. However, developments having taken place after 1992 will be briefly mentioned when this is required to understand the main changes which have occurred since the crisis began.

A preliminary question needs to be settled: how do the 1980s compare with the past? Was that decade a continuation of a longer term trend? The answer is a qualified yes as these years share common features with the period going back to the basic political stabilization of the end of the 1940s (Morlino, 1992; Cotta, 1994), one of the most prominent of these features being the lack of any realistic expectation of alternance in government. The 1980s are in a sense the consequence of the failure of the attempt of the late 1970s to alter these features fundamentally by incorporating the Communist party (PCI) in the governmental majority. The renewed alliance between Christian Democrats (DC) and Socialists (PSI) to which a number of smaller secular parties of the centre were added (Social Democrats – PSDI, Republicans – PRI and Liberals – PLI) which followed that failure can be described as a return to the 'centro-sinistra' formula of the 1960s and early 1970s. Two qualifications have to be made, however. First, there came to be an altered balance between the DC and the other parties of the governing coalition, as a result of both the weakening of the DC and the strengthening of the other partners, especially the PSI: this led to the ending of the Christian Democrat monopoly over the prime ministership. Second, a slow electoral decline of the PCI occurred after 1979 and the party was less perceived as a threat to the democratic system: this was due both to the weakening of the party's links with the Soviet Union and to the cooperative role which it had played in the 1970s in facing extreme left terrorism. As a result of the combination of these old and new features, governing coalitions in the 1980s still lacked realistic alternatives, but they were none the less not as markedly under siege; the opposition had become less threatening and its growth no longer seemed to be inevitable.

Moreover, the traditionally dominant role of the DC had been shaken and a more intense competition for leadership began. This competition was sharpened by the transformation of the second largest party of the coalition, the PSI, whose leader had become prominent both within the party and outside it (Merkel 1987): the alternance between the Socialist leader Craxi and Christian Democrat leaders in the post of prime minister (known as *staffetta*) is a characteristic feature of the period. It is no exaggeration to claim that the competition for leadership among the governing parties was so intense that these did not perceive (or perceived only when it was too late) the importance of the new political challenges coming from the fringes of the political system as a result of the birth of new political movements such as the Northern League, the anti-mafia *Rete*, or the referendum movement.

The political earthquake of 1992–4, which not only brought down the traditional governing parties from power but practically destroyed them, did not come from where it had been expected for more than forty years, that is to say from the Communist opposition. The Maginot line built to contain and then to appease the PCI was entirely ineffective against the new political and extra-political forces which in the early 1990s started the attack on the parties of government.

The 1980–92 period is thus puzzling and paradoxical. It was often perceived as one of political stabilization: yet it ended with an unprecedented earthquake.[1] It was a period of great popularity of the Socialist leader Craxi and of a significant growth of his party which in the elections of 1992 nearly reached (for the first time since 1946) the size of its leftist antagonist (the former PCI now renamed Party of the Democratic Left – PDS); yet it ended with the complete political downfall of that political leader and the collapse of the party. A better understanding of the functioning of party government and specifically of the relationship between government and supporting parties during these years has therefore a double value: it helps to compare and explain similarities and differences in the Italian style of party government in contrast to that of other European countries; it also helps to understand the causes of the breakdown.

## APPOINTMENTS. PARTY CONTROL FROM OUTSIDE AND FROM INSIDE.

The structure of ministerial appointments until 1992 is fairly clear. Party men and women predominate in cabinet positions; ministers without a party background are rare, and can be found in special situations only, for instance in short term transitional governments or in economic ministries.[2] In most cases, as Table 10.1 shows, the party background of ministers included a national party position.

Moreover, the control of appointments was not in the hands of prime ministers but of the party leadership. During the process of cabinet formation, the first stage was one during which ministerial posts were allocated to the parties of the coalition, each party then dealing with the distribution of these posts to its members according to internal party criteria. Indeed the whole government formation process was largely centred on the personnel question, and this was a party question.

Who were then the true 'nominators'? The party chairman always was a central figure in this process; there were variations among parties, however, and these were due to their different structure. In a centralized party such as the Socialist party of the 1980s (Merkel, 1987) and in the smaller parties the role of the party chairman was dominant; in a party with developed factions such as Christian Democracy the balance between these factions had to be taken into account. A special accounting method, known as the *manuale Cencelli*, was used to weigh the ministries and establish a 'fair' representation. In this context the party chairman was largely dependent on the faction leaders who wanted to ensure that their faction obtained an adequate share. The selection process was thus more the result of oligarchic bargaining than of a decision made at the top. Finally, the parliamentary wing of the parties also played a part: the chairmen of the parliamentary groups of the two chambers generally assisted party chairmen in the cabinet formation process and at least in the case of the DC the selection of the ministers would typically follow a meeting of the parliamentary groups which had to provide a list of 'ministrables'.[3]

Table 10.1: *Number and percentage of ministers with a previous National Party Office (Executive or National Council)*

| Cabinet | Duration | DC N (%) | PSI N (%) | All Parties N (%) |
|---|---|---|---|---|
| COSSIGA I | Aug 79–Apr 80 | 17 (85) | – | 21 (85) |
| COSSIGA II | Apr 80–Oct 80 | 14 (87.5) | 7 (77.8) | 24 (82.2) |
| FORLANI | Oct 80–Jun 81 | 15 (88.2) | 7 (100) | 25 (86.2) |
| SPADOLINI I AND II | Jun 81–Dec 82 | 13 (86.7) | 7 (100) | 25 (89.3) |
| FANFANI V | Dec 82–Aug 83 | 11 (78.6) | 8 (88.9) | 26 (89.7) |
| CRAXI I | Aug 83–Aug 86 | 12 (80) | 8 (100) | 26 (89.7) |
| CRAXI II | Aug 86–Apr 87 | 12 (80) | 6 (85.7) | 25 (86.2) |
| FANFANI VI | Apr 87–Jul 87 | 14 (70) | – | 14 (56) |
| GORIA | Jul 87–Apr 88 | 12 (80) | 5 (62.2) | 23 (76.7) |
| DE MITA | Apr 88–Jul 89 | 14 (87.5) | 4 (57.1) | 22 (73.3) |
| ANDREOTTI VI | Jul 89–Apr 91 | 16 (84.2) | 6 (66.6) | 28 (75.7) |
| ANDREOTTI VII | Apr 91–Jun 92 | 12 (75) | 9 (100) | 25 (86.2) |
| AMATO | Jun 92–May 93 | 4 (30.8) | 6 (85.7) | 15 (51.7) |
| CIAMPI | May 93–Apr 94 | 4 (50) | 2 (66.7) | 8 (32) |

Except for the undersecretary to the prime minister, who was also the only undersecretary attending the Council of Ministers, who acted as its secretary, and who always was chosen by the prime minister, the role of the head of the executive in the selection of ministers was therefore limited; to be more accurate it varied according to the weight of the prime minister as party leader. In the case of the DC the prime minister was often one of the faction leaders of the party: he would then select the ministers 'assigned' to his faction; otherwise his role would consist by and large in receiving names and passing them to the head of state for the formal appointment.[4]

Did the stronger profile given by Craxi to the prime ministership alter this situation? When the Socialist leader led the cabinet (1983–7), the role of the prime minister in the selection of ministers appeared larger than in the past, but was this because he was prime minister? The answer is in the end negative, first, as his role was limited to the selection of the ministers assigned to his party and, second, as his strong influence had existed previously and persisted when he left the cabinet and only had his party position. It was essentially his dominant role in the Socialist party that gave him a fairly free hand in the selection of (Socialist) ministers. The case of

Craxi is therefore an exception to the normal pre-eminence of party leadership over government leadership in the selection of ministers, only because he was the leader of a party where factions had been crushed and was successful in combining cabinet and party leadership for a markedly longer period than ever before or afterwards. Clearly one position helped in strengthening the other: a necessary condition (although not the only one) for the long premiership of Craxi was his strong control over his own party while his long premiership further strengthened his hold on his party.

Was there influence in the opposite direction, namely from government to party? Formally, appointments to the party leadership were clearly party matters; they took place at party congresses as a result of a two-stage process: party delegates elected a fairly large party parliament called *Consiglio Nazionale* or *Comitato Centrale* which then appointed the National Executive (*Direzione*). The selection of the party leader (*Segretario*) was previously made by the party parliament, but in the 1980s it became more common for the chairman to be elected directly by the party delegates at the congress.[5] There also was often a smaller body (the *Segreteria*) composed of the collaborators of the party leader in charge of the main central offices of the party (a kind of cabinet of the party). The party leadership also included the leaders of the parliamentary groups of each party, these being elected by the parliamentarians.

Formally the government had no say in these appointments, but the informal picture is less clear-cut. Some evidence can be drawn in this context from the analysis of the background of nominees and of the interlocking of careers, by considering a relatively large circle of party leaders, defined as those who had been members of the party executive and/or had been leaders of one of the parliamentary groups, and examining how many had been ministers. There are two ways of approaching the problem: one consists in considering the first entry into the group, the other in looking at each new renewal in office.[6] The data about first entry in the national party elite show that it typically precedes a ministerial position; but when reappointments are included the percentage of members of the national executive with a ministerial background becomes larger. Yet the number of members of national executives with a ministerial background is smaller than the number of ministers having been members of the executive. There are also significant differences between DC and PSI, a ministerial background being rarer in the Socialist party.

To some extent these numbers are due to size. National executives are larger than party ministerial groups, the ratio being 2 to 1 for the DC, and 6 to 1 for the PSI: being a member of the government is thus more difficult than having a seat on the national executive. Yet, overall, the links between the two types of position are manifest. Thus there is a government–party elite in the governing parties and this elite moves back and forth between the two arenas: it is difficult as a result to determine where the border lies between party and government. The coincidence is not complete between the two branches of the political elite, however: some of its members are more ministerial, having had a longer career in government than in the party, while others tend to have more of a party profile, with shorter periods in government and a longer presence at the top of the party.[7]

Except in the case of the small group of technocratic ministers, it is difficult to find a sharp separation between the two careers, however. No one can aspire to be a minister for very long without belonging to the inner party core, while the opposite is also true to a large extent. A purely party career at the top without experience in government is rather rare.[8] Thus while party dominates the appointment process to the government, being in government is an important resource to prolong and strengthen a career within the party leadership. The influence of government over party does not flow from the government as an institution, but from the individual resources which the government gives to top politicians.

The last part of this picture relates to the interlocking between party and cabinet positions. If one concentrates on the relationship between top party positions and prime ministership and other leading positions in the cabinet, one notes appreciable variations from party to party; there are also political 'rules' regulating the allocation of the prime ministership to members of the coalition. Meanwhile, during the period, the monopoly of the DC was replaced by open competition, while, up to 1981, the leadership of the government had been firmly in the hands of the DC.[9]

If we start from the early years of Italian post-fascist politics, the norm adopted was for the formal and real leader of the largest party of the coalition, the DC, to head the government. Although from September 1946 a formal distinction occurred between the two offices and the prime minister abandoned the position of party chairman (while receiving the honorific title of party president), it did remain the case, almost up to the end of the De Gasperi period (1953), that the party was led from the government and that the prime minister was also the real leader of the party (Baget Bozzo, 1974: 137). After De Gasperi (and the first significant electoral weakening of the DC in 1953) the arrangement was reversed: the chairman of the party became the leading figure and the prime minister, dependent as he was on the growing uncertainty of the governing coalitions, was downgraded to occupying a more limited role and also started lasting in office less long. An attempt was made in 1958 by the then chairman of the party, Fanfani, to restore the unity of the two positions and to add the prime ministership to his leadership of the party:

this arrangement lasted eight months only, resentment in the party against such a concentration of power having produced a successful rebellion of the party 'oligarchs' and only in the 1980s was such a solution experimented again. In the DC the party chairman never was a truly dominant figure; he always had to come to terms with the faction leaders (and to some extent also with the prime minster: more than a leader he was an arbiter).

The other members of the governing coalitions (Liberals, Republicans, Social Democrats, and, after 1963, Socialists) were until the 1980s in a subordinate position: their leaders could not compete for the leadership of the cabinet; at most could they obtain some important ministries. Their participation in the cabinets has been irregular. Some changes occurred in the 1980s as a result of a number of factors. First, the monopoly of the DC over the leadership of the cabinet ended: two other parties, the Republicans and the Socialists, became able to aspire to the prime ministership thanks to their stronger bargaining position in the coalition game. Second, in both these parties the position of party leader was (or had become by then) more dominant. Third, there was a growing feeling in the country that the cabinet should have a stronger role vis-à-vis parliament (Cotta, 1991; 1994) and that coalitions should be more stable. The prime ministership became as a result more important in the political game in the 1980s: small parties conceived it as a crucial instrument to balance the larger size of the DC in coalitions. Especially in the case of the leader of the Socialist party, Craxi, the visibility of the prime ministership seemed to be an important asset in his three-pronged struggle to consolidate his leadership in the party, to establish a kind of duopoly with the DC, and to re-equilibrate the balance between PSI and PCI. Between 1983 and 1987 the fusion of party and government leadership (this time not in the hands of the largest party but of a medium-sized albeit strategically well positioned party such as the PSI) became a significant element in the Italian political system.

This change also forced the DC to depart from its tradition and to follow suit. Thus when the government leadership came back to the DC, its then leader, De Mita, after a short transitional stage (the Goria cabinet) chose to combine the two positions. Yet what had been possible for the leaders of smaller parties proved impossible in the case of the largest party of the coalition. De Mita held both posts for nine months only. The two positions were once more uncoupled afterwards, for two reasons:[10] first, in a factionalized party such as the DC the concentration of power in the hands of the leader raised objections on the part of the other members of the 'oligarchy'; second, the joint holding of government and party leadership aroused the fear within the other parties that there might be a return to DC hegemony in the coalition.[11]

After the elections of 1992 the old mechanisms faced a rapidly developing crisis. The ability of the parties to control appointments to cabinet positions was increasingly in question. First, the Amato (1992–3) and Ciampi governments (1993–4) were markedly less party-based: the number of top ranking party politicians went down and that of technocrats up (Table 10.1);[12] the Ciampi cabinet led by the former governor of the Bank of Italy, one of the few strong technocratic institutions in Italy, was indeed the epitome of the non-party government. Second, particularly with respect to reshuffles in the Amato cabinet and with respect to the composition of the Ciampi cabinet in general, the role of the party leaders in appointments was seriously weakened while the prime minister (in close contact with the head of State) played a greater part.

After the 1994 elections, which brought about a political earthquake, (new) parties temporarily regained control, with three elements characterizing the relationship between parties and government with respect to appointments. First, ministries were allocated among parties of the coalition. Second, in the three major components of the winning coalition (*Forza Italia*, the North League, and the National Alliance) the leader of the party enjoyed a strong position. Third, there was asymmetry between *Forza Italia* and the other parties since *Forza Italia* was the creature of Berlusconi who subsequently became prime minister. The party had no effective structure in the country, as is shown by the fact that a minister was appointed several months after the formation of the government to be its new chairman: the party seemed therefore dominated by the government. In reality, power rested with its charismatic founder and his entourage, a situation which bore some similarity to Craxi governments earlier, although the party of Berlusconi was less of a party than the PSI of Craxi. Thus elements of a dependent party did combine for a while with the prevailing model of a subordinate government, but the collapse of the Berlusconi government in January 1995 led to a return to a technocratic cabinet under Dini, also from the Bank of Italy, an indication that the situation was far from having been stabilized.

## POLICY-MAKING IN A PARTITOCRATIC SYSTEM

With respect to policy-making, the 'partitocratic' label commonly attached to the Italian political system before the crisis of the 1990s suggests that the government depends on the parties: in reality, the picture is less clear. On the one hand, some analyses of the Italian party government show that the intervention of parties is larger in Italy than in other European countries

(Pasquino, 1987 and 1989; Dente & Regonini, 1989); on the other, it has been claimed that the pervasiveness of party intervention does not necessarily mean that parties play a strong part in the definition of policies (Cotta, 1994). One should also not underestimate cases of party neutrality or even absence from the decisional arena (Dente & Regonini, 1987).

Let us first summarize the main characteristics of the Italian political system since the Second World War. These have been defined as being strong polarization and a strong ideological style (Sartori, 1982), an extensive extra-parliamentary apparatus of the largest parties (Bardi and Morlino, 1994), and control of parties over interest groups (Morlino, 1991). These features point in the direction of parties having an elaborate and comprehensive set of preferences and dictating these preferences to a dependent government. Meanwhile, on the government side, the well-known weaknesses of the Italian bureaucracy – in particular the lack of a strong *esprit de corps*, the weak professionalization at the top, the limited resistance to party penetration (Ferraresi, 1980; Regonini, 1993) – combined with high governmental instability tended to increase further the opportunity for parties to dominate.

This picture needs to be somewhat revised, however. First, with the passing of time, the ideological polarization of parties and political life had lost much of its original intensity. Admittedly, the main point remained, namely the permanent exclusion from government of the largest opposition party; but the ideological conflict had ceased to be a clear guide to policy-making. The freezing of the parties into two stable camps (the governing camp and the opposition camp), a situation basically accepted by both sides, meant that ideology had become a ritual. Day-to-day policy-making was less encumbered by ideology, on the contrary: behind the scenes, it tended to focus on (often particularistic) interests, while patronage and clientelism flourished. As a result parties (especially the largest governing party, the DC) had increasingly become diversified coalitions of interests, as the presence of factions indicated. Rather than express well-defined policy lines, parties were engaged in mediating between and balancing different interests in order to maintain party unity. Parties, and in particular their leaders, were therefore not markedly engaged in active policy-making. They reacted rather than initiated: they checked that policy initiatives coming from other actors (including lower-level party leaders) did not endanger the coalition of interests which the party has assembled.

Thus, on the one hand, the intervention of parties in the policy-making processes was pervasive: it was almost impossible to reach any decision without the assent of the parties. Yet, on the other hand, parties were involved only to a limited extent in policy formulation: they were rather continuously interfering guardians. Indeed, the wide diffusion of corrupt practices (*tangenti*) exposed by the judiciary since the early 1990s, was related to the guardian role of the parties, as financial contributions of private businessmen were a 'tax' imposed by parties in their process of monitoring the policy-making process.

The space for government action was both broadened and restricted as a result. It was broadened because the government could have more scope to initiate policies than would have been the case had parties been more cohesive and more ideologically motivated; but the space for government action was also restricted because parties which are coalitions of interests are less likely to leave to the government details of policy-making. It is on these details that the balance of particularistic interests may be most affected: Italian parties tended therefore to interfere more than parties interested in high politics.

There were still policy areas affecting the ideological identities of the parties, but parties were unlikely to promote new policies in such fields, as they would have little chance of success and tensions would be created in government coalitions. Moves of this kind occurred only when parties decided to redefine their political identity: this was probably the case when the Socialist party attempted in the 1980s to move toward the centre to compete with the DC for the support of voters. New policies promoted by the party symbolized the break with traditional socialism.

Yet the government has also to be brought in the picture. Given the nature of the supporting parties (a coalition of coalitions) the political profile was far from well-defined and coherent. As the weaknesses of the state bureaucracy had not disappeared, the administrative identity of the government remained weak; but the government could also profit to some extent from being at the crossroads between parties, administration, and interest groups. Thus it was more likely to act on the basis of initiatives of individual ministers, acting either as party men substituting for their party in devising policies or as representatives of a specific administrative sector together with client interest groups. As a collective body, the government made policies under strong external pressure only, for instance when budgetary cuts had to be introduced to meet the financial standards set by the European Community, when there was an international crisis, or when demographic changes endangered the financial equilibrium of the pension system.

**The case studies**

Ten cases have been selected to examine policy-making in greater depth. These are the limitation of wage indexation adopted by government decree in 1984,[13] four financial bills (*Leggi Finanziarie*) for the years 1983, 1986, 1992, 1993,[14] the '*Achille Lauro* crisis' which began when a Palestinian group hijacked an Italian ship, the *Achille Lauro*, killing an American citizen, and developed when the airplane taking the leader of the terrorist group from Egypt to Tunisia was forced by American military aircraft to land at the Italian airport of Sigonella, the bill which increased aid to developing countries, the creation of an anti-trust authority, the law on radio and television, and the first privatization policies under the Andreotti and Amato governments at the beginning of the 1990s. These cases were selected in order to cover a wide range of policy areas (from foreign policy to financial and budgetary policy, from labour policy to economic regulatory policies), in order to assess whether the weight of government and parties varied, and to examine the different stages of the coalition cycle during the 1980s.

Some cases (those of the *Achille Lauro* crisis and of the financial bills) relate to situations where the government was under an institutional constraint to act; in others, such as privatization, aid to developing countries, or anti-trust legislation, the freedom of action was greater at least in principle. In one case (*Achille Lauro*) the symbolic and ideological aspects (national autonomy *vs*. Atlantic solidarity) were particularly relevant; in the others, down-to-earth interests played a greater part, although 'high politics' could have been invoked, for instance to choose among different budgetary policies or to decide between strongly promoting competition and opting for a more protected market in the anti-trust field.

**Policy initiation. Where were the parties?**

In analysing the role of parties and government in the stage of policy initiation a distinction must be drawn between the cases where there is freedom to act and those where institutional constraints impose action, as in an international crisis and in the budget. In the first type of cases it is easier to evaluate the role of parties in launching a policy; in the other cases initiation is institutionally in the hands of the government: parties can merely formulate policy guidelines either prior to the governmental initiative or as the process develops.

The policies of the first type – wage indexation, development aid, anti-trust, privatizations, TV reform – introduced substantial innovations to the type of legislation prevailing in Italy. In all of them the simplified model of party initiative and government dependence fits imperfectly: even where the party role is more significant the reality involves both the party outside government and the party in government.

In the context of wage indexation the ground for a policy change was prepared by a move away from egalitarianism and a shift towards meritocratic criteria within the parties of the majority and especially the Socialist

Party at the beginning of the 1980s (Mastropaolo and Slater, 1987). The government led by Craxi then exploited a favourable opportunity to launch the policy by decree: dissensions among trade unions and a stalemate in the long negotiations which these were conducting with employers and government provided the prime minister with the occasion to act. The coalition partners were taken somewhat by surprise but followed. Was this action a party or a government initiative? The government clearly did not act under party pressure; yet the partisan character of the policy is manifest. The use by Craxi of his governmental position to redefine the image of the PSI (in the context of a competition for the votes of centrist electors) was a key aspect of this policy.

The pressure to initiate policy on aid to developing countries came from an active campaign of a small opposition party (the Radical party) and from specialist groups in the governing parties. The government stepped in to mediate between political activists and bureaucratic interests and to defend the interests of the ministry of Foreign Affairs in foreign aid (Isernia, 1996).

Anti-trust legislation and privatizations show even more clearly the lack of a strong party initiative on policy: in both cases the role of the government was significant. On anti-trust legislation, the larger parties of the coalition were inactive, while the smaller did more: in fact the legislative initiative was taken by two successive ministers of Industry, one belonging to the Liberal party, the other to the Republican party. The matter did become part of the programme of the De Mita cabinet in 1988, but this was primarily because Italian legislation needed to be adapted to European Community arrangements (La Spina, 1996).[15] Lack of party activism is equally noticeable in the field of privatizations. Unlike parties of the Right in other European countries, Italian parties remained little interested in the matter. Some limited initiatives were taken by MPs of the governing and of the opposition parties, but the parties as such did not take the lead or even push strongly in the direction of privatization. As a matter of fact, nothing happened until the government, under the pressure of the increasing state debt and of the need to move in the direction of European convergence, discovered privatization as a means of raising money: but there never was great enthusiasm for the idea.

Party initiation was probably most marked in the context of television reform. The *Mammí* bill (from the name of the minister who presented it to parliament) settled in 1990 the delicate matter of the relations between State television and the private channels which started to broadcast in the 1980s at the margins of legality; the bill was the result of an agreement between the Socialist party and the new centre-right majority within the DC and it formed part of the compact of a new cabinet under a new prime minister. For the parties television was crucial: they wanted to control it closely.

In the other cases, where initiation was institutionally constrained, the original role of the parties was necessarily limited, while the government was the prime mover. In such cases, however, what is critical is to determine the main goals and content of the policy. Parties can therefore play a part even before the formal initiation of the policy.

In the case of the Finance bills which have to be introduced every year by the government the question which arises is whether the supporting parties did define in advance the budgetary and financial goals to be reached and provided the government with guidelines: such an active role of parties is difficult to detect. In the party programmes and the electoral manifestos there are little more than vague appeals to financial discipline and, on aggregate economic and financial targets, the Bank of Italy (or international organizations such as the IMF) are more likely to determine guidelines. In the initial stage the government, specifically the prime minister and, above all, the Finance minister and the Treasury have the lead. The administrative aspect of the government prevails initially over the party aspect.

In the case of the *Achille Lauro* affair, which was an international crisis, the government (prime minister, minister of Foreign Affairs, minister of Defence) held initially the front of the stage; however, two of the ministers involved were also leaders of their parties (Craxi for the Socialists and Spadolini for the Republicans) while the third (Andreotti) was a major faction leader of the DC.

Two conclusions can be drawn. First, there are variations in the initial stage of the policy making process: these can be related to the nature of the policy field, to institutional constraints, to the changing roles of different parties in the government, and to the timing of a policy within the political cycle. Second, parties as organizations and their leaders do not dominate the policy initiation process as much as might have been expected given the accepted view that Italy has a strongly 'partitocratic' tradition. The government appears to have a greater role, not because of its intrinsic strength, but because of special conditions: thus external or institutional pressures often force the government to take the lead; the parties themselves may even delegate to the government a role which they cannot or do not want to exercise.

Moreover, what is meant by government does vary. At one extreme, the government is at the head of the state machinery. This is particularly the case over budgetary questions and in international crises. At the other, the government is a partisan actor; it represents a political coalition as well as the different components of this coalition: it then conducts essentially a political game: this was the case with respect to the wage indexation question and over television reform.

**Policy development and adoption. The parties as guardians**

Once a theme has come on the political agenda, the parties of the governing coalition are more active: this is so even when they had played no part during the initiation stage, although, at that point, the intervention of parties takes the form of reaction more than of action. The most extreme form of such a reaction consists in killing a policy initiative, a good example being that of pension reform. During the late 1980s and early 1990s, ministers of Labour, faced with the increasing financial imbalance of the pension system periodically launched reform proposals on behalf of the government; these were regularly stopped by parties of the coalition. Other modes of party intervention consist in delaying a policy, in introducing profound changes in content, and even in transforming a policy into an instrument of party politics or of patronage. The cases examined here provide examples of these different modes; they can be arranged along a continuum of greater to lesser government autonomy vis-à-vis parties.

Wage indexation provides the clearest case of government autonomy. There were indeed worries within the parties of the coalition (especially within the DC) about the move itself, not so much on the substance as over the method used, a decree which did not have the full support of the trade unions and of the opposition. The proposals suggested by the party spokesman for economic affairs of the DC were not accepted by the government; in the end, because of the mood of public opinion, of the weakening of trade unions, and also of a generally favourable, albeit not vocal, attitude within the governing parties, the government and in particular the leader of the PSI and prime minister, Craxi, were able to win the day. Supporting parties followed the leadership of the government during the whole process, from the subsequent ratification of the decree by the parliament to a referendum campaign which was forced by the opposition against the decree.

The ability of the government to lead is not usually as marked. In the *Achille Lauro* crisis, the government was at the centre of the decision-making process at the beginning because of its institutional role; yet a conflict developed soon along party lines when the government refused to grant the American military permission to seize the Palestinian hijacker on Italian territory and to take him to the United States. While two parties of the coalition (the Socialist party and Christian Democracy), with a crucial role in the government (holding the positions of prime minister and of minister of Foreign Affairs) wanted to exploit the opportunity to play a 'nationalist' line by following a more independent foreign policy and to develop friendly relations with Palestinians and the Arab world, the Republican party, to which the minister of Defence belonged, wished to maintain its political identity by stressing the case for Atlantic loyalty. The importance of the issue was such that the parties (their executive committees) were quickly brought into play by the members of government in support of their different positions. One of the parties, the Republican party, even threatened to leave the government. Consultations among the parties then took place and a mutually acceptable solution was found. Thus in a sudden crisis the fact that the government had to take the lead can enable parties of the coalition which are strategically placed in terms of ministerial positions to win points. In the end, however, full consultation among the parties had to occur as issues relating to the international alignment of the country were at stake. The ultimate guardians of the foreign policy guidelines which define the limits to the freedom of action of the government are the parties.

In budgetary policy one of two different models might be adopted. There could be either dominance of the state bureaucracy and of the government having some budgetary principles in common or a clear economic philosophy of the governing parties dictating their preferences to the government. We saw already that this second model does not apply to the initiation stage, since government parties do not formulate clear guidelines for budgetary policy and these are left to the Treasury. The intervention of parties is more negative: specific policies can be stopped from being inserted in the financial bills, as in the case of pension reform. Parties act as guardians of the existing equilibrium of interests which they have helped to shape and the government has to work within these explicit or implicit limits. Yet there is no truly coherent budgetary policy of the cabinet: the Treasury has to fight a lonely war against other ministries and it cannot see its views easily accepted in a highly fragmented cabinet. Its main strength is constituted by the external constraints which impose limits on the budget deficit.

During the process of adoption of the financial bills (which with its cabinet and parliamentary stages typically stretches over three or four months) interventions of party authorities at different levels (chairman, party executive, leaders of parliamentary groups) are frequent. They aim both at assuring the government of party support and at ensuring that it does not exceed the limits set by the parties (Verzichelli, 1996); but party intervention often means that the government has to cope with pressures coming from within party groups or with factions fighting for special interests. The result is an intricate bargaining process between government and members of the majority in the parliamentary committees, as well as within the government among ministers: this leads to substantial modifications of the original government bill. The role of the party consists often in striking a balance between these particularistic demands and the global goals of the financial bill. There is also an ambivalence on the part of some of the ministers most involved, as they are both representatives of party (or faction) interests and of their ministry.

The privatization case shows how far parties can act as a brake to governmental initiatives. The governing parties did not reject explicitly the cabinet move to start selling state property; but their official support was timid in the extreme and left in practice plenty of space to the more energetic action of the intraparty groups which opposed this policy initiative. As a result, in spite of having become official government policy, actual privatizations were delayed. For approximately two years (between 1990 and 1992) the Finance minister, who was in charge of the policy, was left more or less alone by his colleagues in the cabinet to fight for the bills required to allow state companies to be sold.[16] Some ministers seemed indeed readier to side with opposition expressed in the parties and in parliament than to support government policy actively. Privatizations took off only in 1993 when the crisis of the traditional governing parties opened the way to a non-party cabinet. This is not surprising: state industries had become a major field of party patronage; privatizations meant therefore a substantial loss of resources for the governing parties.

Party activism was manifest throughout the policy process in the case of the television bill. The close links of the parties (and of different factions within the DC) with state and private television stations easily explain their keen interest in controlling the elaboration of the new rules. The legislative process was paralleled by a continuing debate between the parties of the governing coalition and among the internal factions of the DC. Official party authorities proclaimed the party line asking the government not to betray interparty agreements; intraparty groups pursued their own goals with public declarations and legislative amendments; summits between the leaders of the supporting parties were summoned in order to solve the problems which arose. So tense was the intraparty factional division within the DC that ministers belonging to the left-wing faction of the party eventually resigned from the cabinet.

We had previously seen that the government could play a significant role in policy initiation mainly because the ability and willingness of parties to act as policy initiators was limited. This limitation was due, on the one hand, to the fact that they aimed at defending existing arrangements tailored to the needs of particularistic interests and, on the other hand, to the electoral security which freed them to a large extent from having to be judged on their performance (Cotta, 1994). Yet when it came to finalizing the policy process the weaknesses of the government became immediately apparent and the ability of parties to shape the outcome became obvious. The game played by the government-supporting parties at this point was almost always highly

complex as there was a plurality of supporting parties, as the largest of
them, the DC, was not a monolithic actor, but a coalition of sub-leaders able
to play autonomous games, as there was both a 'partisan' and an 'administrative' side to the government, and as the government itself was far from
being united given potentially conflicting interests among ministers and
between them and the prime minister.

Innovative policies which might have resulted in a significant restructuring of the existing equilibria of interests faced major hurdles as a result. External
pressures might have pushed them high on the political agenda and stimulated
the government to act; but these policies would then be stopped or delayed
or their innovative potential would be blunted. Resistance from one or more
parties of the coalition or from a significant sub-party actor either led to an
explicit veto of government action, as on pension reform, or left the government
without strong support from the parties. In the first case the policy was
dropped; in the latter dissensions in the government appeared, the opposition
of groups of MPs linked to the threatened interests became active in the parliamentary arena and governmental action was weakened. The result was delay,
as on privatization policy, or a significant reduction of the policy goals, as
in the case of attempts to cut the budgetary deficit and to tackle the problem
of the public debt in financial bills. In other cases the government might obtain
a temporary and limited success, but subsequent intervention by the parties
would restate the limits within which a policy can be framed, as in the case
of the *Achille Lauro* crisis.

The action of government was more successful when there was from the
start a basic agreement between party objectives and government interests.
This did not necessarily mean that the government merely implemented party
decisions. The government may have transformed the rather vague policy
orientations of the parties into specific policies and obtained the agreement
of some of the interest groups involved (through a combination of incentives
and threats): the reduction of wage indexation is a good example of such a
development. Parties also tended to support the action of the government
when they foresaw that they might turn the implementation phase of a policy
into opportunities for patronage, as occurred in the case of aid to the
developing countries.

The political events which occurred after 1992 provide the basis for a better
understanding of what was the relationship between government and their
supporting parties in the past. The weakening of the traditional parties as a
result of the political and judicial earthquake led to the appointment of
cabinets which were more independent from the parties and were more
'technocratic'. This greater (albeit temporary) freedom enabled these
governments to take initiatives and to develop policies in areas in which action

could not be taken in the past, as on privatization, pension reform, and substantial budgetary cuts.

The return to political cabinets after the general election of 1994 was too short (April–December 1994) to provide the basis for an accurate evaluation of the new situation. Yet it was apparent that in spite of the electoral alliances forced by the new electoral system and in spite of Berlusconi, the leader of *Forza Italia*, having obtained a strong electoral mandate to become prime minister, some of the familiar problems of Italian governments remained unsolved. A difficult and heterogeneous coalition of parties with the leaders of two of the main parties (the League and the National Alliance) being outside the cabinet quickly put to the test the freedom of action of the government in the field of policy-making.

## PATRONAGE

The importance of patronage in Italian politics does not need to be stressed: it has always been regarded as a major instrument of party government. As a result of the action of the judiciary since the early 1990s, moreover, a large amount of the financial dealings between politicians and businessmen became well-documented and the extent and the working of the phenomenon became widely known.

Patronage has, in the first instance, a key personal dimension. Both at the higher and lower echelons of the vast and diversified public system (from the bureaucracy of the central government and of local government to public or semi-public entrerprises as well as to a large part of the banking system), Italian politicians have enjoyed an extensive power (partly legal and partly para-legal) of appointment: they have used this power to a substantial extent as an instrument of patronage. Yet personal patronage has also gone hand in hand with policy-making. Micro-policies of a distributive character have constituted an important proportion of the legislative activity of governments, not to mention private members' bills (Di Palma, 1977). This type of legislation made it possible to allocate on a particularistic basis a vast amount of resources which thus became a rich instrument of patronage.

It is more difficult to know who controlled patronage and what has been the relative weight of government and of the supporting parties in this respect. Indeed, given the nature of the Italian 'partitocracy', the distinction between the two types of actors is difficult to draw.

Substantial empirical evidence confirms the image of a party-dependent government. Press articles have recurrently stated, for instance, that during the government formation process discussions related not only to policies but also to some important appointments to the large public corporations. Parties continued to be directly involved even when the government was in being, as over top appointments in banks, most of which were until the 1990s in public ownership or under very strong government influence. These appointments which legally had to be made by the cabinet on the proposal of the Finance minister (after consultation with the Bank of Italy and other ministers), were in reality subordinated to a previous agreement among the supporting parties (and within each party where party factions were important) on the basis of a kind of quota system. Such an agreement was typically drawn by the party spokesmen for economic affairs (in close touch with party authorities); when agreement could not be reached, the government would simply wait (sometimes for months or years) even if the terms of office had expired. Top nominations to state radio and television positions also were under strict party control: evidence is provided by the fact that a change in the leadership of the DC generally also brought about a change of the director general of the RAI and of the director of news of the 'Christian Democratic' channel (TG1). The same happened with the other parties (which in this case included also the main opposition party, the PCI).

Yet the party-dependent government image constitutes only part of the reality: in other fields the government or, more accurately, the ministers had more autonomy. The field of micro-policies, of public works, but also of procurements and of prices fixed by the state (for instance in the national health service) provides a large amount of well-documented cases where ministers in charge tended to control patronage. These forms of patronage helped to raise the financial means subsequently used by official party organizations, party factions, and personal electoral campaigns. Ministers have been able in this way to consolidate their popular support and their power base within the party organization.[17]

Thus the widespread image of a party-dependent government must be at least complemented with that of a government-dependent party. In fact the (permanent) governing parties became increasingly dependent on the government for their financial means and for a large part of their electoral support and organizational base.[18] Had the government not distributed patronage and obtained in exchange economic resources for the parties, these would have been unable to maintain the level of organization which they had become accustomed to attain at a time when they ceased to mobilize a large amount of support from members on a voluntary basis. With reduced ideological polarization the need to rely upon clientelistic exchanges to sustain electoral support and party membership also increased. This dependence of the parties on government had a prerequisite: there had to be strong party control on the government in the fields of appointments and of micro policy-making, as parties had to ensure that governmental activity would produce the flow of resources needed. Government dependence and party dependence thus fed on each other.

## CONCLUSION

The picture of party-government relations is somewhat complex in Italy. From many points of view the system could be described as based on a party-dependent government. In the context of appointments, policy-making, and patronage, during the period examined here, the extraparliamentary party organizations were in a position to exercise strong control over the cabinet. Yet there were other aspects. With respect to appointments, a position in the government could help someone to move to the top of the party. With respect to policy-making, the ability of parties to dominate the cabinet was limited by a number of factors. The conservative orientation of parties rendered these better able to preserve the existing equilibria of interests and to adopt a guardian role than to innovate; meanwhile, the dominance of interparty and intrafactional struggles weakened the ability of parties to devote their attention to policy elaboration: both these characteristics resulted in the cabinet having room for action. This room could even become large when the government was institutionally obliged to act. On the other hand, the government was far from being strong because of a weak bureaucracy, an uncertain political standing and the lack of a clear electoral mandate. Thus the government should be regarded not as being a unitary actor but as being composed of a galaxy of actors who could not easily be coordinated. In this respect governments were rather similar to parties in which, too, there were many actors and rarely a strong central authority. Thus government-supporting party relations often took the form of a complex network linking multiple party actors and multiple government actors. Whether subsequent changes in the political system will alter significantly this situation remains an open question.

## NOTES

\*     The writing of this chapter was made possible thanks to the research grant no. 9201650.CTO9 of the Centro Nazionale delle Ricerche. Pierangelo Isernia and Antonio La Spina helped in the analysis of policy cases.
1.     In fact compared with the traditional instability of Italian cabinets the duration of some cabinets was during this period significantly higher (Spadolini 18 months; Craxi I 36 months; De Mita 15).

2.  Between 1979 and 1992 only 4.4 per cent of the ministerial positions were taken by people without a clear party background (but often classified as 'near to party x or y'). Of these positions half were during a caretaker cabinet (Fanfani VI).
3.  In the selection of ministers some balance between members of the two chambers (plus some degree of regional representation) was generally pursued. Parliamentary seniority and a strong electoral basis were also important assets for prospective ministers (Calise and Mannheimer, 1982).
4.  A vivid description of the process is provided by Amato (1994).
5.  In the DC this practice was introduced in the seventies, then abolished and reintroduced again in 1982. The election has always been a contested one. In the PSI the direct election was introduced in 1984; but it became more an acclamation than a true election.
6.  The first point of view attributes more importance to the original background and to the identity defined by this; the second to the ongoing interplay of resources.
7.  To mention a few names among the top Christian Democratic politicians Andreotti holding ministerial positions in most of the post-war cabinets, but never chairman of the party was clearly more a 'government man' than Forlani and De Mita who reached the top of the party hierarchy with a much less rich ministerial background.
8.  All the Christian Democratic chairmen of the last two decades (Zaccagnini, Piccoli, De Mita and Forlani) had previously held some ministerial position. The same can be said of the Social-Democratic (Longo, Nicolazzi, Cariglia and Vizzini) and Republican chairmen (Spadolini and G. La Malfa). The only exception is that of Craxi who in 1976 became the chairman of the Socialist Party without any previous ministerial experience.
9.  The first challenge to the DC monopoly came in 1979 when U. La Malfa (the leader of the Republican Party) was summoned by the head of state. But his attempt to build a government failed. In 1981 Spadolini became the first prime minister that did not belong to the DC.
10. Chairman of the party since 1982, De Mita was nominated Prime Minister in April 1988. After the DC Congress of February 1989 he lost the party leadership which was taken by Forlani, the leader of the centre-right faction. After a few months (June 1989) he was forced to resign also from the governmental position.
11. This coalition was known as the CAF (an acronym of the names of Craxi, Andreotti and Forlani, i.e. the Socialist leader and the chiefs of the two main Christian Democratic factions).
12. The first composition of the Amato cabinet is still predominantly partitocratic, though we find some technocrats personally chosen by the PM (Amato, 1994). During the life of the cabinet the impact of the judicial scandals determined the substitution of many ministers. The choice was then made by the PM without asking the parties. At the end of that governmental experience (April 1993) there were about a third of technical ministers (8 out of 25). In the Ciampi cabinet that percentage rose to 52 per cent.
13. It must be recalled that according to the Italian constitution the government can issue special decrees (*decreti-legge*) which have from the first day the same value as normal laws passed by parliament. The *decreti-legge* become null if

they are not approved by the parliament within 60 days. The decree discussed here reduced substantially the indexation that had been provided by national contracts for dependent workers. The Communist Party and the communist faction of the CGIL, the largest trade union, opposed the content of this measure but especially the fact that it had been decided by the government without much consultation.

14. The Financial bills are the bills which define the basic measures of the public budget (total size of incomes, expenditures, yearly deficit, etc.) and the instruments (cuts in expenditures, new taxes, borrowing, etc.) by which they can be reached.

15. Interestingly enough in the electoral manifesto of the Christian Democratic Party for 1987 anti-trust legislation was proposed not as a value in itself but as a need deriving from the developments of the European market.

16. The minister at the time, G. Carli, a former governor of the Bank of Italy, was a non-party man.

17. Calise and Mannheimer have well documented the correlation between ministerial careers and electoral success (1982).

18. To a lesser but still significant extent also the (permanent) opposition parties through a well established practice of political exchanges with the majority have become 'government dependent' in the sense discussed here.

# 11. The United States: Divided Government and Divided Parties

R.S. Katz

## INTRODUCTION

Questions about the relations between a government and the party that supports it are unusual in the study of American politics. One reason is that the concepts involved, party and government, while central to the parliamentary model of party government characteristic of most western democracies, are foreign to the Madisonian model of liberal democracy around which American government is structured. In contrast to the strong parties and clear lines of authority in the party government model, the Madisonian model is hostile to cohesive parties and is founded on divided and overlapping authority. Most centrally, the independent election, fixed term, and extensive powers of the American president mean that American governments do not require a stable supporting coalition of the kind assumed by the conventional parliamentary model.

The problems of uncritically applying the parliamentary framework in the American context arise immediately if one asks about the majority or minority status of governments. If a general election is a choice of government, then either all post-War American governments have been majority governments (in the sense that the victorious presidential candidate won a majority of the electoral college votes and more popular votes than any single opponent) or else all governments except those based on the elections of 1948, 1968, and 1992 have been majority governments (in the sense that the winning candidate had at least 50 per cent of the popular votes). Alternatively, if one defines the majority status of an American government on the basis of the majority/minority status of the group with the same name in the House of Representatives, then with the sole exceptions of 1947–8 and 1953–4, as well as a result of the 1994 mid-term election, there has been a perfect correlation between party and majority status – all Democratic governments are majority governments and all Republican governments are minority governments. Further complications are added by the equal legislative power of the Senate (in which the Republicans had a majority in 1947–8, 1953–4,

1981–6, and in 1995) and by various features of congressional rules and practices that embody the basic bias of American institutions in favour of the *status quo* and that mean that a simple majority may be inadequate actually to control the result.[1]

The whole concept of majority versus minority government is thrown into further confusion by the problematic status of American parties. On the one hand, it is not clear, for example, that 'the Democratic Party' of a nominally Democratic president is the same entity as 'the Democratic Party' of a nominally Democratic majority in one or both houses of Congress, while on the other hand, it is not clear that congressional parties are sufficiently coherent that the mere fact that those with the same denomination as the president constitute numerical majorities in their respective chambers implies anything important about the status of the government (Katz and Kolodny, 1994).

If the concept of party is problematic in the American context, so too is the identification of government with the president, cabinet, and top advisers. The array of independent agencies (FCC, CAB, FTC, and so on) which have substantial policy-making powers but which are not purely executive in their functions, not under the president's control, and legally required to have bipartisan boards, are only a small part of the problem. Congressional oversight committees, through detailed and direct legislation, as well as through the overt or tacit threat of such legislation, and congressional appropriations committees through micro-level control of the federal budget, may exercise more influence over parts of the civil service than the presidential appointees who nominally are in charge. Moreover, Congress not only limits or amends the legislative proposals of the executive branch, but often simply scraps them and/or legislates on its own initiative, thus sharing, if not in some cases usurping, both the policy-directing and executive management roles customarily associated with 'the government'.

Of course, it is an exaggeration to suggest that the United States has no political parties or that there is no sense in which the president and cabinet constitute a government, just as it is an exaggeration to suggest that European parties may be treated as unitary actors or that a European cabinet is in full and unchallenged control of governmental authority. But while in the European context it may be a useful simplification to attribute collective identities to governments and parties and to assume a clear separation between cabinet and party roles, if not necessarily personnel, and thus to analyse the relationships between governments and the parties that support them, in the American context such assumptions appear more like fantasies than simplifications. Thus, although this essay will follow the same general outline as the other chapters in this volume, its point will be somewhat different; in trying to assess the relationship between parties and governments, its subtext will be that American government is better understood in terms of transitory coalitions. While these coalitions may be in large measure structured by party labels (which themselves reflect significant political affinities and differences), parties as organizations ordinarily have little or no independent impact on the process.

## APPOINTMENTS

### Recruitment of the government

Recruitment of the American government (in the sense in which that term has been used in Chapter 1) can be divided into two steps – the selection of the president and the selection of the remaining members of the government (vice-president, cabinet secretaries, and senior members of the White House staff). Ultimately, of course, the president is chosen by popular election, so the real question in assessing party influence on recruitment is whether the party plays a significant role in the choice of its presidential candidate. And the answer to this question depends on how one understands the word 'party' in American presidential politics.

Formally, of course, the presidential nominee is the choice of his party, decided upon at its quadrennial national nominating convention. But in several respects, there is considerably less substance here than initially meets the eye. The majority of delegates to the national conventions are pledged to support a particular candidate. The last nomination not effectively decided before the convention convened was the 1960 Democratic nomination, and given the explosion of the number of pledged delegates selected in primary elections and the dynamics of the primary process since then, it is unlikely that the effective choice will ever again be made at a convention. The appropriateness of calling the outcome of a convention that merely ratifies the choices made in primary elections and caucuses a 'party' decision depends on one's willingness to equate the primary electorate with 'the party'. Partisan registration, however, is a far cry from party membership as it is understood in most countries, and moreover, even this minimal sense of party affiliation is required for participation in the delegate selection processes of only about half the states.

Winning a presidential nomination requires the building of a coalition of supporters, and individuals who might be identified as party leaders play an important role in this process. But here too there is less 'partyness' than one might naively suppose. The value of these individuals' support comes primarily from their personal political standing and connections (that is, from the extent of their own supporting coalitions), rather than from their formal positions in the party. Indeed, support from the highest position in the party organization per se, the chairman of the National Committee, is generally the least valuable. While the national chairman controls important resources and is in a position to be of considerable assistance to a presidential contender, the chairmanship itself is for this very reason an object rather than an arbiter of the struggle among would-be nominees. Moreover, support from outside of the formal party apparatus – from financial backers, interest groups, the news media (from which simple acceptance as a credible candidate may be more significant than overt support), and ordinary primary voters – is even more important in determining who will be nominated. In the end, the successful candidate takes control of the party almost as a by-product of winning the nomination, rather than being selected by the party organization (Polsby and Wildavsky, 1991, chap. 3).

The lack of party control over recruitment to government office becomes even clearer after the presidential candidate has been selected. The selection of the vice-presidential nominee is the sole prerogative of the presidential candidate. Once elected, the president has sole authority to appoint, and to dismiss, the other members of the government, subject only to the requirement that most senior appointments be confirmed by the Senate. In making these appointments, a president needs to balance a number of possibly conflicting criteria. First, he needs people with the technical expertise to do the job; notwithstanding the sweeping generalizations and assertions of simple solutions for every problem that have become the currency of American electoral politics, managing the government requires skill and expertise that are in relatively short supply. Second, he needs people who will be loyal to him and to his programmes if he is to counter the danger that cabinet members will be captured by the 'sub-governments' that epitomize American national government (Rose, 1991, p. 294). Third, he needs to reward his supporters, and offer inducements to his erstwhile opponents within his party to become supporters. Fourth, he needs to provide symbolic representation for a variety of groups, some of which (for example, African-Americans in the case of Republicans) may not in fact figure prominently in his party's traditional coalition at all. Perhaps most significantly, however, he does not need to satisfy a strong party organization; rather, the other criteria are made particularly salient because he has to build his own substitute for the strong party organization that is lacking in American national politics.

Naturally, the president both takes advice and delegates responsibility in making these decisions. Those involved in the recruitment process generally have long-standing ties to the party, but only in the sense of party as a broad and amorphous umbrella. They are better seen as members of the president's personal coalition which took control of the party organization in the process of getting him elected to office, than as members of a previously existing and independent party organization whose candidate was elected. Even if the national chairman is involved at this stage, it is as a lieutenant of the president, and not as an official of the party.

Table 11.1 examines recruitment during the period 1976–94, which relates to five administrations and to four presidents with regard to the backgrounds of those appointed. The basic unit of analysis is the appointee within each administration, so that when a person changed jobs *within* a government (for example, Patricia Roberts Harris who moved from Housing and Urban Development to Health, Education and Welfare in 1979) this change is noted in the cell marking the intersection of the 'Change of Job Within Government' row and 'Subsequent Appointments' column, but the person's other particulars are not repeated in the second column; the particulars of holdovers from the previous administration, however, are repeated in the 'Initial Appointments' column for the next administration whether the person occupied the same government post or not (for example, the various entries for James Baker, who was White House Chief of Staff in Reagan I, Secretary of the Treasury in Reagan II, and Secretary of State under Bush are repeated for each of the three administrations). When reference is made to a number of individuals, however, each person is counted only once, regardless of the number of administrations in which (s)he may have served.

The rows of Table 11.1 refer to background characteristics of the various members of governments. Each case is entered as many times as is appropriate. These data come from a variety of sources, especially *Who's Who in America, Current Biography*, and the press releases circulated at the time of appointment. It is important to be cognizant of their limitations, especially as regards the holding of minor party positions and the existence of personal ties or patrons. Where these were mentioned, they are included, but there is no way of verifying the absence of a personal tie or failure to have held a trivial party post. In particular, it is likely that many personal connections to congressional and administration insiders have been missed; while politicians appear anxious to announce their ties to the president himself, they are more reluctant to advertise their debts to other people.

The first set of rows addresses the tie between prior occupancy of a post in the formal party organization and membership in one of the governments studied. The evidence of party penetration is striking in its paucity. Excluding the president and vice-president themselves, under 36 per cent of the 103 individuals who held positions in the five governments could be found ever to have held any party office – and this includes cases such as that of Manual Lujan who was once a state party vice-chair and even Margaret Heckler who served as a town committee member 17 years before she became Secretary of Health and Human Services. Those with previous party experience are not randomly distributed among the five administrations, however, but rather are concentrated in the Republican administrations.

The second set of rows reflects the need for experience in the construction of a government, but also shows both the importance and the limitations of party as a criterion for recruitment. On the one hand, a large number of cabinet appointees have experience in previous administrations of the same party: the relatively small number of such appointees in the Clinton administration reflects the long time since the last Democratic administration. On the other hand, there are more than a few cabinet appointees with experience in administrations of the other party. Even more, the importance of the person at the top rather than the party is shown by the small number of members of the Reagan II government appointed to serve in the Bush administration. (And one of these, Lauro Cavazos, was only named by Reagan in August 1988 and was widely regarded as an anticipatory Bush appointee.)

If party is of little significance in government appointments, the third set of rows makes clear what is important – personal ties, especially to the president. While the variety of personal connections is great – personal lawyer, former classmate, state campaign chair, appointee when the President was a state governor – few if any are directly connected to party as an organization.

The next block shows the separation between the 'presidential party' and the rest of American government. Although both Bush and Clinton drew relatively heavily on incumbent members of Congress, what is striking about these data, at least in a context of party government, is the degree to which names *do not* appear in these lists. Membership in government is not in general a 'promotion' from Congress or a gubernatorial office; rather, it appears to represent an alternative career path altogether. Moreover, while those members of Congress who are appointed to government positions may have held important committee positions, they have not held directly partisan positions like majority/minority leader, whip, and so on.

Finally, the last row illustrates that blacks, women, and, more recently hispanics, have acquired a presumptive right to have at least one of their number included in every government. It also reflects Clinton's decision to appoint a 'representative' cabinet, in particular with the inclusion of four women.

To summarize and generalize, the primary pool from which members of American governments are recruited consists of the intersection of two sets of people. The first is the relevant party's group of 'in-and-outers'. These

Table 11.1: *Background of Members of Government*

|  | Carter | | Reagan I | |
|---|---|---|---|---|
|  | Initial Appointments | Subsequent Appointments | Initial Appointments | Subsequent Appointments |
| **Party** | | | | |
| **National Committee** | Andrus<br>Carter<br>Califano<br>Harris | Landrieu | Bush<br>Baldridge<br>Brock<br>Lewis | |
| **Congressional Party; Governor's Association** | Andrus | Muskie | Reagan | |
| **Minor Party Positions** | Berglund | Miller | Baker, J<br>Edwards<br>Haig<br>Schweiker<br>Smith<br>Stockman<br>Weinberger | Heckler<br>Hodel |
| **Identification with Other Party** | Schlesinger | | | |
| **Executive Branch Experience**<br>**Hold Over In Same Job** | | | | |
| **Hold Over Different Job** | | | | |
| **Change Within Government**<br>**Promoted Into Government** | | Harris<br>Civiletti<br>Duncan<br>McIntyre<br>Miller | | Clark<br>Clark<br>Dole, E<br>Hodel<br>McFarlane<br>Schultz |
| **Prior Governments**[2] | Mondale (K,J)<br>Adams (K)<br>Bell (K)<br>Berglund (K,N)<br>Blumenthal (K)<br>Brown (K)<br>Califano (K)<br>Harris (K)<br>Schlesinger (N)<br>Vance (K,J) | Hufstedler (K)<br>Klutznick (E,K) | Bush (N,F)<br>Allen (N,F)<br>Baker, J (F)<br>Bell (N,F)<br>Casey (N,F)<br>Edwards (N,F)<br>Haig (N,F)<br>Pierce (E,N,F)<br>Watt (N,F)<br>Weinberger (N,F) | Dole, E (J,N)<br>Hodel (N,F)<br>Schultz (E,K,N,F) |

| Reagan II | | Bush | | Clinton |
|---|---|---|---|---|
| Initial Appointments | Subsequent Appointments | Initial Appointments | Subsequent Appointments | Initial Appointments |
| Bush | Baker, H | Bush | | Brown |
| Baldridge | | Mosbacher | | McLarty |
| Brock | | | | |
| Lewis | | | | |
| Reagan | Baker, H. | Cheney | Madigan | |
| Bowen | | Kemp | Martin | |
| | | Sununu | | |
| Baker, J | Brady | Baker | Derwinski | |
| Hodel | Verity | Brady | | |
| Weinberger | | Kemp | | |
| | | Lujan | | |
| Bennet | Cavazos | Cavazos | | |
| Baldridge | | Brady | | |
| Block | | Cavazos | | |
| Bush | | Thornburgh | | |
| Casey | | | | |
| Dole, E | | | | |
| McFarlane | | | | |
| Pierce | | | | |
| Schultz | | | | |
| Weinberger | | | | |
| Baker, J. | | Baker | | |
| Brock | | Yeutter | | |
| Herrington | | | | |
| Hodel | | | | |
| Meese | | | | |
| Regan | | | | |
| | Carlucci | | Skinner | |
| | Burnley | | Barr | |
| | Lyng | | Derwinski[1] | |
| | McLaughlin | | Franklin | |
| | Poindexter | | Gates | |
| | Powell | | | |
| | Webster | | | |
| | Wright | | | |
| Bush (N,F) | Brady (R) | Bush (N,F,R) | Alexander (N) | Christopher (J,C) |
| Baker, J. (F) | Burnley (R) | Baker (F,R) | Barr (R) | Reich (C) |
| Bennet (R) | Carlucci (E,N,F,R) | Brady (R) | Franklin (N,F,R) | O'Leary (C,F) |
| Bowen (R) | Lyng (N,F) | Cheney (N,F) | Gates (R) | Shalala (C) |
| Casey (N,F) | McLaughlin (N,F) | Darman (F,R) | Watkins (R) | Woolsey (C) |
| Herrington (R) | Thornburgh (F) | Derwinski (R) | | Panetta (N) |
| Miller (F,R) | Webster (N) | Dole, E (J,N,R) | | |
| Pierce (E,N,F) | Wright (N,F) | Hills (F) | | |
| Schultz (E,K,N,F) | | Scowcroft (F) | | |
| Weinberger (N,F) | | Thornburgh (F,R) | | |
| Yeutter (N,F) | | Yeutter (N,F,R) | | |

Table 11.1 *continued*

| | Carter | | Reagan I | |
|---|---|---|---|---|
| | Initial Appointments | Subsequent Appointments | Initial Appointments | Subsequent Appointments |
| **Personal Ties** | | | | |
| President (Inc. Campaign) | Adams | Duncan | Allen | Clark (2) |
| | Andrus | McIntyre | Baker, J | Dole, E |
| | Bell | | Baldridge | Hodel |
| | Berglund | | Block | Schultz |
| | Blumenthal | | Casey | |
| | Califano | | Donovan | |
| | Jordon | | Edwards | |
| | Lance | | Lewis | |
| | Marshall | | Schweiker | |
| | Turner | | Smith | |
| | Vance | | Stockman | |
| | | | Weinberger | |
| Patron in Administration | | Civiletti (Kirbo) | Regan (Casey) | |
| | | | Pierce (Bloomingdale) | |
| Patron in Congress | | | Block (Dole, R) | |
| Prior Office (President, Vice-President, Congress, Governor, Big City Mayor) | | | | |
| In Office on Appt. | Mondale | Goldschmidt | Schweiker | |
| | Adams | Muskie | | |
| | Andrus | | | |
| | Berglund | | | |
| In Last 2 Years | | Landrieu | Stockman | Heckler |
| Previous | Carter | | Reagan | |
| | | | Bush | |
| | | | Brock | |
| | | | Edwards | |
| | | | Pierce | |
| Representativeness | Harris-black, female | Hufstedler-female | Edwards-south | Dole, E-female |
| | Kreps-female | | Pierce-black | |
| **Total appointees** | 18 | 10 | 20 | 7 |

[1]Derwinski became a member of the government according to the definition employed here when the Veterans Administration, of which he was Administrator, became the cabinet Department of Veteran's Affairs.
[2]Letter codes refer to the prior administration: K – Kennedy; J – Johnson; N – Nixon; F – Ford; C – Carter; R – Reagan.

| Reagan II | | Bush | | Clinton |
|---|---|---|---|---|
| Initial Appointments | Subsequent Appointments | Initial Appointments | Subsequent Appointments | Initial Appointments |
| Baker, J. | Lyng | Baker | Franklin | Espy |
| Baldridge | Verity | Brady | | Brown, R |
| Block | | Darman | | Kantor |
| Casey | | Dole, E | | McLarty |
| Herrington | | Martin | | Albright |
| Hodel | | Mosbacher | | |
| Lewis | | Skinner | | |
| Miller | | Sullivan | | |
| Meese | | Sununu | | |
| Schultz | | | | |
| Weinberger | | | | |
| Yeutter | | | | |
| | Brady (Bush) | | Alexander (Baker, H) | |
| Reagan | | Bush | Madigan | Clinton |
| Bush | | Quayle | Martin | Gore |
| | | Cheney | | Bentsen |
| | | Kemp | | Aspin |
| | | Lujan | | Paneta |
| | | Sununu | | |
| | Baker, H. | | | |
| | Thornburgh | | | |
| Bowen | | Brady | Alexander | Babbitt |
| Brock | | Thornburgh | Derwinski | Cisneros |
| | | | | Peña |
| | | | | Riley |
| Pierce-black | | Cavazos-hispanic | Martin-female | Reno-female |
| Dole, E-female | | Dole, E-female | Franklin-female | Espy-black |
| | | Sullivan-black | | Brown, R-black |
| | | | | Cisneros-hispanic |
| | | | | Peña-hispanic |
| | | | | O'Leary-female, black |
| | | | | Shalala-female |
| | | | | Brown, J-black |
| | | | | Albright-female |
| 20 | 13 | 21 | 7 | 21 |

are individuals who have interspersed periods of service in the executive branch with careers that have primarily developed in the private sector (Mackenzie, 1987). While these may have been active in local politics, they have in general not held important party posts, even at the state level. Thus, while the sets of 'in-and-outers' upon which presidents draw are more or less (but *not* completely) divided by partisanship, this division is not tied to party as an organization. The second set of potential members of government is the early or long-time friends and supporters of the president. A few of these have held important state level party posts, but they are far more likely to have been involved in the personal campaign organizations of individual candidates at both state and national level than to have been in the formal party organizations. The criterion of having held formal party office is striking in its weakness. Indeed, over two-thirds of government members who have held some party office were in at least one of the two main recruitment pools as well, and nearly half were in both. The support or opposition of a state party chair, member of Congress, or other partisan official may have some bearing on the likelihood that a particular individual will be considered seriously, but there is no party clearance, or even review, of potential appointees. While party ties structure recruitment to government, and the party organization provides one of the arenas within which would-be presidents compete, party as an actor either in the selection of the president or in the selection of the other members of the government is virtually an oxymoron.

## Recruitment to party leadership

Not every individual who might be identified as a leader within one of the American parties holds an important (or indeed any) position in its formal organization. Nonetheless, several positions can be identified as roughly corresponding to the formal leaderships of parties in other countries. These include the National Committee Chair and Co-Chair, General Counsel, Finance Committee Chair and Treasurer; the majority/minority leader, whip, caucus chair, policy committee chair, and congressional campaign committee chair in each house of Congress; the chairs of the party governors and mayors conferences. As this list implies, although both American parties have many leaders, there is no collective body that reasonably can be identified as 'the leadership'.

The closest approximation to a single party leader that the president's party has is the president himself, although it must be emphasized that he became party leader because he won the presidential nomination (rather than becoming the presidential nominee because he was the party leader), and retained the leadership because he won the presidential election. Although formally the chair of the national committee is elected by the committee, for the 'in' party the chairmanship in reality is a presidential appointment. The chair then appoints the other officers of the national committee, subject to the formality of committee ratification.

This suggests strong government dominance over the recruitment of party leadership, and so far as the national committee of the president's party is concerned, this is true. The national committees, whose members are based in state politics and over whose recruitment the president has little direct control, are in any event too large (over 160 members for the Republican National Committee and over 400 members of the Democratic National Committee) and meet too infrequently to function as a party leadership. Instead, the staff of the national committee works for the national chairman, and the chairman in turn works for the president.

Presidential domination of recruitment does not extend, however, to the leaders of the congressional parties, or to the mayors and governors conferences. In each of these cases, the leaders either are elected by the members of the caucus/conference, or else appointed by the elected leader. Indeed, as the 1990 challenge to Guy Vander Jagt's re-election as chairman of the National Republican Campaign Committee illustrates, to be perceived to be 'the president's man' actually can prove a liability for an aspirant to leadership within the congressional party (Kolodny, 1991). Given the differing institutional imperatives of the White House and the various state houses, mayors' offices, and the two houses of Congress, each face of the party is protective of its independence from the others and it is not surprising that the leaders of the non-presidential faces of the party often come into conflict with the president.

## POLICIES

### Do American parties have policies?

Policy is as central to partisanship as it is to the functioning of government. Governments are in the business of making and implementing policies, and people choose to become candidates, supporters, and voters of parties in some measure on the basis of the policies with which the parties are associated. To know that a particular individual is a Democrat or a Republican says something about that person's likely orientation in a variety of general respects: in recent years Democrats have been more inclined to use public means to solve economic problems, while Republicans have been readier to use state power to enforce social norms; Democrats have been more receptive to 'trickle-up' economic policies, while Republicans have tended to prefer 'trickle-down' policies; in times of budget cuts, Democrats have been more protective of social spending, Republicans have been more protective of defence spending. Yet while it is relatively easy to identify each party with a general orientation, once one moves to specific policies there rarely is a single or official party position. Rather, there are the personal positions of party leaders. While these positions may become identified in the press and in public perception as the 'party's' positions, members of Congress and state and local officials are free to depart from them whenever their own perceptions of electoral expedience or desirable policy so dictate. Moreover, particularly with regard to Congress, the position enunciated by the leaders is likely to be the result of negotiation and brokerage (trying to find a position that most members will accept) rather than of centralized decision-making and, on many important issues, there is no formal party position at all.

The national parties do take positions on major issues in their presidential platforms. These platforms are drafted by committees of the national conventions, and are debated by the conventions. Three points, however, need to be made. First, like all election manifestos, American platforms tend to be long on platitudes and short on details; in many areas, it is questionable whether they should be called policy documents at all. For example, while the 1992 Democratic platform promised reform of the health care system, it took no position on any of the questions of finance, organization, or control involved. Rather, President Clinton appointed a commission to study the options only after he was in office.

Second, although the platforms are drafted by party committees, these committees are temporary rather than part of a permanent organization. The national party organizations are not intensively involved in policy formulation, and the ideas incorporated into the platforms do not originate with the platform committees. Moreover, because they are committees of the national conventions, whose primary purpose is to select (more recently to ratify the selection of) a presidential nominee, the platform committees are dominated by supporters of the eventual nominee and the results are largely controlled by his handlers. In this sense, it is not clear that the platform should in fact be ascribed to 'party' rather than 'government'.

Finally, the platform is not binding even on the presidential candidate for whom it was written, and certainly not on members of Congress or candidates for subnational office. As a result, the party platform is, at most, a starting point for coalition building rather than a statement of the policy that the government will pursue.

The congressional campaign committees offer advice and counsel to congressional candidates regarding the selection of issues and issue positions. What is most striking about this advice, however, is that although it suggests the existence of a nominal party line, candidates are not punished for deviating from it. Indeed, should a candidate's personal position be different from that of the party, he or she will be given help in developing a strategy to promote that contrary position. Moreover, rather than establishing new positions, the campaign committees' 'issue books' basically package positions that have already been articulated by leaders in the administration or Congress and are more or less accepted by the broad range of sitting members of the party. The rules of the party caucuses take a similarly lax position regarding policy; among the four congressional caucuses, the only rules obligating members to support caucus decisions are the House Democrats' rule requiring party unity on the election of Speaker and other officers of the House, and the House Republican rules obliging the Ranking Republican member of a committee to 'ensure that each measure on which the Republican Conference has taken a position is managed in accordance with such position' and requiring all members of the Republican Leadership 'to support positions adopted by the Conference'. (Note, however, that the Republican rules apply only the to leadership, not to ordinary members.) Thus again it is not clear that it makes sense to talk about the policy position of a party, as opposed to the policy position taken by the individuals who make it up.

Early in 1995, it seemed permissible to suggest that the 1994 Congressional election would constitute a major departure from the picture just presented. In September, more than 300 Republican candidates for Congress agreed to a 'Contract with America', in which they promised a number of relatively well defined policy initiatives. Even more unusually, when the Republicans won control of both houses of Congress, their leader in the House, Newt Gingrich, laid great stress on the binding character of the contract, and in January the Republicans began to enact its provisions concerning the organization and operation of Congress. Whether this unity of action can be maintained with regard to proposals that might have a negative effect on the re-election prospects of individual members remains to be seen.

The sections which follow are derived initially from analysis of 12 specific cases, three from each of the four presidencies considered. They are: (Carter) the 1978 tax cut proposal; the nuclear non-proliferation treaty; energy policy; (Reagan) policy toward Chile; the Caribbean Basin initiative; the intermediate-range nuclear forces agreement; (Bush) the 1990 budget agreement; the anti-flag burning constitutional amendment; education; (Clinton) gays in the military; the economic stimulus package; and health care reform. They span a wide range of policy areas, but they are, of course, atypical at least in the sense of being sufficiently prominent to have been selected for study in the first place. Although the possibility remains that some conclusions are biased by the selection of cases, the consistency of findings over the range of cases suggests that this is not a serious problem. It also means that little of significance would be gained by discussing the details of these policies here.

## Policy initiation

Policy initiation, or policy innovation, is a complex and amorphous process. To understand it, one first must specify what is meant by a policy. Is, for example, deregulation a policy, or is it a policy area encompassing many policies, of which the deregulation of domestic airline fares would be one? Taking the broad definition, and looking for wholly new policy directions or first moves into new policy areas, policy initiation appears to be quite infrequent. Given the diffusion of authority and the structural inertia of the American policy process, most policies necessarily represent incremental development rather than fundamental innovation or change. There are, of course, exceptions. The civil rights policies of the Johnson administration, the foreign policy of *detente* under Nixon, deregulation under Reagan, and perhaps health care reform under Clinton all are examples of policy initiation. Although they all represent responses to pressures from outside of the administration (including, particularly in the cases of civil rights and deregulation, policy initiation by the courts), and all are adaptations of proposals that predated their acceptance by the relevant administration, there is in each case a relatively clear decision to make a whole series of specific proposals that will alter the direction of policy in a broad field. Moreover, the only question on which the propriety of regarding these decisions as government initiatives hinges concerns the status of proposals made by yet-to-be-elected presidents in their campaigns for the White House. Unless proposals of presidential aspirants are regarded as originating in the party (a decision which makes sense only if one identifies as 'party' everything which is not at the time clearly 'government' in the narrowest sense), major policy initiatives do not come from American parties.

Defining individual policies more narrowly, one can reasonably identify two points at which the policy process may be said to have been initiated. The first is the point at which a particular actor (candidate, official, or party) who has or aspires to have the ability to make public policy adopts a problem as his/her/its own, and thus puts the development of a policy on the immediate political agenda. Inclusion of a policy in a party platform or as a significant theme in campaign rhetoric or the articulation of a commitment to take action made in a presidential address would indicate policy initiation in this sense. The second potential point of policy initiation is when specific action is taken to move from a general proposal or commitment to specific government action. In this case, policy initiation would be indicated by the introduction of a bill into Congress, the issuance of an executive order, the dispatching of troops, or the like.

Here again, initiative appears to come primarily from the government or from the presidential challenger who is later elected. Reality is slightly more complicated. In some cases, policy initiative in the first sense comes from presidential aspirants who do not win the nomination or indeed from defeated candidates in previous electoral cycles, whose positions are taken over or adapted by the candidate who is nominated and elected. In other cases, issues that appeared successful in previous congressional or other races are claimed by a presidential candidate. For example, one factor contributing to the emphasis placed on health care reform by candidate Clinton was the success of Harris Wofford in using this issue to win election to the Senate from Pennsylvania defeating President Bush's former Attorney General, Richard Thornburgh.

Congress has been an additional source of policy initiative. Given the power of a presidential veto, congressionally initiated policies rarely are adopted unless and until they are endorsed by the president, at which point a temporally constrained understanding of policy initiation might attribute them to the government. In one set of cases, however, congressional initiation has been clear. These are the cases in which a Congress controlled by one party has passed bills which, although vetoed by the president of the other party, have been adopted by the candidate of the party that controlled Congress and reintroduced immediately after his election. The most prominent recent examples are the Family Leave Act, the Motor Voter Act, and the Brady Act, all of which were passed in the early days of the Clinton administration after having been blocked by Bush. Over the last four decades, this has happened only with a Democratic Congress and a Republican president, and this one-sided pattern of partisan control may account for the apparent leftward bias of policies deriving from congressional initiative.

Straight party line votes on major issues are rare, and indeed many important bills can be passed only with some support from members of the nominal opposition. This is especially true in periods of divided government (which is to say in recent decades under Republican presidents), when no legislation would be possible without significant support from members of the other party, but it is also frequently the case with 'majority' governments. To cite the extreme example, President Clinton described approval of the North American Free Trade Agreement as a make-or-break issue for his administration; yet his initial plan, as well as the ultimate victory, were based on having a majority of supporting votes in Congress come from the so-called opposition. Presidents, of course, anticipate the need to build a coalition that is likely to cross party lines in drafting their original proposals (Mayhew, 1991). On the one hand, these proposals may include items that were inserted only as points to be bargained away, while on the other hand they may also include compromises overtly or tacitly made in advance of formal introduction. In either case, the attribution of initiative is further confused. Nonetheless, given a choice between attribution of initiative to government or to the president's party, all 12 of the policies singled out for specific study appear to have been government initiatives.

**Policy development**

Once legislation is introduced into Congress, whether initiated by the government or by members acting on their own (or potentially as representatives of their parties), it is subject to substantial amendment. While major executive proposals are rarely declared 'dead on arrival' in Congress (although this was the reaction to many Reagan and Bush budgets), the law that emerges from Congress frequently is substantially different from the bill that the president submitted. In some cases, the amendments may be so substantial that the president vetoes what began as his own proposal. Thus, even when it is relatively clear that the government initiated the policy-making process in a particular field, it may be far less clear that the government should be given primary responsibility for the policy that finally is adopted.

Partisanship is significant in the legislative process, and therefore in determining the content of policy, in several ways. First, Congress is organized around party, with all the committee and subcommittee chairmanships in each house going to members of the majority party in that house. Control over the agenda, a strategic location in bargaining networks, and the expectation of leadership and expertise, all can give a skilful chairman great influence over the final form of legislation. Second, copartisans are likely to agree on many questions, making party a natural starting place for the building of coalitions and the trading of favours. Third, party leaders, particularly those of the majority party, have a variety of favours to offer in return for support. But at the same time, commonalities of interest, and likely coalitions, often are defined in ways that cut across party lines (for example, representatives from western states on questions of mining or grazing rights on federal land, or representatives from urban areas on questions of mass transit versus highway construction). Some committees have developed norms of cross party compromise, often accompanied by a norm that the entire committee will stick together when the bill reaches the floor. While the president and party leaders in Congress may prefer to deal with members of the same party, they regularly offer favours across party lines when additional votes are required. And in all of this, as observed above, there rarely is an official party position. Instead, there are only the positions of various party leaders, perhaps reached by mutual accommodation, but perhaps instead in opposition to one another.

**Policy styles**

Given the separation of powers, government policy generally requires the cooperation of both the executive and legislative branches. As a result, there is frequent interaction between the government as embodied by the president and cabinet and the party in Congress. Congressional leaders meet regularly with the president. Cabinet members regularly testify before congressional committees, as well as meeting less formally with party leaders and ordinary members of Congress. While there is some bias in favour of members of the same party, most of these interactions are defined by position rather than partisanship, and so when there is divided government they continue, albeit with greater weight given to meetings with the minority leaders and ranking minority members of committees.

The picture painted above of weak parties in Congress and strong limits on the degree to which one can characterize a party in Congress as supporting a president of the same party (or opposing a president of the other party) reflects the features of the relationship between governments and parties that are most salient in cross-national perspective. At the same time, however, a nationally significant difference between the two American parties should be noted. Perhaps because they perceive themselves to be a permanent minority in Congress, Republicans have tended to act in greater unison to oppose the programmes of a Democratic president, and to support policies of Republican presidents. Also perhaps reflecting their apparent status as a permanent minority, the Republicans in the House became particularly doctrinaire, leading for example to the overt opposition of Republican Whip (now Speaker) Newt Gingrich to the budget agreement struck between George Bush and the Democrats in 1990. Congressional Democrats, on the other hand, have tended to act more like partners in government, cooperating with Republican presidents, but also insisting on the right to leave their own mark on the proposals of Democratic presidents (Ginsberg and Shefter, 1990).

PATRONAGE

The conventional image of American government is that it is a system nourished by patronage. In some respects, this perception is accurate. At the same time, however, it requires some clarification. First, one must decide how specifically targeted a particular 'allocation of values' must be to make it patronage, rather than merely a policy that happens (as virtually every policy does) differentially to benefit one group rather than another. Is, for example, a shift in budget priorities to favour defence spending to be regarded as a change of policy or as patronage in the form of government contracts directed at the very limited number of firms that make military aircraft? What about legislation requiring the defence department to include at least a certain percentage of 'colossal' olives in military salad bars, given that these are only grown in a few, readily identifiable, congressional districts?

Second, one must distinguish between American government writ large and the federal government in particular. For example, while the federal government spends vast sums on highway or mass transit construction, most of this money is channelled to the states in the form of matching grants (with the federal government generally paying 80 per cent of the cost of highway construction and 60 per cent for mass transit). The actual construction contracts, however, are awarded by state and local authorities, so that if there is any patronage involved in the letting of contracts, it is not controlled either by government or by party at the federal level. Similarly, the vast majority of the jobs that might be regarded as patronage appointments are in state and especially local government and are controlled by parties and/or individuals at those levels.

Third, and to some extent running counter to the implications of the first two clarifications, one must remember that the political importance of a variety of patronage is not necessarily commensurate with its magnitude. Thus the ability to name a few people to highly desired patronage positions may be more significant than the power to award thousands of people to jobs like rural postman or railway cleaner. Conversely, it may be possible for some form of patronage to become so widespread that it comes to be expected, and thus loses its power to generate desired patterns of behaviour in exchange.

What then of patronage in American national politics? Looking first at the form of patronage with the deepest resonance in American political culture, 'jobs for the boys', the top executive appointments discussed under recruitment of the government are only the tip of the iceberg of presidential nominees. Altogether, there are approximately 3000–5000 full time federal positions in the executive branch filled by political appointment, plus roughly another 3000 part time or honorific jobs (Beck and Sorauf, 1992, p. 116). While in earlier times, the post office provided many low level patronage jobs (and the Postmaster General often was effective patronage secretary to the President), this ended in 1970 with the creation of the US Postal Service as a government-owned corporation.

To the executive branch jobs subject to presidential appointment may be added roughly 700 federal judgeships, although since these are lifetime appointments the number of vacancies that can be filled by any single president is much smaller. Many of these appointments are subject to Senate confirmation with the attendant public scrutiny, and indeed in some cases, most notably district judgeships, senators from the state in which the appointee would serve have an effective veto power. Both of these limit the president's ability to use the power of appointment purely as a patronage resource. Still, a number of these positions (for example, ambassadorships to European capitals) are widely regarded as appropriate rewards for major political contributors, while others provide 'soft landings' for copartisans defeated in elections. Thus, while the number of patronage jobs available to the government is minuscule (especially if considered in proportion to the total federal workforce or even more in proportion to the labour market as a whole), they can be of great significance in the building and maintaining of a president's supporting coalition. At the same time, however, one must remember that part of the attraction of these jobs is that most have real political significance, so that what appears to one person to be patronage may appear to another as government recruitment. Moreover, as one president is said to have observed, every patronage appointment may lead to 'ten disappointed office-seekers and one ingrate'.

In terms of raw numbers of jobs, the patronage resources available to Congress probably exceed those of the government. In 1990, there were roughly 10000 jobs on the personal staffs of members of Congress (Kolodny and Katz, 1992). In contrast to a decline in presidentially controlled appointments, this is a substantial increase from under 4000 jobs in 1960. Many of these jobs are purely clerical (the equivalent positions in the executive branch are under the civil service system) and also purely patronage appointments. It is important to understand, however, that they are primarily patronage at the disposal of individual members of Congress, not at the disposal of their parties as organizations. While people in leadership positions both have more of this personal patronage at their disposal, and often are able to find jobs for individuals in the offices of other members, the latter in particular is part of the pattern of mutual favour doing that is constantly going on in Congress and does not necessarily respect party lines.

At the same time, the two national party headquarters together employed a total of roughly 500 people. These allow the president to maintain and develop his own campaign organization at the expense of party bank accounts (bearing in mind that much of this money comes from donations intended for this very purpose). The same is true to a somewhat lesser extent for potential challengers in the other party, which is one reason why control of the national chairmanship is regarded as an important sign in the pre-primary jockeying for position.

A second significant area of patronage involves government spending projects (both capital construction like bridges and highways and the location of federal installations that will provide long term employment, the most typical of which are military bases). Three types of decisions potentially contribute to this form of patronage. The first, distinguished from policy-making largely in the mind of the analyst, is the allocation of spending among various broad categories: military spending versus social welfare spending; mass transit versus highway construction, and so on. The second is the allocation of that spending to particular projects, which in the context of American politics means in particular allocation among congressional districts. The third is the awarding of particular contracts to particular firms.

The government has significant influence over the first of these decisions through the drafting of the budget and the threat to veto spending bills that deviate excessively from the president's spending priorities. For example, under Reagan and Bush there was a marked shift in federal spending in favour of defence procurement (such as the 'Star Wars' system) which tremendously benefited industries, and indeed readily identifiable firms that have supported the Republican party (Ginsberg and Shefter, 1990). On the other hand, the power to allocate funds is shared with Congress, which not only can alter the overall spending priorities but also can severely limit executive discretion by mandating that the money appropriated be spent in particular ways.

Obviously funds for projects have to be spent somewhere and in this sense the allocation of money to particular projects is simply an inevitable part of the policy process. Nonetheless, the power to decide where to spend money (or to decide where money will be spent by others) generally is regarded as an important patronage resource. George Bush's September 1992 decisions to proceed with the sale of fighter aircraft to Saudi Arabia (thus preserving thousands of jobs at a McDonnell Douglas plant in St Louis where the announcement was made); to order the rebuilding of Homestead air base in Florida (announced there); and to increase grain export subsidies (announced in South Dakota) all were seen as attempts to use discretionary spending to bolster his own re-election bid. Similarly, Clinton used a variety of spending projects to 'encourage' congressional support for NAFTA. The use of government contracts as a source of patronage is particularly prominent in the defence field, where 'national security considerations' allow the short-circuiting of many procedures designed to limit political considerations (Mayer, 1991).

Despite these prominent examples, the bulk of patronage spending is allocated by Congress rather than the executive. Indeed, one of the dominant themes of American politics has become the conflict between executive and legislative branches over pork-barrel spending. This conflict has been largely independent of party, and is based on the different institutional and electoral imperatives of Congress and the presidency. While members of the majority party, and particularly committee and subcommittee chairs, naturally are in a stronger position to assure the allocation of projects to their own districts, pork-barrel legislation is one of the currencies of interparty coalition building and so the minority party is hardly excluded. Indeed, the distribution of pork is one of the cases in which norms of 'something for everyone' are strongly developed (Mayhew, 1975).

Finally, although it is virtually impossible to assess their true significance, brief mention is required of the host of favors such as special tours of the White House, autographed photographs with the president, sets of presidential cuff links, and so on. Members of Congress have similar resources in private bills, resolutions of congratulation, legislation establishing 'National Pickle Week', and so forth. None of these are likely to be exchanged in a simple *quid pro quo* manner, but they all contribute to a pattern of mutual favour-doing that an actor will be loath to endanger over issues about which he or she does not care deeply.

The beneficiaries of patronage differ depending on whether it is controlled by a Democrat or a Republican, although perhaps not as much as one might expect. The more significant difference is between the use of patronage by the president and by members of Congress. Presidents generally use patronage both to cement their personal electoral coalitions and to secure passage of policies. For Congress, patronage (that is, pork-barrel and other constituency-serving legislation) often is the policy, and a greater premium is placed on the electoral utility both of patronage and of policy stands. There are a number of obvious reasons. In contemporary American politics, presidents are assigned responsibility for policy, and are in a better position to do something about it; while Congress as a collectivity has a strong influence on policy, individual members of Congress generally are neither in a position to have great influence on policy nor to take credit or blame for the influence they do have. A president can stand for re-election only once, and has four years in office before that occasion arises; both senators and representatives can be re-elected repeatedly, and while Senators are on a six-year re-election cycle, the two year term of members of the House means that no sooner are they elected than their re-election campaigns must begin.

CONCLUSION

If American parties were stronger, either in Congress or in society more generally, the patterns described here would be different, and in the nineteenth century they were somewhat different, although this difference is easy to exaggerate (Bartels, 1992). The constitutional principle of separation of powers was introduced to minimize the likelihood that there would be a party in Congress that could simply be described as 'supporting the government'. Moreover, the balance of powers and political opportunities between state and national governments virtually assured that if there were to be strong parties, they would be at the state, not the federal, level.

These basic structural features have been reinforced by developments over the last 100 years. At the state level, civil service reform and the growth of public welfare programs have undermined two of the major patronage resources on which the strong political machines of the nineteenth and early twentieth centuries were based. Even more, the rise of the direct primary greatly lessened the ability of party leaders to reward loyalty and punish defection. In the most recent period, new campaign techniques that both emphasize the individual candidate and require him or her individually to raise substantial sums of money furthered this trend. The more elections became personal contests, the less likely the elected official was to defer to party leaders. Within Congress, there have been a series of changes in rules and procedures, beginning with the 1910 revolt against Speaker Cannon, that have weakened the powers of any collective party leadership.

As all this suggests, while party is significant in the American governmental process, it is party as a summary of policy predilections, as a framework for organizing elections and the institutions of Congress, as a pattern of affinities, and as a starting place for coalition building and the exchange of favours. To look for the influence of party as an actor itself, however, is to ascribe to it an organizational strength and coherence that American parties simply do not have. As David Mayhew concluded on the basis of an extensive analysis of the post-war period, American parties 'seem to play more of a role as "policy factions" than as ... governing instruments' (Mayhew, 1991, p. 199).

## NOTES

Thanks are due to Ben Ginsberg, Sue Hemberger, Robin Kolodny, and Robert Peabody for helpful comments and suggestions.

1.   For example, the votes of three-fifths of the entire Senate (two-thirds of the entire Senate before 1959) are required to end a filibuster.

# 12. India: How a Government Party Decays when Government Swallows Party

## J.W. Björkman and K. Mathur

### INTRODUCTION

For the past half-century, India has displayed a deeprooted yet resilient stability. Since the British Raj ended in 1947, India's constitutional regime has never been threatened by uprisings, military *coups d'état* or revolution, nor do such prospects lie on the horizon. India's parliamentary democracy has a political legitimacy almost unparalleled in the developing world. It has witnessed orderly succession on the death in office of three prime ministers – Jawaharlal Nehru in 1964, Lal Bahadur Shastri in 1966, and Indira Gandhi[1] in 1984 – and it has repeatedly experienced peaceful transitions of political power from one party to another after free and competitive elections at both state and national levels. In short, India has a markedly stable democratic polity with its attendant political parties.

Among these political parties, one has towered over all the others. Founded in 1885 as the Indian National Congress to serve as a spokesman for Indian interests and as a loyal opposition to the viceregal government, this 110 year old party not only successfully led the independence movement against imperial rule but also repeatedly organized itself to contest elections and to form limited governments under the successive Government of India Acts of 1909, 1919 and 1935. Partially before and certainly after 1947, the All India Congress Party had become equated in public opinion with the '*sarkar*' or government of India. It has been, is now, and is likely to remain inextricably entwined with the politics of India.

In this chapter, we will emphasize the structure and processes of the Congress Party as a political party and its relationships to the Government of India, when in or (more rarely) out of power. To do so, we will sketch the post-independence history of the Congress Party and its transformation over time in relation to executive leadership. By focusing on the quarter-century after the death of Jawaharlal Nehru in 1964, we shall examine patterns of appointments and patronage as well as selected policies in several national cabinets. It may be noted in advance that, despite a free press as well as many self-serving memoirs of political actors during this period, data are remarkably scarce – particularly quantifiable data about the degrees of autonomy or dependence in party/government appointments and about the amounts of patronage dispensed by government, party or other bodies. Nonetheless there are overarching patterns of relationships which reveal the dramatic decline over time of Congress Party influence over government and the corresponding rise of prime ministerial leadership, whoever was the incumbent.

Since independent India's first elections were held in 1951, the Congress Party has formed the national government, except between 1977 and 1979 and between 1989 and 1991. Moreover, the Congress Party has played a significant role in the socio-political development of the country by commanding large majorities in Parliament on most occasions and by having a strong organizational network. These two characteristics led Rajni Kothari (1964) and W.H. Morris-Jones (1978) to describe India as a 'dominant party system' that is a multi-party system in which free competition among parties occurred but in which the Congress Party dominated all political action. The continuation of Congress dominance depended on the efficient functioning of the party organization.

Without oversimplifying Mahatma Gandhi's reorganizational reforms of 1920, the party's structure has always been markedly centralized. Based on a series of elections through levels of political activity that began with direct elections of Congress Party leaders at the grass-roots and then indirectly elected party leaders at successively higher levels of party activity, a representative body called the All India Congress Committee (AICC) was constituted while a Congress President was elected. The apex organization comprised the AICC, a Congress Working Committee (WC), and the Congress Party President. The preferences of the latter weighed heavily in selecting the former, and the system (independently from Leninist formulations) was characterized by 'democratic centralism'.

When independence was achieved in 1947, the Mahatma urged the Indian National Congress to 'dissolve' as a political movement and to reconstitute itself instead as a society for social service. He explicitly argued against the continuance of the Congress as a political party but his major lieutenants, in particular Jawaharlal Nehru and Vallabhbhai Patel, disagreed as did most other Congress leaders. Consequently, although some committed Gandhians resigned their memberships and left the party, the Indian National Congress continued its politically partisan activities. Indeed, based on the elections of 1946 under the 1935 Government of India Act, the Congress provided the transitional government and then the first post-Raj government of India. At

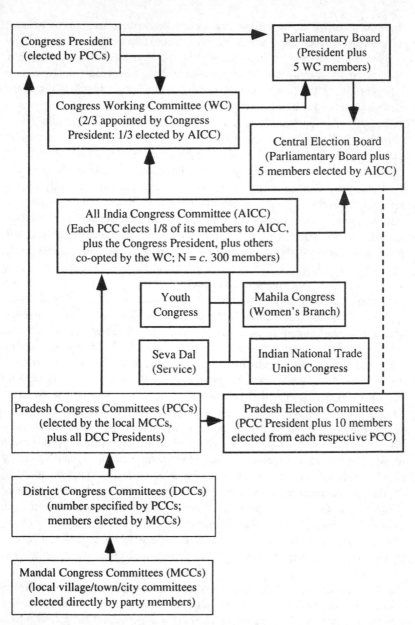

Source: Björkman, 1987:53

Figure 12.1: *Classic organization of the Congress Party in India*

the same time, all the Indian members of parliament elected in 1946 became a Constituent Assembly in order to draft a constitution for the newly independent 'dominion'. On 26 January 1950 the Constitution of the Republic of India was promulgated: it terminated India's dominion status (with its inherent link to the British Crown) but retained India's membership in the British Commonwealth of Nations.

Because the Constituent Assembly simultaneously served as India's postpartition parliament and because the Congress Party had a preponderant majority in this bi-functional entity, the government of India remained under the control of the Congress Party. Jawaharlal Nehru, as leader of the Congress Parliamentary Party, continued to serve as prime minister. Equally importantly, he continued to serve as president of the All Indian National Congress which did *not* revise its party constitution while otherwise democratizing the regime. Nehru and particularly Patel – the iron-willed *apparatchik* who almost single-handedly 'integrated' the 562 erstwhile princely states into the Indian Union (Menon, 1957) – argued on behalf of a strong disciplined political party not only to organize the government but also to contest the elections scheduled for 1952, the first ever held in India under universal adult suffrage.

Nehru's personal domination of the party and the government, however, did not overly constrain inner party democracy. Internal democracy was maintained for at least two reasons. First, Nehru took his role of implanting parliamentary and democratic institutions on to the Indian soil rather seriously. Second, his colleagues – both in government and in party – were those with whom he had had personal relationships from the days of the freedom struggle when they were also companions in British jails. It was possible for them to disagree with Nehru or offer him candid advice without threatening his leadership. In addition, anyone who had been imprisoned by the British during the freedom movement commanded respect in society and had some kind of right to air their dissent, even if such dissent was expressed publicly. The organizational strength emanated from the way the party was structured from the local level upwards, with appointees elected and nominated at each point. Parliamentary and organizational wings worked together within all the committees. Such cooperation was also reflected in the Central Election Committee formed during the election years which chose the candidates of the Congress Party.

This structure provided Congress with the strength to transform itself successfully from a national movement into a party of governance. It also helped in creating a conciliatory machinery within the party at various levels which prevented local conflicts from becoming issues of national moment. As Manor (1988) points out, the management of resources – at which many in the Congress organization excelled – was essential to achieve reconciliation, to mediate in factional disputes, and to influence political decisions at state and district levels. Manor further described the Congress Party as a giant system of 'transactional linkages', a mechanism for the distribution of spoils in return for political support and organizational loyalty. The main integrating ideas were opportunism, self-aggrandizement, the impulse to enter patron-client relationships, and to forge deals. As a consequence the role of the party in policy-making gradually diminished while its place as an integrating mechanism in society came to be strengthened.

During the 1960s observers attributed much of the success of Congress to its ability to forge widespread patronage networks which provided a crucial linkage between local demands and central responses (Weiner, 1967; Kothari, 1975). These naturally helped to solve a variety of power conflicts. Gradually, however, these links were destroyed. No elections were held within the party after 1972 as Mrs Gandhi started to appoint persons to both governmental and organizational positions for their personal loyalty and not for their ability to articulate grass-roots demands. These appointees did not have the capacity to influence local behaviour and could not mediate in social and political conflicts. As a result, Congress gradually lost its pre-eminent role in the Indian political system. In his presidential address to the 1985 Bombay session of the Congress(I) Party, Rajiv Gandhi referred to this decline when he complained that

> ... millions of ordinary Congress workers throughout the country are full of enthusiasm for the Congress policies and programmes. But they are handicapped for on their backs ride the brokers of power and influence, who dispense patronage to convert a mass movement into a feudal oligarchy. There are self-perpetuating cliques who thrive by invoking the slogans of caste and religion and by enmeshing the living body of the Congress in their net of avarice ...

## APPOINTMENTS

### Selection of prime ministers

After the British government agreed to terminate the Raj and began the transfer of power, elections were held in 1946 under the 1935 Government of India Act. Based on their results, an interim government was formed with Nehru chosen by his colleagues to head the government as he was the then President of the Congress Party. His successor as President of the Congress Party was Acharya Kripalani who insisted that all important decisions should be made only in consultation with the Congress President and the party's Working Committee; Nehru and his government colleagues, however, consented only to keep them informed; they argued that discussions often could not be made public. A struggle ensued and, after a bitter debate, Kripalini resigned the Congress Presidency.

Nehru was challenged again in 1951 when conservative elements attempted to capture party positions just before the First General Elections. Purshottam Das Tandon's election as Congress Party President marked the second effort by the party to exercise organizational control over the government. In the ensuing struggle, Nehru asserted that the party had no special responsibility in policy making. Tandon resigned after conceding that Nehru was more important than he was himself and that the country needed Nehru's services more than his own. Nehru became again party president: when he subsequently relinquished the presidency of the party, the principle had none the less been established that no person could become Party President if he or she did not command the confidence of the Prime Minister. The party had been thoroughly governmentalized or, one might say, domesticated.

In 1963, in order to revitalize the Congress Party at its grass-roots and incidentally to constrain the clear ambitions of Morarji Desai (who had been chief minister of the enormous Bombay state), Nehru invented the 'Kamaraj Plan'. This device 'requested' volunteers from among those party members then serving as cabinet ministers or as chief ministers to 'resign' and to serve instead in party posts only. Kamaraj, being the chief minister of Madras state, resigned to become Congress President, a post which Nehru himself vacated; and about a dozen other state and national Congress leaders – including Morarji Desai – felt compelled to devote themselves exclusively to regeneration of the party. Among those 'selflessly' resigning was a Minister without Portfolio in the Union cabinet, Lal Bahadur Shastri.

Given Nehru's overwhelming pre-eminence in both government and party, it is impossible to judge which of his roles had priority. Clearly Nehru was prime minister because he was leader of the Congress, but his concern for government duties over party prerogatives was well-known and intrinsically accepted. The pre-eminence of party over government became evident when Nehru was no longer on the scene, however. When Nehru died in May 1964, the cabinet members who had resigned to take over party posts (who later came to be known as the Syndicate) presided over the selection of his successor as prime minister; meanwhile, party and parliament adopted a convention whereby the most senior member of the Cabinet, in this case the home minister, became acting prime minister while the selection process was underway. The Congress Parliamentary Party – the Congress members of the Lower House (*Lok Sabha*) and of the Upper House (*Rajya Sabha*) – had the responsibility of choosing as prime minister one of the Lok Sabha members or someone who could become a member of that body within six months; but the parliamentary party could only act on the advice of the party 'High Command'. Since this High Command has always been a euphemism for the party president (who in 1964 was Kamaraj Nadar from Madras) and the Congress Working Committee (comprised largely of the other state party bosses), the real power of selection of the Congress Party leader in parliament and therefore of the next prime minister of India lay with the incipient 'Syndicate'.

At the time of Nehru's impending departure from the political scene (his deteriorating health was well-known), it was widely rumored that Kamaraj himself wanted to become the national leader. Had he done so, another political convention might have been established whereby leadership of both the Congress Party and the nation would rotate among the major regions of India. The Nehru family came from Allahabad in Uttar Pradesh, at the centre of the Hindi-speaking region; but Kamaraj could speak neither Hindi nor English, respectively the national and associate (or so-called 'link') languages of India; and the other state Congress bosses were predictably wary of his ambitions. So the Syndicate selected a mild-mannered and modest member of the party with a reputation for honesty but for little else to become the second prime minister of independent India. As Lal Bahadur Shastri also came from Hindi-speaking Uttar Pradesh – which, having been the Nehruvian power base, lacked a Syndicate member – power relationships among the major state Congress bosses were not disturbed.

Shastri died less than two years later: at that point the procedures closely followed those initiated in 1964. The Home Minister again became acting prime minister while the Congress High Command and the Congress Parliamentary Party deliberated on the choice of successor. The Syndicate remained powerful but its members were wary of one another; their only point of unanimous agreement was to prevent Morarji Desai from assuming party leadership. Kamaraj was still Congress President and is largely credited with orchestrating the selection of another mild-mannered, modest, almost inconsequential party member who had been Minister of Information and Broadcasting in the Shastri cabinet. His choice had one additional virtue: she was the only child of Jawaharlal Nehru and, as such, continued the tradition of selecting the supreme Congress leader from Uttar Pradesh. Indira Gandhi had been selected by the Syndicate primarily because she blocked the rise of Morarji Desai. Unlike his grudgingly self-effacing behaviour in 1964 when Shastri's election was 'unanimous', Desai contested the 1966 election within the Congress Parliamentary Party but lost resoundingly.

The elevation of Mrs Gandhi was interpreted as further evidence that power was shifting even more sharply toward the Congress President and his allied group of state party leaders. The expectation that she would rely on these leaders was amply fulfilled when she consulted many of them before finalizing her first cabinet; indeed, the changes that she made were minor and her cabinet mostly comprised Shastri's colleagues. However, she did not consult them when on 5 June 1966 the government announced a 35 per cent devaluation of the rupee. This decision proved very unpopular throughout the country. An incensed Kamaraj blamed himself for having put Mrs Gandhi in power, muttering 'big man's daughter, a small man's mistake'. At his instance the Congress Working Committee passed a resolution denouncing the Government of India for its decision on devaluation. The rift between Mrs Gandhi and the organizational wing of the party began to manifest itself.

The conflict between Mrs Gandhi and the Syndicate intensified after the 1967 elections. The Congress Party had fared poorly and many Syndicate members were defeated. With the support from the Chief Ministers of those states where Congress had won, Mrs Gandhi was elected leader of the Congress Parliamentary Party and became Prime Minister for a second time on 12 March 1967. She then announced her cabinet without consulting the Syndicate, which further reflected her independence from party guidelines. Senior organizational party leaders realized that their influence under the principle of collective leadership, which had been established during the Shastri years, was severely eroded. As a countermeasure, the Syndicate secured the induction of Morarji Desai into the Cabinet as Finance Minister as well as Deputy Prime Minister. Although not a member of the Syndicate, Desai had challenged Mrs Gandhi for election as the parliamentary leader and harboured unmistakable ambitions for the top office. With this manoeuvre, the battle of wills had begun.

During the following two years relations between the organizational wing and the governmental wing of the Congress Party were characterized by an uneasy truce while Mrs Gandhi improvised her policy of 'garibi hatao' (see below). The next confrontation occurred over the nomination of a candidate for the post of President of India, whose powers were largely symbolic but could be enhanced through a creative interpretation under new management. Through the Congress organization, the Syndicate had secured endorsement for one of its own members, but Mrs Gandhi refused. She urged an open 'conscience vote' by members of the electoral college in order to 'further the progressive cause' and her nominee won. The final blow came on the issue of controlling organizational matters; when parallel meetings at the Bangalore AICC session were held by Mrs Gandhi and by the party president on 12 November 1969, the Congress party effectively split, Mrs Gandhi was popularly perceived as a champion of the poor and as espousing the traditional goals of the Congress Party. She claimed continuity with her father's thinking which still commanded tremendous credibility, while Syndicate members came to be regarded as entrenched conservative party bosses.

Mrs Gandhi then revived Nehru's practice of uniting top government and party posts in herself: she was simultaneously prime minister and party president or allowed only her confidants to serve in that post. On the assassination of Mrs Gandhi in 1984, Congress had once more to choose a successor as national leader; it had been 18 years since she had been selected by the Congress High Command; in the interim the Indian National Congress had split. The Congress Parliamentary Party existed, but the party organization was extremely weak.

Rather than appointing the most senior cabinet minister to serve as acting prime minister while deliberations were held to select an appropriate successor, the President of India (Giani Zail Singha, a Sikh Congressman who had previously served in several of Mrs Gandhi's cabinets) appointed her son Rajiv as Prime Minister. Zail Singh then summoned whichever members of the Congress Parliamentary Party could be located during the post-assassination confusion and directed them to confirm his choice. With even less than half of the Congress(I) elected leaders present, Rajiv Gandhi was chosen by the Congress Parliamentary Party to succeed his mother and was at once sworn in as prime minister. His position was later ratified by the fully assembled party in both its legislative and organizational versions, but the haste with which the decision was taken was justified on the grounds that an imminent breakdown of law and order required rapid action to reassure the Indian people that a reliable Congress central government continued to exist. In point of fact, the Congress(I) Party had no collective nor organizational leadership which could take the decisions with dispatch, much less due process.

Seven years later, in 1991, the assassination of Rajiv Gandhi occurred on the campaign trail during the Tenth General Elections as the Congress(I) sought to return to power. Therefore decisions about who would become president of the party and then who would become leader of the parliamentary party (and thus potential prime minister) awaited the outcome of the elections themselves. For a time, there were strong pressures on Rajiv's widow – Mrs Sonia Gandhi – to become Congress President and even perhaps accept appointment as Prime Minister under the constitutional provision that cabinet members have up to six months in which to secure an elected seat in parliament. As she firmly refused to countenance any active political role, the leaders of the party eventually persuaded another mild-mannered Congressman, not only elderly but in relatively poor health, to accept interim prime ministerial responsibilities. Although the Congress(I) did not obtain an absolute majority in the Lok Sabha, it was the largest single party and so the mild-mannered stop-gap politician, PV Narasimha Rao, was asked by the President of India (another Congressman) to attempt to form a government. Narasimha Rao and his colleagues decided to form a 'minority' government which to date (three years later) is still in office and which, through by-elections and through skilfully inducing other MPs back into its fold, holds a small majority.

Rao subsequently displayed his influence in the party when, after 20 years, elections took place within Congress. In April 1992 the AICC elected ten members to the Congress Working Committee, but these included several leading dissidents as well as some outspoken critics of Narasimha Rao. This obvious threat led Rao to act: he commented on the surprising absence on the new committee of either women or members of the Scheduled Castes and Tribes. Five of the ten elected members resigned and publicly urged Rao to reconstitute the CWC in order to include representatives of these minorities. The other five elected members also felt compelled to resign to avoid being labelled as social reactionaries: the election was in practice a non-event. Thus the party did, in some fashion, once again influence the appointment of the prime minister, but the prime minister in turn, as head of the government quickly succeeded in influencing the party (if not yet in fully dominating it).

## Appointment of ministers

The selection of members of the Cabinet is a prerogative of the Prime Minister, but invariably some consultations go on within the top leadership. This consists of seasoned politicians in whom the PM has confidence, with senior or retired bureaucrats participating sometimes in giving this advice. PV Narasimha Rao reputedly sought advice from a retired bureaucrat and asked him to make initial contacts with those who could possibly be included in the Council of Ministers. It is difficult to know whether a person included in the Cabinet was a choice of the party or not or whether he/she represented a particular constituency. However, the inability of the Prime Minister to appoint a Cabinet in one single attempt or the lack of stability in the cabinet (that is, turnover of ministers) may indicate major difficulties in arriving at a successful balance.

From Nehru to the Gandhis, prime ministers have used various techniques to appoint ministers who would be unable to hold their own (Mathur and Björkman 1994). They chose increasingly politicians who had little or no prior experience in the Union Council of Ministers. In the Rajiv Gandhi cabinet, more than two-thirds of the ministers had less than five years' experience in any level of government. The so-called 'youthfulness' of that cabinet was thus not so much a matter of age as of lack of experience. Those who entered the cabinet increasingly were Chief Ministers or state-level political leaders. This process reflected the fact that prime ministers felt threatened by leaders who attempted to develop or maintain local bases of support: thus Mrs Gandhi appointed state Chief Ministers to the cabinet and removed these from the local scene. The coherence of the cabinet came to be gradually eroded as the perspectives of most cabinet ministers were limited by their local experience: meanwhile, the prime ministers – especially Mrs Gandhi and Rajiv Gandhi – could assert themselves as their colleagues carried on their squabbles.

Frequent reshuffling of the cabinet and changing portfolios were other methods adopted by both Mrs Gandhi and Rajiv Gandhi. The proportion of cabinet ministers who completed full terms with the Prime Minister was low; the smallest number was during Mrs Gandhi's second cabinet of 1971–7. In this period Mrs Gandhi had a very large majority in Parliament and reached the pinnacle of her popularity. While the Indira and Rajiv cabinets always lasted more than four years, ministers served terms averaging less than three years; duration even did not exceed two years in some important ministries such as defence or home affairs between 1967 and 1989. The lack of concern for the effectiveness of leadership in ministries is evident from the fact that a portfolio such as education was headed for long periods by a junior minister and not by a cabinet minister. Ministerial tenure was even shorter in the Rajiv Gandhi cabinet.

The Upper House of Parliament is indirectly elected by representatives of the states. This practice provides some opportunity for professionals or men and women of outstanding merit to be brought into Parliament without going through popular election campaigns. This enables prime ministers to include persons in the cabinet who are not true politicians: this role of the upper house has diminished, however. Meanwhile, the cabinet gradually became more political and it lost administrative experience and professional training, while the public interest at large became less important in allocating portfolios.

Cabinets have been unstable during the period when both Mrs Gandhi and Rajiv Gandhi commanded large majorities in parliament and were undisputed leaders of their party, being also party presidents. Conflicts between the organizational wing and the parliamentary wing of the party were minimized, but the Gandhis were not able to avoid regional or factional pressures. Party as such did not limit the prime ministers' action; what did limit their power were personal, factional, caste-based and regional divisions, while there was little ideology to bind the cabinet together.

## POLICIES

### Statist economic planning

After independence in 1947, there was a high degree of consensus about the need for an active role for the state in promoting economic development. Investment planning and financial controls were widely accepted as methods of building a modern infrastructure for rapid industrialization and there was comparatively little controversy about the management of industrial policy. India enjoyed initially a comfortable foreign exchange position and regulations about the private sector were applied with relative flexibility. The first five-year plan, issued in 1951, was moderate in that it attempted detailed planning only for a few selected industries which India lacked and which the private sector could not be expected to provide. The First Five-Year plan did not derive from Congress party debates: it was rather imposed by Nehru who had been impressed by the rapid results of state planning in the Soviet Union.

The Second Five Year Plan (1956–61), authored largely by PC Mahalanobis, a statistical adviser to the Planning Commission which was chaired by prime minister Nehru, was markedly more ambitious. It sought to transform India from an agricultural into an industrial economy by channelling investment to the production of capital goods. To achieve these goals, the government nationalized most major industries and established a system of licences and direct controls to regulate what remained of the private sector.

The planners recognized that rapid rates of industrialization could be achieved only if adequate financial resources were available to turn the public sector industries into the 'commanding heights' of the economy and if radical institutional change occurred in agriculture in order to obtain sufficient agricultural surpluses which could keep inflation in check. Because of his unique position in both party and government, Nehru was able to secure broad agreement on these social goals of economic planning; the party raised stiff oppposition to the implementation of the programmes designed to achieve these goals, however. This was particularly true of the changes proposed in agriculture: in 1956, Nehru and his supporters could not obtain the party's endorsement of cooperative farming. The implementation record on the grading of food grains by the state was hardly more encouraging: state-level chief ministers who belonged to Congress and were members of the policy-making organs of the party strongly opposed the scheme presented in 1959. Political dissatisfaction within the party led Nehru to withdraw the proposals. The food minister was forced to resign and the new incumbent, who was head of the Congress Party organization in Bombay, was quick to announce that he would not implement state trading in food grains.

The lack of financial resources was what started dissension within the party and the subsequent demand to reduce Third Plan goals. The chief ministers of the states who gathered for the November 1962 meeting of the National Development Council to discuss the Annual Plan for 1963–4 were therefore confident in arguing for a substantial reduction in Plan outlay and much greater reliance on the private sector to carry out development schemes while stepping up public outlays on defence. Nehru refused to give way and his finance minister proposed steep increases in taxation to raise the necessary revenues.

The problem of increased international aid remained and, because the major donors were chary about requests of the Indian government for further assistance to finance its Fourth Five Year Plan (1967–72), a special World Bank mission conducted in 1964 a six month study of the economy policy under the Third Plan. Although commissioned when Jawaharlal Nehru was alive, the study-team submitted its report several months after his death in May 1964. By then, the political scenario had markedly changed and Lal Bahadur Shastri had become prime minister. India had already fought an embarrassing border war with China and war clouds were gathering again over the Indo-Pakistani border. These events had an incidence on the development budget while there were increased criticisms of the planned approach to economic development. The political leaders who took control of the Congress Party after Nehru and who influenced the choice of Shastri as Prime Minister were also at variance with Nehru's stated ideals of economic self-sufficiency, which included replacing imports by domestic production and discouraging foreign investments. Left-oriented groups which had previously endorsed Nehru's ideals for a 'socialistic pattern of society' criticized the Plan for creating greater concentrations of wealth. On the other hand, the private sector was critical of its economic politics which stifled growth and efficiency.

Personally without very strong views, prime minister Shastri inclined toward the private sector's perceptions of Indian economic policies. To head his secretariat, Shastri appointed a senior ICS official, L.K. Jha, previously Governor of the Reserve Bank of India, who favoured dismantling many of the restrictions placed on the economy; the crucial economic ministries also began to be headed by civil servants with similar views. The bureaucratic advisers of the prime minister were therefore more flexible about planning and economically more liberal than the members of the Planning Commission, which Nehru had established by administrative fiat rather than through parliamentary legislation. Significantly, while Congress broadly accepted the macro-economic policies proposed by Nehru and his planners, it effectively blocked their implementation by reducing most 'socialist' programmes.

## Devaluation of the rupee, 1966

The package of policies recommended by the World Bank mission included proposals for a relaxation of industrial controls, import liberalization, and the stimulation of investment in private industries. The chronic trade imbalance was attributed to an overvalued exchange rate which reduced competitiveness in export markets: the Indian rupee needed therefore to be devalued. This package of economic reforms contrasted sharply with the policies being pursued by the Planning Commission. It was, however, presented to the Government of India as the precondition for substantial inflows of aid which could rise from about $1.1 billion per annum to around $1.7 billion per annum during the period of the Fourth Five Year Plan. This suggested increase of external capital assistance paralleled the Planning Commission's estimate that the Fourth Plan could be financed only if external assistance on that order of magnitude were available. The Prime Minister's Secretariat as well as the senior officials in the ministries concerned appeared to be in broad agreement with the policy package. Speaking to the National Development Council in September 1965, the prime minister said that India's ability to attract external resources of such magnitude 'depended on the goodwill of the countries that had been helping India and also on institutions such as the World Bank etc'. However, the World Bank and the IMF made it clear that increased aid flows depended on the devaluation of the rupee. On the other hand, there was no specific statement by the party organization.

Yet, within Congress, many expressed strong resentment at foreign pressure on matters considered to be part and parcel of national sovereignty as well as of self-reliant development. Among them were those for whom acceptance of this reform package was a confession of failure of the previous decades and a denial of Nehru's dream. A prime example was T.T. Krishnamachari, Shastri's minister of finance, who refused even to consider the devaluation of the rupee. However, extraneous events then played a part. First, the war between India and Pakistan had occurred in late 1965 and, after some months of stalemate, it was agreed that negotiations towards a settlement would take place in Tashkent. Second, Shastri referred some allegations which had been made against the finance minister to an independent judicial enquiry. The finance minister felt that, by taking this action, the prime minister had lost confidence in him and resigned. An important dissenter had left the government.

Events then moved quickly. In early January 1966 B.K. Nehru, India's ambassador in Washington, returned to Delhi for advice about devaluation. The Prime Minister had appointed a cabinet committee comprised of Ashok Mehta, deputy chairman of the Planning Commission, Sachin Chaudhri (the new finance minister), and Chidanbaram Subramaniam, minister of agriculture to recommend a decision, Shastri's Secretary, L.K. Jha, being the committee's rapporteur. All four were known to support devaluation, while none represented the organizational wing of Congress. Despite the importance of macro-economic policies, there were no debates nor any resolutions in the party on the subject. Shastri then went to Tashkent where, shortly after signing a peace agreement negotiated with President Ayub Khan of Pakistan, he suffered a heart attack and died on 11 January 1966.

Shastri's successor as Prime Minister, Mrs Gandhi, accepted the briefing of the *ad hoc* cabinet committee. Without consulting party leaders, some of whom had expressed reservations about devaluation of the rupee, she agreed to proceed with a negotiated devaluation. B.K. Nehru returned to Washington, carrying a report initialled by the Finance Minister, which clearly indicated the intention to devalue the rupee. After several months, the International Monetary Fund began to put pressure on the Government of India to follow up its decision by announcing the devaluation. Despite continued differences within the Congress Party, the announcement was made on 6 June 1966 and, within ten days, the US announced resumption of its economic aid which had been suspended during the Indo-Pakistan war. This sequence clearly suggests that the Government had devalued the rupee in response to pressures by the aid-giving agencies in order to obtain further external assistance. Mrs Gandhi discussed the matter with the party *after* the decision had been taken: the Congress Party president was outraged not to have been consulted and stated that the question should have been put before the relevant party bodies. Mrs Gandhi wavered but B.K. Nehru went ahead in Washington.

The 1966 decision to devalue the rupee set in motion serious debates on the government's economic policies since 1952. The Planning Commission came under attack. The devaluation of the rupee resulted in a sharp decline in popular support for the Congress Party. Mrs Gandhi had to resort to shrewd political strategies to stay in power. Little change occurred in overall economic policies, however; indeed the regulation and control of the private sector increased. The political rhetoric for equity and justice even received greater prominence.

## Devaluation of the rupee, 1991

The second major devaluation of the rupee in 1991 was a culmination of expectations about a complete shift in economic policies by the government of India. It was part of a package of economic reforms initiated by the minority Congress government which came to power in 1991. An economist was appointed finance minister, one of his first acts being the devaluation of the rupee. There seems to have been little discussion of these reforms in the party organization although several senior leaders expressed concern about the abandonment of the economic approach which had hitherto been adopted.

The fact that Congress did not have a majority in 1991 resulted in conflict being limited, as it was feared that the government might otherwise fall. The political situation was in flux, however. Already, during his 1984–9 tenure of office, Rajiv Gandhi had begun to move towards a more liberal economy. He had appointed three committees of experts and civil servants to examine issues of trade, of finance, and of the restructuring of the public sector. Imports had also been liberalised. In 1989, however, Congress (I) lost its massive majority and a coalition of opposition parties came to power, which, in turn, was so divided that new elections took place in 1991.

The Narasimha Rao Congress minority government assumed office on 21 June 1991. As an immediate response to the financial crisis, it announced devaluations of the rupee in discrete steps on 1 and 3 July 1991; other changes were also announced, indicating that a major shift in economic policy was to occur. Imports were deregulated; industrial licensing was abolished in all but a few sectors, restrictions on investments were removed, the participation of foreign capital was allowed up to 51 per cent in general and up to 100 per cent in export-oriented industries. The new government thus supported an open economy, with the deregulation of trade and industry, the reduction in the size of the public sector, and a tight monetary policy.

These decisions were consistent with the IMF's structural adjustment programmes and the conditions it required for extending loan facilities. Critics on the left attacked the shift as a supine surrender to international aid agencies; but the large amount of support for these policies, including for the decision to devalue the rupee, can be seen by the fact that the other political parties did not choose to bring down the minority Congress government by a combined action. As its 1966 counterpart, the 1991 devaluation of the rupee was strongly supported by government economists and civil servants. A small core group in the finance ministry had seized the initiative and had had intensive negotiations with IMF and World Bank officials, while the Planning Commission had ceased to be at the centre of economic policy-making.

Congress itself played no appreciable part in initiating the policy of devaluation: its role was confined to supporting the government in parliament and, much later, in the Working Committee and in the AICC. While some critical voices were raised in this last body, their impact was symbolic rather than substantial. Once the Prime Minister had acted on the advice of his technical advisers, the party could oppose his decision only at the cost of its own self-destruction. In an ironic twist of fate, the weaker the Congress Party was in parliament, the stronger its leader became with respect to the party organs.

### 'Garibi Hatao': the policy to 'abolish poverty'

The devaluation of the rupee by Mrs Gandhi in 1966, shortly after she succeeded as prime minister, led to fundamental questions being raised again about the economic and social transformation of India and about the appropriate strategy to be adopted to fulfil the goals advocated by Congress since independence. Renewed demands by ginger groups in the party that Congress implement its longstanding commitments to social and economic equity coincided with Mrs Gandhi's efforts to secure her position both as prime minister and as party leader. These economic demands helped to draw political battle lines. At one level, the struggle was between the newly-appointed Mrs Gandhi and the entrenched party organization which – personified by the Syndicate of regional Congress bosses – was seeking to have a greater say in governmental decision-making. At another level, a younger group of socialist radicals was determined to wrest control of the party from the 'reactionary' leaders of the Syndicate to turn into an effective instrument for radical economic reform.

In order to isolate the party leaders and to establish her pre-eminence in policy-making, Mrs Gandhi used the economic issues and the populist claims about unfulfilled party goals. She proposed a ten-point programme to demonstrate the party's continued commitment to its historic mission. Apart from a proposal to remove the privileges of the former princely rulers, the ten points merely reiterated long-standing policies of the Congress Party. These were, at least in principle, noncontroversial. Yet they provoked a sharp debate when submitted for approval to the All India Congress Committee. The issue of bank nationalization was initially presented in diluted form as 'social control' of banking, but the proposed withdrawal of privileges from the ex-rulers generated strong emotions. It was argued that such a decision would break a promise solemnly made by the government and specifically by its Congress leaders (notably Sardar Vallabhbhai Patel who, until his death in 1950, had been Deputy Prime Minister in Nehru's cabinet) when the princely states had been integrated into the Indian Union. Meanwhile, however, the debate strengthened the resolve of the radicals to implement fully the ten-point programme and thereby to reduce the strength of the conservative wing of the party.

The ten-point programme was formally endorsed by the AICC in June 1967; but, during the following two years, little was done to implement it. The relationship between the organizational and parliamentary leaders of the Congress remained uneasy until 1969 when, following the presentation of the outline for the revised Fourth Draft Five Year Plan, a further debate on the economic situation occurred. The issue centred this time around the role of the public sector, which the Syndicate criticized but which Mrs Gandhi supported. Gradually she came to align herself with the radicals and then actively sought their support in her fight against the Syndicate. Events then moved quickly. In a swift move, Mrs Gandhi relieved Morarji Desai from the finance portfolio and on 12 July 1969 nationalized the banks by presidential ordinance. The letter she wrote to Desai and her defence of the decision to nationalize all major banks set an ideological framework which established the tone of all subsequent moves which she took against the Syndicate: bank nationalization was described as a progressive measure which would transfer national resources to the people rather than allow them to remain in the hands of the big business houses. The popularity of such arguments was such that it constituted a tactical victory against the Syndicate.

The reason why economic issues were used to fight political battles and why Mrs Gandhi could mobilize support through radical rhetoric was the way in which the economic crisis had been handled after Nehru's death in 1964. Shastri had assembled political and bureaucratic advisers who were known critics of the planning model adopted in the Second and Third Five Year Plans. The Planning Commission had been eclipsed as a policy-making body while power shifted to those civil servants and those cabinet ministers who were critical of what planning and the public sector stood for. Indeed, great credence was given to the argument of the business community that economic problems were largely due to the predominance of left-wing planners favouring massive investment in industrial projects which took a long time to mature and who neglected agriculture as well as consumer industries. While the financial and economic reforms recommended by the World Bank represented a radical departure from the planning principles adopted by Nehru, those liberal reforms had been favourably regarded by expert opinion in the finance ministry and by the secretariat of the then prime minister. A shift in economic strategy began also to be noticeable in a number of other changes of agricultural and food policies. For many, as a result, the 1966 devaluation of the rupee was viewed as the culmination of a policy of surrender to the pressures of international aid-giving agencies. Political opposition had already begun to be built against these measures when Mrs Gandhi came on the scene. Although she had been the Prime Minister when devaluation was announced, she was absolved of any personal blame for it.

On the economic front, the liberal economic policies did not have much favourable result. The new agricultural strategy led to rapid production gains only in those areas of the country in which there was already a good infrastructure. Despite incentives to the private sector, industrial production had not gathered pace nor had more investment been generated. Concentration of agricultural growth in certain areas and the concentration of wealth in few firms heightened perceptions of inequalities. Distributive justice became a major political issue, and popular discontent began to turn into public violence.

During the 1960s, the issue of the concentration of wealth had been examined by a number of committees. All of these bodies inclined toward the view that failures were largely due to ineffective implementation of the industrial licensing and regulating system and that, rather than being weakened, the system needed to be strengthened to achieve the goals of the plan. In agriculture, a 1968 Reserve Bank of India Report pointed out that the landless and near-landless, who were being bypassed by the prosperity accruing to farmers through the new agricultural strategy, needed special help; in 1970 several new development agencies were established to help the small and marginal farmers as well as landless agricultural labourers.

The process of confrontation within the All India Congress Party, which ultimately led to its split, began on these substantive political and economic issues. The 1967 ten-point programme represented the views of the so-called socialists in the Congress Party, whose support Mrs Gandhi chose to seek in order to fight her intra-party battles. She also used promises about the removal of poverty to mobilize a large constituency among the poor and the deprived. The nationalization of the banks, the abolition of special privileges of former princely rulers, the appointment of a Monopolies and Restricted Trade Practices Commission, and a new Industrial Policy to tighten controls over the private sector, all were part of this general strategy; that strategy of Mrs Gandhi's became formalized as the official programme of both her party and her government at the national election of 1971. Opposition parties allied merely to achieve what they themselves called their one-point programme of 'Indira Hatao', namely to remove Mrs Gandhi from office. Her characteristic reply was:

> Kuch log kehtai hain, Indira Hatao;
> Mai kehti hun, *garibi hatao*!
> (Some people say, get rid of Indira;
> I say, *get rid of poverty*!)

In a deft turn of phrase, Mrs Gandhi had not only almost accidentally coined an election-winning slogan but had made herself a symbol of radical social change. She had also removed almost every remaining vestige of independent power within her own political party.

In 1969 Mrs Gandhi seemed intent on revitalizing the All India Congress party organizationally and ideologically when she chose these radical issues to purge the party from its conservatives. By freeing herself from party-imposed personnel and policy constraints, she appeared to attempt to reform a rather sclerotic 84-year-old political institution. With the advantage of hindsight, one can see that her efforts led to rewarding personal allegiance rather than organizational loyalty and caused party disintegration rather than renewal. 'Garibi Hatao' marked the beginning of Mrs Gandhi's 15 year campaign against her own political party although she had it fully under control.

## PATRONAGE

The change from the Congress Party of the early years to the one criticized by Rajiv Gandhi in his 1985 presidential address in Bombay came about in several ways. There are finite limits to the resources that any state, even a highly interventionist state like India, can control. As long as that control was growing, as during the first two decades after independence, and as long as those contending for resources were limited in number, patronage played a positive part in helping Congress to build support. When resources began to be limited while contenders increased in number, not only was Congress weakened but the State became a wider arena of conflict among politicians who did not belong to the Congress Party but joined or developed their own parties (Kohli 1991).

The rise of the new 'contenders' was partly a result of the state policies themselves. The new agricultural strategy adopted in the 1960s led to the emergence of a class of rich farmers who had prospered under this strategy: because of subsidies designed to reduce input-costs and because of assured prices for outputs, this class became dependent on the state for its prosperity. Having become rich, it asked for political power to take greater advantage of what the state could provide, such as education, government jobs, or urban consumer goods.

On the other hand, democracy and the soliciting for votes at the elections held regularly raised awareness of state benefits among groups hitherto deprived. These began to enter the political arena to demand the resources which they thought were due to them, while some regions felt left out as the effects of development policies were uneven and regional demands began to be made.

Political representation also underwent a change. Parties began to be formed for specific constituency interests, while existing parties, such as Congress, started to be fragmented internally through factional groups based on caste, community or region. The national leadership became a coalition of these competing interests and state institutions became arenas where the battles were played out. The leaders of the early period had acquired a national perspective through its participation in the freedom movement; although their original power base was in different regions, they were not just local or regional leaders. They had risen to a national level both in visibility and in commitment. As resources dwindled, however, the nature of national leadership changed (Bardhan 1986).

Consequences followed in terms of recruitment to the cabinet and to policy-making. Cabinets came to reflect the political power of each specific group. Between 1967 and 1977, Mrs Gandhi relied heavily on minorities, religious groups as well as scheduled castes and tribes; however, during her last term in office (1980–4), she began to lean towards the Hindu majority.

The result was a growing interest in holding government office *not* for policy-making or goal-setting (nor for debates over policies per se), but rather in order to penetrate the government machinery and thereby control the allocation of resources held by the central government and, to a lesser extent, by the state governments. Most party leaders strove for positions in the cabinet not in order to provide executive leadership for agencies but in order to be in a strong position to affect implementation in favour of their constituencies. These positions were under the close control of the prime minister.

Another important part of the dismantled structure once supplied a financial base for the party. In the pre-independence era as well as during the Nehru-Shastri years, Congress membership meant payment of annual dues. These dues were modest, but millions of members provided a financial base to which were added (almost invariably secret) campaign contributions from commercial and business interests. As the party's organizational structure decayed, so did its membership, while persistent inflation eroded the value of the small sums still being collected. Fund raising from private sources was never readily traceable but, with the rise of Sanjay Gandhi, charges and counter-charges were made about payoffs, kickbacks from government contracts, external sources (the 'foreign hand'), and outright protection money. Huge amounts of unaccountable cash drew people of dubious character into the Congress Party in every region of the country: as Manor commented, 'the ability to deliver money to party coffers has taken precedence over a person's links to reservoirs of popular support' (1981:28–9).

India's policies of economic development had relied heavily on supporting the state sector and on regulating activities of the private market. Insurance companies and the banking industry were nationalized while new heavy industries were state-run. Both in terms of capital and of employment, these public enterprises dominated the organized economy. Managerial positions in these enterprises were used extensively to provide benefits and opportunities for patronage income for members of parliament, for political leaders who needed to be rewarded, or for dissidents who had to be won over.

Various measures were introduced to restrict the role of the private sector. New industrial units could not be set up nor capacity for production of existing units be expanded without government approval in the form of licences and permits. Decisions of this kind sometimes reached the cabinet or the prime minister. Imports were restricted and the availability of foreign exchange was regulated. A vast network of administered prices and financial incentives had developed, most of them during Mrs Gandhi's periods in office. All these regulatory mechanisms proved to be a potent formula for political corruption. Large amounts of money were required for elections and were usually contributed by the private sector which sought to subvert government regulations and/or obtain special licences.

In the Indian context, patronage, particularly in terms of its amounts and dimension, involves an examination of the functioning of the entire political and economic system. The exchange of goods and services in terms of social patterns and dependency relationships is pervasive, yet difficult to document in detail. Everyone assumes that '*sifaris*' (personal 'pull') causes things to happen, what people believe to be real being often more real than what is real. Yet it is impossible to determine accurately who controls patronage in the country and what is its amount. The government clearly plays a major part in determining the allocation of goods and services in society, particularly because these are scarce. Leaders of the ruling party which supports the government of the day also have a role, but must act through government agencies and their administrators.

CONCLUSION

Other than its annual all-India session, the Congress party has two arenas for policy debates: the Congress Working Committee (CWC) and the

Congress Parliamentary Board. The CWC sets the policy agenda for the government while the Parliamentary Board decides on the strategy to counter the opposition in Parliament. Under Mrs Gandhi the CWC became packed with nominated members while the selection of parliamentary candidates was decided by a Central Election Committee which was also a nominated body: thus only those candidates who were acceptable to what came to be known as the 'High Command' were selected. The result was that policy debates were devoid of much meaning and the party degenerated in sycophancy.

Policy-making clearly followed the needs and demands of the prime minister. During the tenure of office of Mrs Gandhi and of Rajiv Gandhi, party organization was deliberately weakened to make it subservient to the government. This was done in two ways at least. First, no elections to party posts took place after 1972. All office-bearers were nominated or appointed by the central leadership; no local leader could ever claim to be legitimized by an election. Under its pyramidal structure of party authority, Congress was wholly dominated by its national leader, a prime minister who was simultaneously party president. At the time of Nehru, it had become a convention that the party president needed the confidence of the prime minister (*not* the other way around): this was also the pattern under Mrs Gandhi, while, during Rajiv Gandhi's tenure in office, the two posts were never divided.

Second, those who were appointed to represent 'constituencies' in the cabinet were loyalists and not independent articulators of the demands of these constituencies. Both cabinet and party organization lost much of their meaning in carrying on policy debates. Disagreements did not come out in the open nor receive public scrutiny. One could only surmise about the influence of a constituency by the way a policy was formulated and particularly how it was implemented.

The Congress(I) Party of the 1970s and 1980s was – unlike its previous incarnation under Nehru and Shastri – not only unable to influence the government but also uninterested in doing so as long as the flow of patronage continued. Patronage clearly compensated for the loss of policy influence, with appointments to lucrative posts in public enterprises often being a major form of patronage. Party organization has had a limited influence on policy-making, which has remained the exclusive preserve of the government. The executive takes upon itself not only the right to make policy choices but also the right to reveal as little or as much of these policies as it chooses and to defend them with all the confidence of the numerical strength which it enjoys in the legislature (Mathur and Jayal 1993). The stronger Congress(I) became in parliament, the less influence the party was able to exercise over the government. The relationship between the Government of India and the

Congress Party which supports it has therefore been, and remains, of the party-dependent and government-dominant type.

## NOTE

1.  There is *no* kinship nor family relationship between Mahatma Gandhi and Indira Nehru Gandhi, the only child of Jawaharlal Nehru. Her husband, Feroz Gandhi, was a Parsi who had been active in the nationalist movement, became a member of parliament, and later became an outspoken critic of Nehru and his policies. Before an unamicable separation in the early 1950s, Feroz and Indira Gandhi had two sons – Rajiv and Sanjay – who represented the fourth generation of the Nehru family to have been at the centre of Indian politics since their great-grandfather, Motilal Nehru, held office in the Indian National Congress.

# 13. Conclusion
## J. Blondel and M. Cotta

### INTRODUCTION

The examination of the 11 countries discussed in the previous chapters supports the claim, made in the Introduction, that there is a need to study the relationship between governments and their supporting parties in greater depth. That relationship is more complex and varied than is often assumed. There is in particular a strong case for exploring the impact of government on supporting parties, a matter which is less often examined. Interpreting the government as a purely executive tool in the hands of the parties is an oversimplification: the government is not merely a dependent variable. Governments enjoy a significant extent of autonomy vis-à-vis parties in many cases; they also exercise influence on the parties.

There are enough variations among the countries covered in this book for a first test of the explanatory factors to be undertaken. Among the nine European and two non-European countries analysed here, one is presidential (the US), another semi-presidential (France), and the rest are parliamentary systems. The parliamentary systems include both one-party and coalition governments; party types vary from organizationally strong to organizationally weak, from ideological to pragmatic; one can also distinguish among different policy fields or policy types. On this basis it is possible to summarize findings and thus achieve a more realistic intepretation of the workings of democratic government.

### APPOINTMENTS

Appointments to ministerial positions are probably the most visible aspect of party government. A 'pure' model entails that parties provide the pool of eligibles, the people with long party careers among whom candidates for government positions are to be selected, while they control also the selection (and deselection) process (Katz; 1986, 1987).

Ten of the cases provide substantial empirical evidence for the part played by this model in mass democracies of the twentieth century: the exception is the United States. As Katz states, the United States is an exception, not because another principle prevails, but because of what might be called the 'implosion' of party. Strong federal decentralization, presidentialism, and the democratization of party life through primaries have turned the parties into what might be better described as galaxies with no clear centre. Within a very thin, albeit resilient traditional frame (Republican or Democratic) a plurality of 'lower-level parties' based on different institutional loci and/or personal coteries operate with a very large amount of autonomy. Rather than the traditional two parties, these 'lower-level parties' play a part in the appointment process: thus it is dubious whether the notion of party government still obtains. It is even difficult to identify clearly what is the party. Autonomy of the government (and its 'lower-level party') vis-à-vis the other 'lower-level parties' is a better way of describing the situation.

In the ten other countries, on the other hand, the organizational substance of parties has been preserved to a much greater extent. Parties are fairly easily identifiable actors and play a significant part in the selection of prime ministers and of the other cabinet members (Blondel & Thiébault, 1991). Yet the question arises whether the 'pure' model of party government, which stresses influence from party to government, and the corresponding image of a party-dependent government fully capture the reality. This model fits political life best when party influence is coupled with a separation of roles, namely when the leaders of the parties keep their position in the party organizations and nominate their 'delegates' to the cabinet. The party is thus the 'real' political government while the government is a subordinate body. This hierarchy, to which we shall also refer when discussing policy-making, is based on an imbalance between party and government: a strong party organization with a clear ideological identity faces a relatively weak government. It presupposes that the party keeps some distance from the government as if to preserve its ideological purity against the inevitable compromises of daily political life.

To what extent do these conditions obtain in the 1980s and 1990s? Our cases show that the model of the dependent government does not truly prevail and that it is even losing ground in the countries where it used to prevail. We have in many cases to relax the model and look towards the idea of *fusion*, to some extent at least, between party and government leadership: in such a case the direction of influence and the nature of the political hierarchy become rather uncertain.

The closest approximation to a dependent government is to be found when two factors are at work. The first factor relates to the features of the party system and to the political basis of governments. Where the party system requires coalition governments, where coalitions are heterogeneous and expectations about their duration low, there is a strong probability that party leaders will prefer to remain in their party position, that they will keep the government at arms length, and that ministers will be subordinated to party authorities. On the contrary, where a party is able to win control of the cabinet on its own in single-party government, the fusion of party and government leadership and even the control of the former by the latter are easier to achieve; the same can occur when the coalition is homogeneous.

The second factor is the strength of party organization. The stronger and more developed the structure of a party, the clearer the identity of the leadership of that party, the more it controls autonomous resources, and the more it can dominate the government. With few exceptions the large mass parties of the Left tend to fit this model better. Their anti-establishment origin also plays a part. 'Bourgeois' parties have a generally weaker organization; they are – or were traditionally – the 'in' parties and have – or had – easier access to government; the leadership of these parties is also usually less clearly identified with the leadership of the membership organization. Other 'faces' of the party, such as the parliamentary component or the ministers tend to play a greater part. There are exceptions in both directions: some socialist parties have a weaker organization such as the French or the Italian parties; some 'bourgeois' parties have a developed structure, such as the Austrian Populists or the Swedish Moderates. We should expect in such cases different characteristics to obtain.

The general hypotheses which have just been put forward are supported by substantial empirical evidence. The split between party and government leadership can be found more often in countries, such as Belgium, Finland, Italy, the Netherlands, where coalitions have been comparatively more heterogeneous; cabinets have also tended to last less in these cases. Fusion of party and cabinet leadership tends to exist in the other countries: this arises where single-party cabinets are the norm, as in Britain or India, and where they have alternated with coalitions, as in Austria or Sweden. Stable and politically homogeneous coalitions also generally result in a fusion of the two positions: the cases of Austria, during Populist-Socialist coalitions, of Germany, of France under governments of the Right, and of Sweden under 'bourgeois' coalitions are cases in point.[1]

The factor of party strength appears to play less of a part. Thus fusion prevails in single-party governments even where the party is well-organized, as can be seen by the examples of Socialist cabinets in Austria and Sweden. The effect of this variable may be larger with coalitions, especially when the coalition is weak: in the stronger parties the positions of prime minister or deputy prime ministers and of party leader remain split while there tends to be fusion in the weaker parties.

There have been some interesting changes in this respect in the 1980s, with innovations taking place in countries where party and government leadership positions were traditonally split and where governmental subordination used to be the rule. Party leaders have moved into the cabinet in Finland and the Netherlands and to some extent even in Italy. In this last country the trend has been more pronounced in the smaller parties (Socialists and Republicans), when they came to lead the government, than in the larger party (Christian Democracy) where the attempt to combine the two positions quickly proved unacceptable. This development seems linked to the variables which were mentioned earlier. The greater stability of coalitions has been one element in Finland and also to some extent in Italy; the internal party factor has also played a part. The ideological and organizational decline of many traditional parties may have made the leaders of these parties realise that they needed to draw advantages from the resources to which they could have access when in government.

The fusion of leadership positions is only one part of the picture of party-cabinet relations with respect to appointments. For a comprehensive picture to be drawn, the extent of overall overlap has to be studied. The role of parties in controlling governments is obviously enhanced when politicians with a long career of top positions in the party organization provide the bulk of ministers and when party authorities play a decisive role in the selection of these ministers. The substantial 'weight' of parties in Western parliamentary systems is confirmed by the fact that party authorities play in all cases a crucial part in the selection of ministers. Yet behind this picture which is consistent with the model of party government (and more specifically of the party-dependent government) there exists a more complex reality. The frequent and growing fusion between government and party leadership positions means that often nominators or those who are influential in nominations are *both* party leaders and prime ministers or key ministers. In such cases, the selection of ministers becomes the means by which the government leader enhances his or her control over the party which supports the government. The appointment of ministers is then an instrument to control the party from the government. Since government leaders are still party leaders, we remain within the realm of party government, but the reality becomes less simple than the 'pure' model suggests. This complexity increases when a party leader stays for a long time at the head of the government. Admittedly, this does not mean that he or she loses partisan identity, since in a parliamentary system the government needs a disciplined parliamentary majority to remain in office and since elections have to be fought under party banners: the political survival of a government leader who stopped being a party leader would be at risk.

These cases show the importance of fusion between party and government roles, not only in Britain but also, at least during the period examined in this book, in Austria, Finland, France, Germany, India, the Netherlands, Sweden; even in Italy its effect has been significant when it has occurred. Obviously the role of these party-cum-government leaders varies when we move from single-party cabinets, where their influence extends to all the government, to coalition cabinets where it is limited to the ministers of their party. There are also everywhere variable limitations to their independence, such as traditions of internal party democracy, or the existence of party factions. These limits exist even in Britain, although many conditions, from single-party governments to the weakness of the parties in the country especially in the case of the Conservatives, contribute to enhancing the predominance of the party-cum-government leader. But even a cabinet and party leader such as Margaret Thatcher found in the end that the (parliamentary) party decided who should be the leader.

The analysis of the relationship between parties and government is comprehensive only if one also assesses how the party leadership is selected. A direct and formal impact of the government in the process of selection of party authorities is rare: European parties have generally well established internal procedures of leadership appointment and these procedures conform to some extent to norms of party democracy and thus entrust selection to a section of the membership and at least to parliamentarians. A formal intervention of the cabinet is therefore unlikely; but where the party has a less democratic structure and is essentially an instrument of political action, the leader of the cabinet may play a part in appointing those who run the organization, as in the British Conservative party where the cabinet and party leader controls party headquarters and appoints the party chairman. The situation is not very different in the German CDU: although the secretary general of the party is formally appointed by the party congress, he has come to be in practice chosen by the Chancellor under Kohl's leadership. Moreover, there are often informal and subtle forms of influence and these should not be underestimated: oligarchical practices thus often set limits to democratic principles. For instance the candidate to the post of party chairman may be unopposed, as is often the case in Belgium: this means that party leaders have reached an agreement in advance and these include the prime minister and some of the senior ministers. Moreover, a successful cabinet career may constitute a stepping stone for a party career, as long-term ministers tend to become part of the party oligarchy.

The American case is exceptional from this point of view as well. While the party (or to be more accurate the 'non-presidential' part of the party) has little influence on cabinet appointments, the president has little impact on the selection of much of the party leadership. The president is involved in his part of the 'galaxy' (the presidential party) but not in the other parts (the congressional parties, the state parties): there is autonomy among the different 'parties'. The separation between institutions is paralleled by a separation between different sections which are the instruments of many independent political competitors. The overall party is reduced to being a framework for coordination.

## POLICIES

Policies are typically regarded as either alternative or complementary to appointments in the definition of party government. Without entering the debate about the relative importance of the two elements, it is sufficient to note that policies may parallel appointments (Budge & Keman, 1991). The 'pure' party government model assumes that the party is able and wishes to take a position on all issues and to see that these positions are adopted by governments, a characteristic which entails that the party must be a unitary actor.

There is ample evidence about the policy-seeking role of parties and about the influence which these bring to bear on governments in Western European countries. There are electoral manifestos, government compacts in coalitions, summits of party leaders, meetings of party representatives with ministers. Yet it would be a serious mistake to view government as being purely passive and subordinate to parties. It is not difficult to find policy initiatives originating from the government without or before an action by parties, to see governments play a major role in transforming vague ideas advanced in party programmes into concrete policies, resist party initiatives, arbitrate between conflicting party proposals; it is even less unusual to discover that members of the government play a significant (albeit informal) role in the formulation of the policy platforms of parties. The overall picture that can be derived from the empirical analyses is that policy-making has to be interpreted much more as a two-way than as a one-way process and as a process in which the government is a far more significant actor than the 'pure' party government model would suggest.

This finding leads back to the question raised in the introductory chapter: what is government? While it is relatively easy to identify in the policy-making process *who* the government is (both as a collective group and as a set of individuals), it is more difficult to understand *what* it is, and therefore what is the meaning of its influence in this field. It is interesting to note that while we have theories of parties, of what they are, of their goals and of their behaviour, we do not have comparable theories of governments. We will return to this point at the end of this chapter.

A comparative look at the country studies shows that there are significant variations in party-government relations with respect to policy-making. There are variations across countries; there are also variations within countries because of changes in the political nature of the government and because of changes in the nature of the political system. There is evidence sustaining the view that the factors discussed in the introduction of this book play a part, whether these are institutional (presidential versus parliamentary system) or result from party characteristics, such as structure, ideology, or leadership. The single-party or coalition character of cabinets, their duration in office, and the fields and types of policy-making are also associated with variations in the relationship between government and supporting parties.

The role of parties in the formulation of policies tends generally to be increased in coalition parliamentary governments; in such cases, the government comes to be in a position of dependence. The life and authority of the cabinet depend in such cases on agreements negotiated among the parties which typically cover policy issues. The existence in some countries (Belgium, the Netherlands) of detailed coalition agreements means that cabinet action is strongly determined by party guidelines. Indeed the dependence of the government may be further manifested by other instruments of party control, such as regular meetings of ministers with party chairmen, national executives, leaders of the parliamentary parties: these are common practice in Austria, Belgium, the Netherlands, Finland) (De Winter, 1993). Summits of party leaders are more irregular and are used to solve policy problems which are new or had not been adequately clarified in the coalition agreements, as in Belgium or Italy (Criscitiello, 1993).

Yet even in coalitions the instruments of party control are not always as strong. Coalition agreements are often filled with rather general statements about policy goals and lack specificity about implementation. The reasons for such vagueness vary. Parties may not see the need to enter into details and leave further work to the government: this was seemingly the case in the Netherlands in the past and is still the case in Finland; alternatively, because of ideological differences, parties are unable to reach a definite agreement and they make do with ambiguous expressions which in practice give the government the responsibility of finding solutions: this seemed to have been the case in Italy. Indeed, in coalition agreements, policies excluded because of the specific opposition of a party may be more important than stated agreements about policies to be pursued: in such cases, if it steers away from dangerous areas, the government will have at least a greater leeway to initiate policies; but it may also face angry reactions from parties which are unhappy with the choices having been made.

Moreover, the relationship between party and government can be more ambiguous than it appears at first sight with respect to coalition agreements, because of the fusion between the two elements at the top. Fusion entails that the party representatives negotiating the coalition agreement have often been members of past governments and/or expect to be ministers in the new government: they are thus often likely to introduce in the agreement elements which suggest a 'governmental' rather than a party perspective. They will not only take into account party preferences but also what is practical from the point of view of government. This point of view may be strengthened by the involvement of experts in the drafting of particular aspects of the coalition agreement, as in the Netherlands. The length of the participation in the government of a party plays a major part in this respect, as the distinction between party and governmental points of view tends to become blurred as time passes. There are many cases, such as those of the Liberal Party in Germany, of the Christian Democratic parties in Belgium, Italy, the Netherlands, of the Congress Party in India, and of the two main Austrian parties where there have been permanent or near-permanent governing parties.

While coalition agreements are ostensibly an instrument of party control over the government, they may perform, in a more subtle way, the opposite function as well: the government may use them in the course of its action to discipline the supporting parties. If the government acts along the lines defined in the agreement, it is in a position to ask parties and specifically the parliamentary parties to remain loyal to the cabinet.

There is a paradox in the case of single-party governments. On the one hand, the government is 'taken over' by a party, but, on the other, parties exercise less control over the cabinet than in other cases. Such a situation seems to provide ideal conditions for full government dependence on the party, as the party does not need to negotiate the programme with others. Yet, because it has 'won' the government, the party has a less urgent need to exercise marked control over the government: there is implicit rather than explicit control. Moreover, in single-party governments, there is generally fusion between party and government at the personal level. The party leader becomes government leader and holds both positions, as can be seen in Britain, Austria, and Sweden, and, with some exceptions, in India; or a subordinate party leader takes the cabinet leader's place as in France under Socialist governments, and on occasion in India. The leadership of the party thus moves in a sense from the party to the government.

Such an institutional transfer has important consequences in terms of resources and constraints. By being at the head of the cabinet, the party leader gains access to the full resources of his position, indeed more so than prime ministers in coalition governments, because these do not have the same hierarchical authority vis-à-vis other ministers. The prime minister has at his or her disposal the civil service; there are also less tangible but politically significant resources of prestige, visibility, and information. There are also constraints under which the head of a party does now operate: budgetary and administrative, internal and international responsibilities fall on the government. The combination of resources and constraints is likely to give to a party leader who is also government leader a different perspective and detach him or her from the party to an extent. This leads to a political dialectic between the party organization and the party (leadership) in government, a dialectic which is at the same time within the party and between party and government.

This situation is in part merely an extension of the normal problems arising between the different levels of any party; but an institutional dimension is also introduced. To assert its position, the party leadership can use the resources of the institution of government but it must also face the responsibilities of government and keep party followers in line. As the cases examined in this volume indicate, the party-cum-government leadership does not only implement the original party manifesto: it also acts autonomously. Since it needs to maintain support in the party, it has to cajole, manipulate, put pressure, in order to bring the party to accept its positions: governmental resources will be used in this process. This is why the party becomes to an extent government dependent.

The particular characteristics of the party are an important variable in this context. In general, the weaker the organization of the party, the more easily that party will be dependent on the government as the party-cum-government leadership can use institutional resources that overshadow those of the party: there is thus a marked difference between the British Conservative party, on the one hand, and the Swedish or Austrian Socialist parties, on the other. In the first case the government fully controls the Central Services of the party; in the others there is a need to pay greater attention, in the name of party democracy, to the preferences of members, although, admittedly, the parliamentary party probably also plays a greater part in the first case than in the others. Yet government leadership remains party leadership. If it forgets it, a rebellion within the party is likely to occur: this is probably why even in as deferential a party as the British Conservative party the leadership must sometimes give way to policy initiatives coming from the grassroots even if it does not approve of them.

What are then the differences between single-party and coalition governments in this respect? Single-party governments enjoy more loyalty on the part of the parties supporting them; they are 'their' governments rather than governments resulting from compromises reached with other parties at the price of variations from party preferences. The policy initiatives of single-party governments will therefore be less subjected to party scrutiny, the expectation being that these initiatives naturally follow the party line. This contrast with coalition governments is less marked where there are clearly defined wings in the party and these are based on policy orientations, as in the British Labour party for instance: one wing may feel underrepresented in the government and is consequently likely to be appreciably less loyal.

As far as the government is concerned, the most important difference between single-party and coalition cabinets is manifestly the fact that the cabinet is more self-assured vis-à-vis the party in single-party governments, as the party would wound itself and endanger its future if it were to bring down a government whose policies are held not to be satisfactory; in coalitions, on the contrary, such an action against the government can be regarded as being directed at the other parties and thus to some extent as part of the normal process of political competition. Moreover, single-party governments can typically count on direct popular support: the party-cum-government leader has won the election; his or her authority does not derive merely from the party, as tends to occur in coalitions. This relative disadvantage of coalition governments is reduced, however, if the coalition has received an electoral mandate, as has occurred in Germany or France, or if, as in France, the direct election of the real leader of the government gives him a special status.

What then is government autonomy in the field of policy-making and can governments act without an input from the supporting parties? The greatest amount of government autonomy is found in the United States, in large part as a result of the institutional structure and of the character of the parties, these two factors being indeed associated. At the level of the presidential convention, policies remain vague and are also largely the result of the presidential candidate's own thinking. At the congressional level the separation of powers system enables the president to remain independent while the parties are typically too undisciplined to be able to act as leading forces in the field of policy-making, though there may be exceptions. Autonomy means therefore essentially autonomy between the different 'parties', those of the president, those of Congress, those of the individual states, each of which tends to be confined to the boundaries of its institutional arena. Yet there is a limit to the autonomy of the president: he needs Congress for many, indeed most of his policies. He has therefore to strike compromises with the legislators of his party and of the other party: this is when the different segments of the American parties have to come together. Thus, in a highly pluralistic and fragmented political system, policy initiation is markedly autonomous but there has to be interdependence at later stages of the decision-making process.

In the parliamentary and semi-presidential systems which predominate in Western Europe and the Commonwealth, interdependence between party and government is the basis on which the system works. This does not preclude the existence of significant areas of autonomy, areas of autonomy which result partly from the intrinsic limitations of the instruments of party scrutiny and partly from the specific resources and assets of the government.

Whatever the nature of coalition agreements or of party manifestos, there is always a gap between a policy drafted in a document and a policy initiated concretely. The government may also enjoy a substantial amount of autonomy to decide when to make a move on an aspect of the programme; indeed delays in the implementation of a political programme can also come from the party, either because the party changes its mind or because the matter was mentioned in the programme primarily for symbolic purposes. Delays due to the government have many origins: it may be that the government has doubts about an idea; it may also be that needs change with the passing of time or as a result of unexpected events. In many cases, if programmes or manifestos and coalition agreements are vague on some points, the government has to spend time in giving shape to these points. The parties may in turn react and further delays may be incurred. A dependent government may prefer to wait; alternatively the parties may prefer to leave to the government the responsibility of finding a solution, for instance because they are afraid of the unpopular decisions which might have to be taken. Overall there is a different state of affairs once the government is in existence: so long as it is being built, the parties confront the problems alone; later there are two actors, the government and the parties, one of which, the government, has at its disposal important resources to deal with new problems and even manipulate them to an extent. Indeed, the greater the success of a government, the more important and frequent will there be renegotiations of the original agreement with the supporting parties.

As many cases have shown the autonomy of governments vis-à-vis supporting parties in the context of new issues tends to be strengthened by the external commitments and responsibilities of these governments. This is manifest in foreign affairs and in many economic matters. Even in strongly 'partitocratic' systems international commitments and decisions taken in supra-national arenas often enable governments to free themselves from party constraints.

Yet parties will react when the autonomous initiatives of the government touch on issues which are central to their policy profile and their political identity. Sometimes publicizing dissent vis-à-vis the cabinet may be a sufficient remedy: a kind of division of roles may emerge, the government choosing that of realism and the party that of principle. The matter may be too important for such an arrangement, however: autonomy will then be once more restricted and give way to interdependence.

## PATRONAGE

Patronage is still the less well-known of the three dimensions of party-government relations, even if it is not the least important. The nature and the normative implications of the phenomenon naturally induce those involved to conceal their actions and their motivations: accurate evaluations are inevitably difficult. Moreover, the boundary between patronage, on the one hand, and appointments and policy-making, on the other, is often imprecise, in part because the actors themselves camouflage patronage under nobler labels.

Even if we take into account all the evaluation problems it is pretty clear from the country studies that the extent of patronage varies significantly across countries. On the one hand, in the Netherlands, Sweden, Finland and Britain, patronage is rather limited; on the other, in Austria, Belgium, India, Italy, the United States, its scope is such that it becomes a central element of political life, while France and Germany should probably be located somewhere between these two groups. In the countries where patronage is widespread, it also is an important aspect of the relationship between government and supporting parties. Except for the United States, these are countries where parties are strongly organized: they may remain rather passive on policies, but they have a keen interest in seeing the fruits of patronage reaching their members, followers, and friends.

It is more difficult to establish who is in control of the processes of distribution of the different types of benefits. While some of these can be obtained from other channels, for instance through parliament where parliament can act independently from the government, it is the government which is generally the crucial channel through which patronage is dispersed.

The question remains as to whether the government and specifically the ministers act under party orders or have enough freedom to use patronage as a means of controlling parties. The main variable appears to be the strength of party organizations: the larger and the more autonomous the party organization, the more patronage will be in reality controlled by party authorities while being formally distributed by the government; ministers act then as the instruments of the party. In such cases, the control by the party of ministerial appointments and of policy-making is indeed primarily aimed at ensuring control over patronage resources. This is probably the best way of interpreting the traditional situation in Austria, Belgium, and Italy. Where the party structures have been weaker, as in France, or have become recently weaker, as in some of the countries mentioned above, patronage is controlled on a more individualistic basis: ministers who are also party bosses use patronage to reinforce their position both in the party and in the government. More than a resource for the party, it becomes a resource for power struggles within the party.

## CONCLUSION: BEYOND A SIMPLE INTERPRETATION OF PARTY-GOVERNMENT RELATIONS

In the introductory chapter of this volume we remarked that the 'pure' model of party government, which views government as subordinate to the supporting parties, points to an important aspect of democratic political life; we also noted that such a model has normative implications for democracy. Yet we also suggested that the model may not provide a wholly satisfactory representation of the reality. It seemed to overestimate the 'weight' of parties and underestimate the role of governments as well as the ability of these governments to resist the influence of parties and in turn exercise influence on parties. It was claimed that variations in party-government relations could be interpreted more realistically in terms of a two-dimensional space where the first dimension assessed the degree of autonomy or of interdependence between the two elements and the second the direction of influence existing between the two of them. It was then proposed to analyse party-government relations on three distinct planes, those of appointments, policy-making, and patronage.

The empirical study of eleven countries during the 1980s and early 1990s has provided support for the view that government-party relations needed to be explored in a more balanced way; it also provided support for a scheme which helped to analyse variations both across and within countries. The importance of the influence of parties on governments cannot be denied, especially in European political systems; but there are also substantial areas of autonomy of governments vis-à-vis the parties supporting them; there is also ample evidence that governments influence parties.

A truly satisfactory understanding of democratic government thus means not just looking at the role of parties, as has been typically the case, but at the role of governments as well. This leads back to a question raised earlier, however: what is the government? That question is still unanswered: there are many theories about parties; there is little about governments. The studies of appointments, policy-making, and patronage which have been conducted in this volume provide the first steps towards filling that gap.

Government, more than parties, is multi-faceted. First, it is a part of party: it is the top party stratum which acquires a new role by having won an election or a parliamentary majority; from this point of view party-government relationships are simply relationships between different strata of the party. Second, the government is a representative actor: this is especially important when government faces directly the electoral challenge, as there is then a contrast between the party oriented towards its members and the government towards its voters. Third, the government is an institution representing the state in both external and internal affairs: while parties may pursue their goals, the government has to ensure that the state is maintained and that answers are given to the issues which cannot be shelved. Fourth and as a consequence of this state role, the government is the head of the central administration: it leads the civil service but also tends to become its representative. These different faces of government could be translated into the language of resources, responsibilities and constraints, with each face being characterized by a different mix of these three elements. To look at the working of democracy from the point of view of government influence is therefore not the end of an old story: it is the beginning of a new one.

## NOTES

1. In the case of coalitions, fusion has different meanings for the parties. Obviously one party only can have the position of prime minister; for the other parties there will be positions of vice prime ministers or of 'first ranking' ministers. Such a situation will also be considered to be fusion.

# Bibliography

## GENERAL

Blondel, J. *Political Leadership* (1986), London and Los Angeles: Sage.
Blondel, J. 'Ministerial careers and the nature of parliamentary government: the cases of Austria and Belgium', *EJPR* vol. 16, (1) (1988), pp. 51–71.
Blondel, J. and F. Müller-Rommel, eds, *Governing Together: The Extent and Limits of Joint Decision-Making in Western European Cabinets* (1993), London: Macmillan.
Budge, I. and H. Keman, *Parties and Democracy* (1991), Oxford: Oxford University Press.
Bunce, V. *Do New Leaders Make a Difference?* (1981), Princeton, N.J.: Princeton University Press.
Cameron, D.R. 'The Expansion of the Public Economy: a comparative analysis', *American Political Science Review* v.72, (1978), pp. 1243–61
Castles, F.G. and R. Wildenmann, eds, *Visions and Realities of Party Government* (1986), Berlin: De Gruyter, European University Institute Series.
Criscitiello, A. 'Majority Summits: Decision-Making inside the cabinet and out: Italy 1970–1990', West European Politics, (1993), vol. 16, 581–94.
Döring, H. ed., *Parliaments and Majority Rule in Western Europe* (1995), NYC: St Martin's Press.
Flora, P. and A. Heidenheimer, eds, *The Development of the Welfare state in Europe and America* (1981), New York: Transaction Books.
Gallagher, M., M. Laver and P. Mair, *Representative Government in Western Europe* (1992), New York: McGraw-Hill.
Katz, R.S. ed., *Party Governments: European and American Experiences* (1987), Berlin: De Gruyter, European University Institute Series.
Katz, R.S. 'Party Government: A Rationalistic Conception', in F.G. Castles and R. Wildenmann, eds, *Visions and Realities of Party Government* (1986), Berlin: De Gruyter, pp. 42 and foll.
Katz, R.S. and P. Mair, eds, *Party Organizations: A Data Handbook on Party Organizations in Western Democracies 1960–1990* (1992), London and Los Angeles: Sage.
Katz, R.S. and P. Mair, eds, *How Parties Organize; change and adaptation in party organizations in Western democracies* (1994), London: Sage.
King, A. 'Executives', in F.I. Greenstein and N.W. Polsby, eds, *Handbook of Political Science*, Vol. 5 (1975), Reading, Mass.: Addison–Wesley, pp. 173–256.
Lane, J.E. and S.O. Ersson, *Politics and Society in Western Europe* (1991), London and Los Angeles: Sage.
La Spina, A. 'Some Reflections on Cabinets and Policy-Making: Types of Policy, Features of Cabinet, and Their Consequences for Policy Outputs', *EUI Working Papers SPS*, N. 90/5 (1990), Florence: European Univ. Institute.
Laver, M. and N. Schofield, *Multiparty Government: The Politics of Coalition in Western Europe* (1990), Oxford: Oxford University Press.

Lehner, F. and K. Schubert, 'Party Government and the Political Control of Public Policy', *EJPR*, (1984), vol. 12, 131–46.

Lijphart, A. 'Democracies: Forms, Performance, and Constitutional Engineering', *EJPR* (1994), 25, 1–17.

Luebbert, G.M. *Comparative Democracy: Policymaking and Governing Coalitions in Europe and Israel* (1986), New York: Columbia University Press.

Mintzel, A. and H. Schmitt, (1981), 'How to investigate the future of party government' (unpublished), in R.S. Katz, 'Party Government: A Rationalistic Conception', F.G. Castles and R. Wildenmann, eds, *op.cit.* (1986), p. 42.

Nousiainen, J. 'Ministers, Parties and Coalition Policies', *Studies on Political Science* (1990), No 10, Turku: Department of Political Science, Univ. of Turku. Juva: WSOY.

Peterson, R.L. *et al.*, 'Government Formation and Policy Formulation', *Res Publica*, vol 25, (1983), pp. 49–82.

Strom, K. 'Minority Governments in Parliamentary Democracies', *Comp. Pol. Stud.* vol. 17 (2) (1984), pp. 199–228.

Strom, K. 'Deferred Gratification and Minority Governments in Scandinavia', *Legislative Studies Quarterly* (11), 4, November 1986, pp. 583–605.

Strom, K. *Minority Government and Majority Rule* (1990), Cambridge: Cambridge University Press.

Wiberg, M. *The Public Purse and Political Parties: Public Financing of Political Parties in Nordic Countries* (1991), Helsinki: The Finnish Political Science Association.

## AUSTRIA

Gerlich, P. and W.C. Müller, 'Austria: Routine and Ritual', in J.Blondel and F.Müller-Rommel, (eds), *Cabinets in Western Europe* (1988), London: Macmillan, 138–50.

Gerlich, P., E. Grande, and W.C. Müller, 'Corporatism in Crisis: Continuity and Change of Social Partnership in Austria', *Political Studies* (1988), Vol. 36, pp. 209–23.

Gerlich, P., W.C. Müller, and W. Philipp, 'Potentials and Limitations of Executive Leadership: the Austrian Cabinet since 1945', *European Journal of Political Research* (1988), Vol. 16, pp. 191–205.

Khol, A. 'Österreich und Europa im Annus mirabilis Europae 1989', *Österreichisches Jahrbuch für Politik* (1989), 813–41.

Kiesenhofer, T.P. '"*Europapartei*" SPÖ?', *University of Vienna*: MA Thesis (1994).

Lehner, G. 'Ökonomische und steuerpolitische Auswirkungen der Steuerreform 1988', *Österreichisches Jahrbuch für Politik* (1988), 591–613.

Meth-Cohn, D. and W.C. Müller, 'Looking Reality in the Eye: The Politics of Privatization in Austria', in V.Wright, ed., *Privatization in Western Europe* (1994), London: Pinter, 160–79.

Müller, W.C. 'Die neue große Koalition in Österreich', *Österreichische Zeitschrift für Politikwissenschaft* (1988a), Vol. 17, pp. 321–47.

Müller, W.C. 'Privatizing in a Corporatist Economy: The Politics of Privatization in Austria', *West European Politics* (1988b), Vol. 11, No. 4, pp. 101–16.

Müller, W.C. 'Party Patronage in Austria', in A. Pelinka and F. Plasser, eds, *The Austrian Party System* (1989), Boulder: Westview Press, pp. 327–56.

Müller, W.C. 'Regierung und Kabinettsystem', in H. Dachs, ed., *Handbuch des Österreichischen politischen Systems* (1991), Vienna: Manz, pp. 110–25.

Müller, W.C. 'Austrian Governmental Institutions: Do They Matter?', *West European Politics* (1992), Vol. 15, pp. 99–131.

Müller, W.C. 'Executive–Legislative Relations in Austria: 1945–1992', *Legislative Studies Quarterly* (1993), Vol. 18, pp. 467–94.

Müller, W.C. 'Models of Government and the Austrian Cabinet', in M. Laver and K.A. Shepsle, eds, *Cabinet Ministers and Parliamentary Government* (1994a), Cambridge: Cambridge University Press, pp. 15–34.

Müller, W.C. 'Koalitionsabkommen in der Österreichischen Politik', *Zeitschrift für Parlamentsfragen* (1994b), Vol. 25, pp. 346–53.

Müller, W.C. and W. Philipp, 'Parteienregierung und Regierungsparteien in Österreich', *Österreichische Zeitschrift für Politikwissenschaft* (1987), Vol. 16, pp. 277–302.

Müller, W.C., W. Philipp, and B. Steininger, 'Wie oligarchisch sind Österreichs Parteien? Eine empirische Analyse 1945–1992', *Österreichische Zeitschrift für Politikwissenschaft* (1992), Vol. 21, pp. 117–46.

Ofner, G. 'Der Weg zur großen Steuerreform', *Österreichisches Jahrbuch für Politik 1987* (1987), pp. 331–56.

Nowotny, E. 'Die große Steuerreform 1988 – Analyse und Bewertung', *Österreichisches Jahrbuch für Politik 1988* (1988), pp. 571–89.

Tades, H. and J. Stabentheiner, 'Das 3. Wohnrechtsänderungsgesetz. Bemerkungen zu seinen miet- und wohnrechtsändernden Teilen', *Österreichische Juristenzeitung* (1994), Vol. 49, Sonderheft, pp. 1–34.

Tálos, E. ed., *Sozialpartnerschaft* (1993), Vienna: Verlag für Gesellschaftskritik.

Vodopivec, A. *Wer regiert in Österreich?* (1960), Vienna: Verlag für Geschichte und Politik.


## BELGIUM

Compiled with the help of T. Laurent FDS assistent.

Ackaeart, J. and L. De Winter, 'Het geld van de CVP en de anderen', *De Nieuwe Maand* (1984), XXVII, pp. 485–93.

Alen, A. 'De bijzondere machten: een nieuwe "besluitregering" in Belgie?', *Tijdschrift voor Bestuurswetenschappen en Publiek Beleid* (1986), 41, 123–59.

Beuls, L. 'De aankoop van gevechtsvliegtuigen: analyse en evaluatie van de besluitvorming', pp. 441–96, in L. Reychler et al., *Een onvoltooid beleid. De Belgische buitenlandse en defensiepolitiek 1830–2015* (1993), Kapellen: Pelckmans.

Brassinne, J. *Les nouvelles institutions politiques de la Belgique* (1989), Dossier du C.R.I.S.P., n. 30, Bruxelles.

Brassinne, J. 'La Belgique fédérale', *Dossier du C.R.I.S.P.* (1994), n. 40, Bruxelles.

Coolsaet, R. *Klein land, veel buitenland* (1992), Leuven: Kritak.

De Ridder, H. *Leo, Mark, Wilfried, et les autres* (1987), Bruxelles: Duculot.

De Ridder, H. *Sire, donnez-moi 100 jours* (1989), Bruxelles: Duculot.

De Ridder, H. *Le cas Martens* (1992), Bruxelles: Duculot.

De Ridder, H. *De strijd om de 16* (1993), Tielt: Lannoo.

Dewachter, W. and E. Das, *Politiek in Belgie. Geprofileerde machtsverhoudingen* (1991), Leuven: Acco.

Dewachter, W. *Besluitvorming in politiek Belgie* (1992), Leuven: Acco.

De Winter, L. 'De partijpolitisering als instrument van de particratie: een overzicht van de ontwikkeling sinds de Tweede Wereldoorlog', *Res Publica* (1981), 23: 53–107.

De Winter, L. 'Belgium: Democracy or oligarchy?', in: M. Gallagher and M. Marsh, eds, *Candidate selection in comparative perspective: the secret gardens of politics* (1988), London: Sage, 20–46.

De Winter, L. 'The selection of party presidents in Belgium in the postwar period', *Joint Workshops of the ECPR* (1989a), Paris.

De Winter, L. 'Parties and policy in Belgium', *European Journal for Political Research* (1989b), 17: 707–30.

De Winter, L. 'Parliamentary and party pathways to the cabinet', pp. 44–69, in J. Blondel and J–L. Thiébault, eds, *The profession of government minister in Western Europe* (1991), London: Macmillan.

De Winter, L. *The Belgian legislator* (1992), Florence: European University Institute.

De Winter, L. 'The selection of party presidents in Belgium: rubberstamping the nominee of the party elite', *European Journal of Political Research* (1993a), 24: 233–56.

Eyskens, M. *Buitenlandse zaken* (1992), Lannoo: Tielt.

Frognier, A.P. 'Belgium: a Complex Cabinet in a Fragmented Polity', pp. 68–85, in J. Blondel and F. Müller-Rommel, eds, *Cabinets in Western Europe* (1988), London: Macmillan.

Gabriel, O. ed., *Die EG-Staaten im Vergleich. Strukturen, Prozesse, Politkinhalte* (1992), Westdeutscher Verlag: Opladen.

Hondegem, A. *De loopbaan van de ambtenaar. Tussen droom en werkelijkheid* (1990), Leuven: Katholieke Universiteit Leuven.

Huyse, L. *De verzuiling voorbij* (1987), Leuven: Kritak.

Lemaitre, H. *Les gouvernements belges de 1968 à 1980. Processus de crise* (1982), Stavelot: Ed. Chauveheid.

Lijphart, A. ed. *Conflict and Coexistence in Belgium. The Dynamics of a Culturally Divided Society* (1981), Berkeley: Institute of International Studies, University of California.

Maes, M. 'De formele aanstelling van de partijvoorzitters in Belgie, 1944–1990', *Res Publica* (1990), 32: 3–62.

Martens, W. *Parole donnée* (1985), Bruxelles: Hatier.

Mottard, G. *Ministre enfin* (1992), Liege: Ed. du Perron.

Platel, M. 'Martens IV – Eyskens I – Martens V', *Res Publica* (1982).

Rihoux, B. 'Ecotaxes on the Belgian political agenda. The Greens versus the established political parties and interest groups', *Joint sessions of workshops of the ECPR* (1993), Leiden (unpublished).

Rihoux, B. 'Les écotaxes-produit sur la scène politique Belge I', *Courrier Hebdomadaire du C.R.I.S.P.* (1994a), Bruxelles, n. 1426.

B. Rihoux, 'Les écotaxes-produit sur la scène politique Belge II', *Courrier Hebdomadaire du C.R.I.S.P.* (1994b), Bruxelles, n. 1427–8.

Rihoux, B. 'Ecotaxes on the Belgian Agenda, 1992–1994: A Green Bargain?', *Environmental politics*, 1994/3, 513–18.

Tegenbos, G. 'Politieke benoemingen in Belgie en Vlaanderen', *Ons erfdeel* (1992), XXXV, pp. 553–60.

## BRITAIN

Artis, M. & D. Cobham, eds, *Labour's Economic Policies* (1991), Manchester: Manchester Univ. Press.

Bagehot, W. *The English Constitution* (1964 ed.), London: Watts.

Benn, T. *Against the Tide: Diaries, 1973–6* (1989), London: Hutchinson.

Benn, T. *Conflicts of Interest: Diaries, 1977–80* (1990), London: Hutchinson.

Burch, M. 'The United Kingdom', in J. Blondel & F. Müller-Rommel, eds, *Cabinets in Western Europe* (1988), London: Macmillan, pp. 17–32.

Budge, I. & H. Keman, *Parties and Democracy* (1990), Oxford: Oxford Univ. Press.

Butler, D. and D. Kavanagh, eds, *The British General Election of 1979* (1979), London: Macmillan.

Coates, K. ed., *What Went Wrong* (1979), London: Institute of Workers' Control.

Conservative Party Conference Reports, 1979–91.

Conservative Party Campaign Guide, 1979, 1983, 1987.

Donoghue, B. *Prime Minister* (1987), London: Cape.

Farnham, D. & J. Pimlott, *Understanding Industrial Policy* (1990), London: Cassell.

Hennessey, P. *Cabinet* (1986), Oxford: Blackwell.

Holmes, M. *The First Thatcher Government* (1985), Brighton: Wheatsheaf.

James, S. *British Cabinet Government: The role of Politicians in Elective Office* (1992), London: Routledge.

Kelly, R.N. *Conservative Party Conferences* (1989), Manchester: Manchester U.P.

Labour Party Conference Reports, 1974–9.

Labour Party Programme, 1973.

McKenzie, R.T. *British Political Parties* (1963), London: Heinemann.

Minkin, L. *The Labour Party Conference* (1980), Manchester: Manchester U.P.

Norton, P. *Dissension in the House of Commons 1974–1979* (1980), Oxford: Oxford Univ. Press.

Pryor, (then Lord) J. *A Balance of Power* (1986), London: Hamish Hamilton.

Ramsden, J. *The Making of Conservative Party Policy* (1980), London: Longmans.

Rush, M. *The Cabinet and Policy Formation* (1984), London: Longman.

Savage, S.P. & L. Robins, eds, *Public Policy under Thatcher* (1990), London: Macmillan.

Smith, G. & D. Squire, *Local Taxes and Local Government* (1987), London: Institute of Fiscal Studies.

Travers, T. *The Politics of Local Government Finance* (1986), London: Allen and Unwin.

Veljanovski, C. *Selling the State* (1987), London: Weidenfeld.

## FINLAND

Anckar, D. 'Finland: Dualism och konsensus', in E. Damgaard, ed., *Parlamentarisk forandring i Norden* (1990), Oslo: Universitetsforlaget, 131–75.

Arter, D. *Politics and Policy-Making in Finland* (1987), Sussex: Wheatsheaf Books.

Hakovirta, H. and T. Kosiaho, eds, *Suomen hallitukset ja hallitusohjelmat 1945–1973* (1973), Helsinki: Kirjayhtymä.

Immonen, K. ed., *The Long Perspective: Kauno Koivisto, Statesman* (1993), Helsinki: Kirjayhtymä.

Laakso, S. *Hallituksen muodostaminen Suomessa* (1975), Vammala: Suomalainen lakimiesyhdistys.

Murto, E. *Pääministeri: Suomen pääministerin rooli 1917–1993* (1994), Helsinki: Painatuskeskus.

Nousiainen, J. 'Finland', in J. Blondel and F. Müller-Rommel, eds, *Cabinets in Western Europe* (1988), London: Macmillan, 213–33.

Nousiainen, J. *Ministers, Parties and Coalition Policies* (1991), Turku: Department of Political Science, University of Turku.

Nousiainen, J. *Politiikan huipulla* (1992), Juva: WSOY.

Nousiainen, J. 'Finland: Ministerial Autonomy, Constitutional Collectivism, and Party Oligarchy', in M. Laver and K.A. Shepsle, eds, *Cabinet Ministers and Parliamentary Government* (1994), New York: Cambridge University Press, 88–105.

Nyholm, P. 'Finland: A Probabilistic View of Coalition Formation', in E.C. Browne and J. Dreijmanis, eds, *Government Coalitions in Western Democracies* (1982), 71–108.

Tiihonen, S. *Hallitusvalta: valtioneuvosto itsenäisen Suomen toimeenpanovallen käyttäjänä* (1990), Helsinki: Valtion painatuskeskus.

Wiberg, M. ed., *Parliamentary Control in the Nordic Countries* (1994), Jyväskylä: The Finnish Political Science Association.

## FRANCE

Avril, P. '"Chaque institution à sa place ..." – Le Président, le parti et le groupe', *Pouvoirs*, 20, (1981).

Avril, P. 'Le Président et le parti non présidentiel de la majorité', *Commentaire*, (1983), (22).

Bigaud, C. 'La pratique parlementaire sous la cohabitation', *Regards sur l'Actualité*, 191, May 1987.

Braud, P. 'Etre le parti du Président – Délices et maléfices', *Projet*, 209, Jan–Febr 1988.

Cabannes, J. 'Les deux gouvernements Rocard constitués en mai et juin 1988', *Revue de Droit Public*, Jan–Febr 1989.

Charlot, J. 'Le Président et le parti majoritaire: du gaullisme au socialisme', *Revue politique et parlementaire*, n. 905, Juil.–Août 1983.

Dagnaud, M. and D. Mehl, 'L'élite de la cohabitation – Enquête sur les cabinets ministériels du gouvernement Chirac', *Pouvoirs*, 42, (1987).

Dagnaud, M. and D. Mehl, *L'élite rose – Sociologie du pouvoir socialiste* nouvelle édition augmentée (1988), Paris: Ramsay.

Dagnaud, M. and D. Mehl, 'L'élite rose confirmée', *Pouvoirs*, 50, (1989).

Dupin, E. *L'après Mitterrand – Le Parti Socialiste à la dérive* (1991), Paris: Calmann-Lévy.

Gaffney, J. 'The Emergence of a Presidential Party: The Socialist Party', in A. Cole, ed., *French Political Parties in Transition* (1990), Dartmouth.

Hainsworth, P. 'From Opposition To Office: The French Right After The March 1986 Legislative Elections', *Contemporary French Civilization*, 11(1), Winter 1987:26–38.

Limouzy, J. 'Les rapports du ministre avec le Parlement et les partis', *Pouvoirs*, 36, (1986).

Mendel-Riche, F. 'L'activité du Parlement de 1981 à 1985', *Regards sur l'Actualite*, 121, May 1986.

Mény, Y. *La corruption de la République* (1992), Paris: Fayard.

Payen, A. 'Les modes d'action du Parti Socialiste sur le gouvernement Rocard', *Mémoire de DEA*, Université de Lille II, (1992).

Portelli, H. 'L'intégration du Parti Socialiste à la Cinquième République', in J.L. Parodi and O. Duhamel, eds, *La Constitution de la Cinquième République* (1985), Paris: Presses de la FNSP.

Portelli, H. 'Les partis et les institutions', *Pouvoirs*, 49, (1989).

Portelli, H. *Le Parti Socialiste* (1992), Paris: Montchrestien, Coll. Clefs.

Quermonne, J.L. 'Un gouvernement présidentiel ou un gouvernement partisan?', *Pouvoirs*, 20, (1981).

Quermonne, J.L. *L'appareil administratif de l'Etat* (1991), Paris: Seuil.

Ross, G. and J. Jenson, 'Pluralism and the Decline of Left Hegemony: The French Left in Power', *Politics and Society*, 14(2), 115–46, (1985).

Schonfeld, W.R. *Ethnographie du PS et du RPR – Les éléphants et l'aveugle* (1985), Paris: Economica.

Suleiman, E. 'The Politics of Corruption and the Corruption of Politics', *French Politics and Society*, Vol. 9(1), Winter 1991.

Thery, J. F. 'Les gouvernements Mauroy de mai et juin 1981', *Regards sur l'Actualité*, 73, July–Aug 1981.

Thiébault, J.L. 'Party leadership selection in France – Creating a "president party"', *European Journal of Political Research*, 24: 277–93, (1993).

## GERMANY

von Beyme, K. *Die politische Klasse im Parteienstaat* (1993), Frankfurt: Suhrkamp.

Dyson, K. 'West Germany: The Search for a Rationalist Consensus', in J. Richardson, ed., *Policy Styles in Western Europe* (1982), London: George Allen and Unwin.

Haungs, P. 'Parteipräsidien als Entscheidungszentren der Regierungspolitik – Das Beispiel der CDU', in Hartwich and Wewer, eds, *Regieren in der BRD* (1983), 2.

Katzenstein, P. *Policy and Politics in West Germany: The Growth of a Semi-sovereign State* (1982).

König, T. 'Decision-making in the German Labor Policy Domain: A Model for Analysis', (1992), Paper presented at the Second European Conference on Social Networks.

Liebert, U. and W. Merkel, eds, *Die Politik zur deutschen Einheit. Probleme – Strategien – Kontroversen* (1992), Leverkusen.

Liebert, U. *Parlamentarismus und organisierte Interessen im Aufbau der Demokratie: Bundesrepublik Deutschland, Italien und Spanien im Vergleich (1948–1990)*, Opladen (forthcoming).

Mayntz, R. and U. Derlien, 'Party Patronage and Politicization of the West German Administrative Elite 1970–1987 – Toward Hybridization?', in *Governance*, Vol. 2, No. 4; Oct. 1989: 384–404.

Niedermayer, O. 'Innerparteiliche Demokratie', in O. Niedermayer and Stöss, eds, *Stand und Perspektiven der Parteienforschung in Deutschland* (1993), Opladen.

Perschke-Hartmann, C. *Die doppelte Reform. Gesundheitspolitik von Blüm zu Seehofer* (1994).

Putnam, R.P. *The Comparative Study of Political Elites* (1976), Englewood Cliffs, N.J.: Prentice Hall.

Scharpf, F., B. Reissert, and F. Schnabel, *Politikverflechtung: Theorie und Empirie des kooperativen Föderalismus in der Bundesrepublik* (1976), Kronberg.

Scharpf, F. 'Verhandlungssysteme, Verteilungskonflikte und Pathologien der politischen Steuerung', in M. Schmidt, ed., *Staatstätigkeit: International und historisch vergleichende Analysen* (1988), PVS-Sonderheft 19, Opladen.

Schindler, P. *Datenhandbuch zur Geschichte des Deutschen Bundestages 1983–1991* (1993), Baden Baden.

Schmidt, M. *Wohlfahrtsstaatliche Politik unter bürgerlichen und sozialdemokratischen Regierungen. Ein internationaler Vergleich* (1982), Frankfurt.

Schmidt, M. *Regieren in der Bundesrepublik Deutschland* (1992), Opladen.

Wewer, G. *Richtlinienkompetenz und Koalitionsregierung: wo wird die Politik definiert?* (1990), ebd.

Wildenmannn, R. *Volksparteien, Ratlose Riesen?* (1989), Baden-Baden: Nomos.

# INDIA

Alexander, P.C. *My Years with Mrs Gandhi* (1991), New Delhi: Vision Books.

Bardhan, P. *Political Economy of India's Development* (1986), New Delhi: Oxford University Press.

Björkman, J.W. 'India: Party, Personality and Dynasty', in A. Ware, ed., *Political Parties: Electoral Change and Structural Response* (1987), London: Blackwell, 51–71 and 251–3.

Chopra, P. *Uncertain India: A Political Profile of Two Decades of Freedom* (1968), Cambridge, Mass.: The MIT Press.

Gautam, O.P. *The Indian National Congress* (1985), Delhi: B R Publishing.

Hardgrave, J.L. Jr. *India: Government and Politics in a Developing Nation* 3rd edition, (1980), N.Y.: Harcourt, Brace Jovanovich.

Hardgrave, J.L. Jr. 'India on the Eve of Elections: Congress and the Opposition', *Pacific Affairs* (1984), 57: 406–18.

Hartmann, H. *Political Parties in India* (1982), Delhi: Meenakshi Prakashan.

Kochanek, S.A. *The Congress Party of India* (1968), Princeton, N.J.: Princeton University Press.

Kochanek, S.A. 'Mrs Gandhi's Pyramid: The New Congress', in H.C. Hart, ed., *Indira Gandhi's India* (1976), Boulder, Colo.: Westview Press.

Kohli, A. *Democracy and Discontent: India's Growing Crisis of Governability* (1991), Cambridge: Cambridge University Press.

Kothari, R. 'The Congress System in India', *Asian Survey* (1964), 4:1161–73.

Kothari, R. *The Politics of India* (1975), Boston, Mass.: Little Brown & Co.

Manor, J. 'Party Decay and Political Crisis in India', *The Washington Quarterly* (Summer 1981): 25–34.

Manor, J. 'Parties and the Party System', in A. Kohli, ed., *India's Democracy* (1988), Princeton, N.J.: Princeton University Press.

Mathur, K. and J.W. Björkman. *Top Policy Makers in India: Cabinet Ministers and Their Civil Service Advisors* (1994), New Delhi: Concept Publishers.

Mathur, K. and N.G. Jayal, *Drought, Policy and Politics* (1993), New Delhi: Sage.

Menon, V.P. *Transfer of Power: The Story of the Integration of the States* (1957), Princeton, N.J.: Princeton University Press.

Morris-Jones, W.H. *The Government and Politics of India* (1967), London: Hutchinson.

Morris-Jones, W.H. *Politics, Mainly Indian* (1978), Madras: Orient Longmans.

Nandy, A. 'Indira Gandhi and the Culture of Indian Politics', in *At the Edge of Psychology: Essays in Politics and Culture* (1980), Delhi: Oxford University Press. Pages 112–30.

Rudolph, L.I. and S.H. Rudolph, *In Pursuit of Lakshmi: The Political Economy of the Indian State* (1987), Chicago, Ill: University of Chicago Press.

Sisson, J.R. *The Congress Party of Rajasthan* (1972), Berkeley, Calif.: The University of California Press.

Sisson, J.R. and R. Rameshray, eds, *Diversity and Dominance in Indian Politics* (two volumes) (1990), New Delhi: Sage.

Venkateshwaran, R.J. 'PM and His Deputy: A Rival Near the Throne', *The Statesman* (13 September 1990).

Weiner, M. *Party Building in a New Nation* (1967), Chicago, Ill.: University of Chicago Press.

Weiner, M. 'Party Bureaucracy and Institutions', in John Mellor, ed., *India: A Rising Middle Power* (1981), Boulder, Colo.: Westview Press.


ITALY


Amato, G. 'Un governo nella transizione. La mia esperienza di Presidente del Consiglio', in *Quaderni Costituzionali* (1994), a. XIV, n. 3, pp. 355–71.

Baget Bozzo, *Il partito cristiano al potere. La DC di De Gasperi e Dossetti, 1945–1954* (1974), Firenze: Vallecchi.

Bardi, L. and L. Morlino, 'Tracing the Roots of the Great Transformation', in R. Katz and P. Mair, eds, How Parties Organize: *Change and Adaptation in Party Organizations in Western Democracies* (1994), London and Los Angeles: Sage.

Calise, M. and R. Mannheimer, *Governanti in Italia. Un trentennio repubblicano* (1982), Bologna: Il Mulino.

Cotta, M. *Classe Politica e Parlamento in Italia* (1979), Bologna: Il Mulino.

Cotta, M. 'Italy: a fragmented government' in J. Blondel and F. Müller-Rommel, eds, *Cabinets in Western Europe* (1988), London: Macmillan.

Cotta, M. Il Parlamento nel sistema politico italiano. Mutamenti istituzionali e cicli politici, *Quaderni Costituzionali* (1991), v. 11, 201–24.

Cotta, M. 'Il governo di partito in Italia. Crisi e trasformazione dell'assetto tradizionale', in M. Caciagli, F. Cazzola, L. Morlino, S. Passigli, eds, *L'Italia tra crisi e transizione* (1994), Roma: Laterza.

Cotta, M. and P. Isernia, eds, *Il gigante dai piedi di argilla. La crisi della partitocrazia italiana* (1996), Bologna: Il Mulino.

Dente, B. and G. Regonini, 'Politics and policies in Italy', in P. Lange and M. Regini, eds, *State, market and social regulation: new perspectives on Italy* (1989), Cambridge: Cambridge University Press.

Di Palma, G. *Surviving without governing: the Italian parties in Parliament* (1977), Berkeley: University of California Press.

Ferraresi, P. *Burocrazia e politica in Italia* (1980), Bologna: Il Mulino.

Isernia, P. 'Bandiera e risorse: la politica estera italiana negli anni ottanta', in M. Cotta and P. Isernia, eds, (1996).

La Spina, A. 'Partiti e mercato. Le politiche di regolazione', in M. Cotta and P. Isernia, eds, (1996).

Leonardi, R. and D. Wertman, *Italian Christian Democracy, the politics of dominance* (1989), London and Los Angeles: Sage.

Mastropaolo, A. and M. Slater 'Italy, 1946–1979: party platforms and electoral programmes under the republic', in I. Budge, D. Robertson and D. Hearl, eds, *Ideology, strategy and party change: a spatial analysis of post-war election programmes in 19 democracies* (1987), Cambridge: Cambridge University Press.

Merkel, W. *Prima e dopo Craxi. Le trasformazioni del PSI* (1987), Padua: Liviana.

Morlino, L. ed., *Costruire la democrazia. Partiti e gruppi in Italia* (1991), Bologna: Il Mulino.

Morlino, L. ed., *Costruire la democrazia* (1992), Bologna: Il Mulino.

Pasquino, G. 'Party Government in Italy: Achievements and Prospects', in R.S. Katz, ed. *Party Governments: European and American Perspectives* (1987), Berlin and New York: de Gruyter.

Pasquino, G. 'Unregulated regulators: parties and party government', in P. Lange and M. Regini, eds, *State, market and social regulation: new perspectives on Italy* (1989), Cambridge: Cambridge University Press.

Regonini, G. 'Politici, burocrati e politiche pubbliche', in G. Pasquino, ed., *Politici e Burocrati* (1993), Roma: ISTAT-CNR.

Sartori, G. *Teoria dei partiti e caso italiano* (1982), Milano: Sugarco.

Suleiman, E. and J. Waterbury, eds, *The political economy of public sector reform and privatization* (1990), Boulder, Colo.: Westview Press.

Verzichelli, L. 'Le politiche di bilancio: il debito pubblico da risorsa a vincolo', in M. Cotta and P. Isernia, eds, (1996).

## THE NETHERLANDS

Ammerlaan, R. *Het Verschijnsel Schmelzer* (1973), Leiden: Sijthoff.

Andeweg, R.B. 'Less than Nothing; Hidden Privatisation of the Pseudo-Private Sector: the Dutch case', *West European Politics* (1988), v.11:4, 117–28.

Andeweg, R.B. 'Institutional Conservatism in the Netherlands: proposals for and resistance to change', *West European Politics* (1989), v.12, 42–60.

Andeweg, R.B. 'The Dutch Prime Minister: not just chairman, not yet chief?', *West European Politics* (1991), v.14:2, 116–32.

Andeweg, R.B. 'Privatization in the Netherlands: the result of a decade', in V.Wright, ed., *Privatization in Western Europe: Pressures, Problems and Paradoxes* (1994), London: Pinter, 198–214.

Andeweg, R.B. and W. Derksen, 'The Appointed Burgomaster: appointments and careers of burgomasters in the Netherlands', *Netherlands Journal of Sociology* (1978), v.14, 41–57.

Andeweg, R.B. and G.A. Irwin, *Dutch Government and Politics* (1993), London: Macmillan.

Daalder, H. (1964), 'Leiding en Lijdelijkheid in de Nederlandse Politiek', reprinted in H. Daalder, *Van Oude en Nieuwe Regenten: Politiek in Nederland* (1995), Amsterdam: Bakker, 11–39.

Hillebrand, R., G.A. Irwin, and M.L. Zielonka-Goei, *Seeing Double: Identifying the Political Leader of Dutch Political Parties*, paper presented to the workshop on 'Leadership Selection in Western Political Parties in the 1980s', ECPR Joint Sessions, Paris, 10–15 April, 1989.

Lijphart, A. 'Op Weg naar een Presidentieel Stelsel?', *Socialisme en Democratie* (1970), v.27, 140–1.

Lijphart, A. *The Politics of Accommodation; pluaralism and democracy in the Netherlands* (1975), sec. ed., Berkeley: University of California Press.

Lijphart, A. 'Time Politics of Accommodation', *Acta Politica* (1984), v.19, 9–18.

Lijphart, A. 'From the Politics of Accommodation to Adversarial Politics in the Netherlands: a reassessment', *West European Politics* (1989), v.12, 139–53.

Mair, P. Party Democracies and Their Difficulties, inaugural lecture, Leyden University, 11 March, 1994.

Oerlemans, J. 'Nederland één-partijstaat', *NRC-Handelsblad* (1990), 14 Februari.

Outshoorn, J. 'The Rules of the Game: Abortion Politics in the Netherlands', in J. Lovenduski and J. Outshoorn eds, *The New Politics of Abortion* (1986), London: Sage, 5–27.

Petersen, R.L., M. de Ridder, J.D. Hobbs, and E.F. McClellan, 'Government Formation and Policy Formulation; patterns in Belgium and the Netherlands', *Res Publica* (1983), v.25, 49–82.

Rehwinkel, P. and J. Nekkers, *Regerenderwijs; de PvdA in het kabinet-Lubbers/Kok* (1994), Amsterdam: Bakker.

Secker, W.P. *Ministers in Beeld; de sociale en functionele herkomst van de Nederlandse ministers (1848–1990)* (1991), Leiden: DSWO Press.

Terlouw, J. *Naar Zeventien Zetels en Terug; politiek dagboek 9 Maart 1981 – 5 November 1982* (1983), Utrecht: Veen.

Visscher, G. *Parlementaire Invloed op Wetgeving*, (1994) The Hague: SDU.

## SWEDEN

Bergström, H. *Rivstart? Från opposition till regering* (1987), Stockholm: Tidens Förlag.

Bäck, M. and T. Möller, *Partier och organisationer* (1990), Stockholm: Allmänna Förlaget.

ESO (Expertgruppen för studier i offentlig ekonomi), *Det offentliga stödet till partierna. Inriktning och omfattning* (1990), Stockholm: Finansdepartementet (1994: 31).

Feldt, K.O. *Alla dessa dagar ... I regeringen 1982–1990* (1991), Stockholm: Norstedt.

Isberg, M. and J. Johansson, 'Ledningsrekrytering i riksdagens Partigrupper' in von Sydow, B., Wallin, G. and Wittrock, B., eds, *Politikens väsen. Idéer och institutioner i den moderna staten* (1993), Stockholm: Tidens Förlag.

Johansson, J. *Det statliga kommittéväsendet. Kunskap, kontroll, konsensus* (1992), Stockholm Studies in Politics: 41.

Larsson, T. *Regeringen och dess kansli* (1986), Lund: Studentlitteratur.

Larsson, T. *Det svenska statsskicket* (1994), Lund: Studentlitteratur.

Pierre, J. *Partikongresser och regeringspolitik: en studie av den socialdemokratiska partikongressens beslutsfattande och inflytande 1948–1978* (1986), Lund: Kommunfakta Förlag.

Ruin, O. 'Sweden in the 1970s: Policy-Making Becomes More Difficult', in Richardson, J., ed., *Policy Styles in Western Europe* (1982), London: George Allen & Unwin.

Ruin, O. 'Sweden: The New Constitution (1974) and the Tradition of Consensual Politics', in Bogdanor, V., ed., *Constitutions in Democratic Politics* (1988), Aldershot: Gower.

Ruin, O. *Tage Erlander Serving the Welfare State, 1946–1969* (1990), Pittsburgh: University of Pittsburgh Press.

Ruin, O. 'The Duality of the Swedish Central Administration: Ministries and Central Agencies', in Farazmand, A., ed., *Handbook of Comparative and Development Public Administration* (1990), 2, New York: Marcel Dekker.

Ruin, O. 'Three Swedish Prime Ministers: Tage Erlander, Olof Palme and Ingvar Carlsson', in Lane, J-E., ed., *Understanding the Swedish Model* (1991), London: Frank Cass.

## UNITED STATES

Bartels, L.M. 'The Impact of Electioneering in the United States', in D. Butler and A. Ranney, eds, *Electioneering: A Comparative Study of Continuity and Change* (1992), Oxford: Clarendon Press.

Beck, P.A. and F.J. Sorauf, *Party Politics in America* (1992), New York, N.Y.: Harper Collins.

Ginsberg, B. and M. Shefter, *Politics by Other Means: The Declining Importance of Elections in America* (1990), New York, N.Y.: Basic Books.

Katz, R.S. and R.A. Kolodny, 'The United States', in R.S. Katz and P. Mair, eds, *Party Organisations: A Data Handbook on Party Organisations in Western Democracies* 1960–1990 (1992), London and Los Angeles: Sage.

Katz, R.S. and R.A. Kolodny, 'Party Organization as an Empty Vessel: Parties in American Politics', in R.S. Katz and P. Mair, eds, *How Parties Organize: Change and Adaptation in Party Organizations in Western Democracies* (1994), London and Los Angeles: Sage.

Kolodny, R.A. 'Congressional Party Politics and the Congressional Campaign Committees: The Leadership Challenge to Rep. Guy Vander Jagt' Paper presented at the 1991 Annual Meeting of the American Political Science Association (1991).

Mackenzie, G.C. ed., *The In-and-Outers: Presidential Appointees and Transient Government in Washington* (1987), Baltimore, Md: Johns Hopkins University Press.

Mayer, K.R. *The Political Economy of Defense Contracting* (1991), New Haven, Conn.: Yale University Press.

Mayhew, D.R. *Congress: The Electoral Connection* (1975), New Haven, Conn.: Yale University Press.

Mayhew, D.R. *Divided We Govern: Party Control, Lawmaking, and Investigations 1946–1990* (1991), New Haven, Conn.: Yale University Press.

Polsby, N.W. and A. Wildavsky, *Presidential Elections: Contemporary Strategies of American Electoral Politics* (1991), New York, N.Y.: Free Press.

Rose, R. *The Postmodern President* (1991), Chatham: Chatham House.

# Index